Told to Be Small. Born to Be Boundless.

She Wasn't Supposed to Fly

A MEMOIR

S. T. GRIFFON

GAMSHOM PRESS

Published by Gamshom Press
12787 Booker T Wash Hwy | Suite 104 | Hardy, VA 24101 | USA
www.gamshompress.com

Printed in the United States of America.
Library of Congress Control Number: 2026906168
ISBN-13: 979-8-9949031-1-7 (paperback)
ISBN-13: 979-8-9949031-0-0 (ebook)

Author's Note

This work is a memoir. It reflects key aspects of my journey and life experiences over several years. Some names and identifying details have been changed, and some individuals portrayed are composites. For narrative purposes, the timelines of certain events have been altered or compressed.

Foreword

In a world determined to tell us who we are and where we belong, the most radical act is choosing for yourself. But that choice, to flip the script from surviving to thriving, doesn't come easily. Most of us are taught to prioritize everything and everyone else, and S.T. Griffon did just that, until the weight of it all became too much to carry. Only then, in a courageous act of self-reclamation, did she begin to choose herself, and that's when everything changed.

This story begins in darkness, as most authentic transformations do, because we spend so much time waiting for grace to find us when the truth is more straightforward and more complicated: we must find it within ourselves. We tell ourselves that life happens to us, but S.T.'s story reveals a deeper truth. Each experience, no matter how brutal, becomes a thread in the larger tapestry leading us home to who we truly are. Our most painful chapters often become our greatest victories when we learn to transform life's hardest blows into pathways toward healing.

That transformation—from wound to wisdom, from surviving to flourishing—is what S.T. offers us in these pages. She doesn't just share her story, she reminds us that our most uncomfortable moments can become sacred portals to the life that awaits us when we become our authentic selves—and sometimes, it's through our deepest struggles that we learn to fly.

Her bravery offers something invaluable: proof that rising is possible, even when everything suggests otherwise.

May her story permit you to write your own.

Dr. Tomi White Bryan
Author of *Emotional Intelligence 3.0: How to Stop Playing Small in a Really Big Universe*

Introduction

According to the laws of physics, the bumblebee shouldn't be able to fly. Its wings are too small, its body too round, its lift too low. And yet, it flies, without hesitation, without apology. Because the bee doesn't measure its potential by someone else's rules. It simply takes flight.

I've always held on to that story, not because I cared whether it was scientifically accurate, but because it mirrored my own impossible truth. Like the bumblebee, I wasn't supposed to fly.

I was born into a world that made sure I knew my place. A place where people like me: shaped by trauma, raised in chaos, forged in silence, weren't expected to rise. Not from a fractured home. Not through poverty. Not with scars too deep to name and two babies clinging to a paratrooper's rucksack filled with grief and grit. Everything said I'd fail. Every voice echoed, you can't.

But here I am. And here is this book, a chronicle of what it means to rise when the world tells you to stay grounded. It's about defying the rules that were never meant to protect you. About the strength to carry your story, and the courage to believe you're allowed to soar.

To the reader who has ever been told you can't, shouldn't, or won't, this story is for you. Let's fly anyway.

Chapter 1

Forces beyond your control can take away everything
you possess except one thing, your freedom to
choose how you will respond to the situation.

—Viktor E. Frankl

The CEO called it "restructuring," but corporate jargon couldn't soften the blow. I was being fired.

"We have eliminated your role."

"I'm sorry, what did you say?"

"We have eliminated your role," he repeated.

"Eliminated? Am I being fired?" My heart sank.

"Your role as it exists today isn't workable, so it's being eliminated."

"What does that mean?" I said, my voice rising.

"It means that, after a brief transition, you will no longer work for this company." His tone was firm, making it clear his words were final.

"Could you tell me why?" I asked, my voice cracking.

"Look, the market isn't great, and we have to make some tough business decisions ..."

He kept talking, but his voice faded into the background as my mind spun in confusion.

What's happening? How could he eliminate the job I worked so hard for, after only six months? Did I do something wrong?

"We have different priorities," I heard him say. His voice was flat and emotionless, like he was reading from a script.

The meeting was being held over Zoom, and I couldn't help but wonder why a conversation like this wasn't happening in person. Still, I was grateful to avoid facing anyone or being escorted from the building.

I stared into the camera, gripping the arms of my chair as I fought to hold myself together. My chest burned and my body trembled, but I refused to let the tears fall.

I will not cry. I will not cry. I will not cry, I repeated silently. There would be time for tears later—but not now. Not in front of him.

His voice pulled me back to the moment.

"Do you have any questions for me?"

I had plenty. *Why am I being fired? What changed after eight successful years with the company? Why did you promote me to the leadership team six months ago, only to humiliate me?* But I didn't ask any of them. I was fighting to keep it together, and I knew his decision was final. Wanting the conversation to be over, I simply said, "No, I don't."

He left the meeting, leaving me alone on the call with the human resources manager.

"I'll go over COBRA benefits and your vacation balance with you," she began. "And then we can discuss turning in ..."

"Just email me anything you need me to know," I interrupted, my voice sharp. I leaned forward and clicked "End" to disconnect from the meeting.

I rested my elbows on my desk and buried my face in my hands. The tears I'd been holding back broke free. My chest heaved, and my breath came in sharp, ragged bursts. I pounded my fists on the desk and screamed.

In over two decades of working, no one had ever fired me. The CEO had reduced my loyalty, my hard work, and everything I'd poured into my career to nothing more than a cold business decision.

The sting of betrayal burned deep in my chest. Work had been my refuge, my purpose, my meaning. It had defined who I was and was proof that I had kept the promises I'd made to myself so long ago. As the tears flowed, grief turned into anger.

"*Fired!*" I screamed, my voice raw. "I did everything they asked and sacrificed so much for this company!" I swept my arm across my desk and watched stacks of papers scatter to the floor. Finally, anger gave way to exhaustion as I slumped in my chair. *What am I going to do?*

As my sobs slowed, I felt an unexpected warmth on my cheek. I turned toward the window, squinting against the bright afternoon sun as I gazed out at the endless blue sky. I pinched the bridge of my nose and drew in slow, deep breaths.

"Get it together, Shonna," I whispered to myself. The words felt more like a plea than a command.

I closed my eyes, and slowly, my heartbeat steadied, and my breathing calmed.

Being fired wasn't part of my plan, and it was terrifying, but this wasn't the first time something had challenged me. I had faced seemingly insurmountable odds before—escaping a dysfunctional home, joining the 82nd Airborne Division, losing my mom, and navigating an abusive marriage. Each challenge had threatened to break me, but I'd survived them all.

"And I'll survive this too," I said firmly.

The words lingered as a hint of doubt invaded my thoughts. *Will you?*

Chapter 2

I am what survives of me.

—Erik Erikson

"I just want to survive."

The words left my mouth before I realized I had spoken out loud. The teacher had asked the class to write about their plans for the future.

"What did you say, Shoshanna?" the teacher asked, and my cheeks flushed with embarrassment.

"I just want to survive," I whispered.

"Is that really your answer?" she asked, with an edge to her voice.

The rest of the class was staring at me. *Why would I say something so stupid out loud?*

When I didn't respond, she continued. "There is so much more to life than just surviving. The world is a big place, and ..."

"Not for me, there isn't. Everywhere I look, there is bad stuff happening. Gang fights. People selling drugs. Someone trying to steal your stuff. Around here, people are committing crimes or trying not to be the victim of one."

She rose from her chair and stepped closer. "What you say may be true, but know this: your current circumstances don't have to define your future."

"What does *that* mean?"

"It means that with determination and hard work, you can do almost anything. The key is working hard to make it happen."

"How do I do that?"

"You start by dreaming bigger. If your only goal is to survive, that's all you'll achieve. Education is also important. The more you learn, the more doors will open for you. Focus on school and let your imagination soar. OK?"

I nodded.

The sound of the bell signaled the end of the day. I stepped outside and squinted. The bright sun was a stark contrast to the gray hue of the fluorescent lights. I began walking toward the bus stop.

Dream bigger and focus on school. The school part is straightforward because I love learning. But what did she mean by letting my mind soar? Could I really have a better life? Lost in thought, I hadn't noticed the male figure.

"Where you going, lil momma? You wanna hit this?" The foul smell of marijuana smoke invaded my nose as I turned to see an older man with wild eyes emerge from a nearby alley.

Damn it! Why didn't I wait a little longer to leave? I scolded myself. Leaving school too early meant waiting for the bus, and waiting alone on any corner in the city was never safe.

"Leave me alone!"

"Leave you alone? I ain't even begun messing with you yet."

I walked faster, but the sound of shuffling feet was getting closer, and the bus was nowhere in sight.

"Where are you going so fast? I'm trying to talk to you," he slurred.

My eyes frantically searched the ground for anything I could use as a weapon. The sun glinted on a piece of glass, a beer bottle. Two quick strides, and the bottle was in my hand.

"What you think you gon' do with that bottle, bitch?"

I gripped the strap of my backpack with my left hand and the neck of the beer bottle with my right. I turned toward him and raised the bottle. His dark eyes widened in surprise. I balanced my weight evenly on my legs and prepared to hurl the bottle in his direction.

The sharp squeak of brakes broke through the tension. I turned and saw the bus coming to a stop behind me. The doors swung open, and I dropped my hand, letting the bottle fall as I turned and walked onto the bus. My hands trembled as I fumbled for my bus pass. I took the seat closest to the driver and looked out the window. The menacing-looking man was stumbling away, growing smaller as the bus moved forward. I closed my eyes and let out a heavy sigh, releasing the breath I hadn't realized I'd been holding.

When I finally got home, I slipped through the front door and took the stairs two at a time to get to my room. I fell on the bed and tried to force my shoulders to relax, but the tension remained. I feared more than just the streets. Fear followed me home, always present and inescapable. I lived with the fear of my older brother's abuse; I worried that my mother's shifting sense of morality would land her in jail; and most of all, I feared being trapped in an endless cycle of poverty and chaos.

"My teacher is right, I need to dream bigger," I said. "I deserve more than a life filled with violence in the streets and dysfunction at home. To survive, I have to become more, do more, and want more."

The tension eased as a tear slowly slid down my cheek. The tear wasn't a sign of sorrow, but a quiet testament to the realization that I deserved better.

"*I will not fail.*" My voice cracked.

"*I will not fail.*" The determination rose within me.

"*I will not fail.*" My resolve strengthened.

The door slammed against the wall, startling me. My mother was standing in the doorway, staring at me.

"What's going on in here, and who are you talking to?"

"I'm not talking to anyone."

"I heard you talking."

"I was talking to myself."

"What were you saying?"

"Nothing."

"You were saying something."

"I was trying to memorize something."

She looked at me with a long stare, her eyes searching for cracks in my story.

"Get up and come and go to the grocery store with me."

"OK," I said, and jumped to my feet to follow her out of the room.

Chapter 3

The time is always right to do what is right.

—Martin Luther King Jr.

I sat in the car, waiting for my mother. It felt strange that she had asked me to go to the store with her, only to leave me waiting outside. Still, I didn't mind. I welcomed the quiet solitude.

My thoughts drifted as I waited. Why hadn't I shared my plans with my mother when she'd asked what I was saying? Maybe it was fear of her reaction. She would have likely dismissed my ideas, pointing out the pitfalls and obstacles I'd face. Maybe she would've been right, but my newfound hope was too fragile to endure her scrutiny. I needed to hold on to the belief that the future I wanted was possible.

My mother was beautiful. Her almond-shaped eyes, golden brown skin, and voluptuous figure were breathtaking. She was intelligent too, her mind sharp and curious. However, she was also a whirlwind of extremes. For instance, her strength often seemed unbreakable, yet there were moments when a hidden fragility surfaced. Similar to the time my grandmother had reprimanded her for refusing to eat pork.

"Ma, is there pork in those greens?" my mother had asked cautiously. Dinner at my grandmother's house was always tense. She openly disapproved of my mother's religious beliefs and refused to adapt her cooking to accommodate them.

"Pork? Child, they're greens, and there's nothing in them you haven't eaten before."

"I know, Ma, but you know I don't eat pork."

"I know you grew up eating pork, and now you're too good for the food I cook."

"That's not it. I just can't go against my faith."

The spoon in my grandmother's hand came down hard on the counter.

"You'll eat the food I cooked, or you can take your kids and leave my house!"

Startled, my mother took a step back before leaning toward me and whispering, "Don't eat the meat, just pick it out."

There were also moments of tenderness, like the time she sewed a version of the latest fashion trend so I would have something nice to wear to school.

As an avid believer, she read her Bible daily, fraying the pages. However, her moral compass didn't always point true, as she sometimes adjusted her definition of right to justify her inconsistent actions.

"Ema, doesn't the Bible say you're not supposed to steal?" I'd once asked her.

"It isn't stealing if you're taking something that is owed to you."

Her love of learning was contagious. She cultivated my hunger for knowledge through countless games of chess, where she and I battled in strategy and will. She patiently taught me the game, never once taking it easy on me.

"Are you sure that's the move you want to make?" she once said as she raised her eyebrows in mock curiosity.

"I'm not falling for your tricks," I replied. But I still hesitated, lifting my hand from the knight I was about to move and instead moving the bishop—a decision that had paid off.

There were also many not-so-fun moments when …

"Stop, thief!"

A sudden commotion grabbed my attention.

I turned toward the sound and froze as I saw my mother frantically running toward the car. Her arms clutched something tightly to her chest, and she had a panicked look on her face. Just a few feet behind her, a man was in fast pursuit, his fist waving in the air.

"Open the door, Shoshanna!" I heard her say.

I stared at the chaotic scene, trying to put the pieces together. *Why had he yelled, "Stop, thief?"*

"Open the damn door," she huffed out breathlessly.

I remained still, my limbs refusing to move. I could hear heavy boots pounding the ground as the man closed in. He was going to catch her. Cans and a loaf of bread tumbled from her arms to the pavement. *Why was she running with food in her arms?*

The car door swung open, and she dove in, tossing the remaining groceries into the passenger seat. Her hands gripped the steering wheel tightly as she slammed the gearshift into place.

"Ema!" I yelled.

The man was standing directly in front of the car. She pressed the accelerator anyway. The car jolted forward, slamming me back into the seat as the seat belt bit sharply into my shoulder. Barely able to move, I strained to peek through the back window, where I saw the man scrambling to his feet, fury etched across his face.

"Why did you do that? You almost hit him!"

"Why didn't you open the damn door?"

"I didn't know what was happening. Besides, you were in the car before I could get to it."

"What if he had caught me?"

"Why was he chasing you? What did you do?"

"I didn't do shit. And you should have opened the door like I told you to."

"I couldn't reach it in time," I said, my voice trembling.

"I'll see how fast you can move when we get home." Her words carried an unspoken promise of punishment.

My body stiffened. What had I done to deserve to be punished? She was the one who appeared to have been stealing. I sighed and looked out the window, silently praying that she would calm down before we got home.

Chapter 4

What matters in life is not what happens to you
but what you remember and how you remember it.

—Gabriel García Márquez

My earliest memories are from when I was around seven years old. No matter how hard I try, I can't remember anything prior to that. When I look at earlier photographs, I see myself in them, but they don't look familiar. One thing that stands out to me about those pictures is that I am never smiling. My expression is an emotionless, blank stare.

One of the most vivid memories is of an incident that happened when I was in third grade. I accidentally bumped into another student during a fire drill, and my teacher, Mrs. Graves, began yelling at me.

"What did you do?!"

I stared up at Mrs. Graves, paralyzed with fear. When I didn't respond, she slapped me across my face, the sting of the blow burning my cheek. But before I could react, she grabbed my arm, dragged me across the room, and shoved me to the floor. The last thing I saw before my vision blurred with tears was the cold, hard look on her face—her lips curled into a sneer—just before spit landed on my cheek. A stunned silence filled the room as my classmates watched in disbelief. Paddling was common, but striking a child and spitting on them? That was unheard of. Heat flooded my face, a mix of humiliation and grief.

When class ended, Mrs. Graves called me to her desk. My legs felt heavy as I hesitantly made my way to the front of the room. She grabbed my hand and shoved a crumpled piece of paper into my palm.

"Give this to your parents and have one of them sign it. Don't come back to school until you do," she said, her voice flat.

A note? As if the humiliation hadn't been enough, now I had to explain everything to my parents?

I clutched the paper in my hand as I walked home, my mind racing. Why had she treated me that way over an accident? Then I remembered the note. *Oh my gosh ... what am I going to tell Ema? How could I have been so clumsy?*

I saw the front door to my house and cringed. When I walked inside, I saw Betsy, my older sister, sitting on the couch. I handed her the note.

"What is this?"

"It's a note that I have to get signed and take back to school."

"I can see that it's a note, but why do you have to get a note signed? What did you do?"

"I didn't do anything. Will you sign it for me?"

"Why should I sign it for you? Besides, it says it has to be signed by a parent."

"You sign your school notes all the time," I said. "Can you just sign this one for me?"

"Tell me what happened, and I'll decide whether I'll sign it."

I told Betsy what had happened. "I accidentally fell into another student. The teacher accused me of shoving her down, and then she slapped me."

"Your teacher slapped you?!"

"Stop yelling. Ema will hear you. It was my fault. I shouldn't have been so clumsy. Will you sign the note?"

"No. Ema needs to know about this." Betsy took off running with the note in her hand, and it wasn't long before I heard my mother approaching.

"Shoshanna. What is Betsy talking about? Did someone slap you?"

"Yes. My teacher did. I accidentally fell into a girl, and Mrs. Graves thought I shoved her on purpose."

"I don't give a damn if you did it on purpose or not. She is not allowed to slap you."

"I didn't do it on purpose. It was an accident."

"I said I don't care. Tell me exactly what happened."

I repeated the same thing I had told Betsy. "I accidentally fell into another student. The teacher accused me of shoving her down, and then she slapped me."

"There is no way a teacher would do that. Stop lying!"

My mother was furious. One thing that angered her faster than anything else was being blindsided because she had partial or incorrect information. Because of that, she wanted to make sure I was telling her everything.

"I'm telling you the truth," I pleaded.

"I'll tell you one last time. Stop lying!"

I didn't know what else to say, so I said nothing.

My mother pulled me down to the couch and sat next to me. She still looked angry, but her voice was soft.

"Shoshanna, if you tell me the truth right now, I won't be mad."

Staring at my feet, I said, "I'm telling the truth."

"OK, maybe you're not lying. Maybe you're just exaggerating so you won't get in trouble."

I thought for a moment, replaying the events in my mind. "I'm not exaggerating."

"OK, then," she said. "I am going to go up to your school tomorrow to talk with Mrs. Graves. If she confirms that what you said is true, I'll deal with her. But if her story is different, I'm going to beat your ass right there. Do you understand?"

Horror swept over my face. Maybe I shouldn't have told her about Mrs. Graves slapping me. At least then, the slap would have been the worst of it. Getting a beating at school would be an unprecedented level of humiliation.

I nodded.

"Go to your room. We'll deal with this tomorrow."

The tension in her voice told me she was still skeptical, but she was no longer yelling, which meant she hadn't dismissed the possibility that my story might be true.

The next day, my mother walked me to school. She held my hand as we walked. We made small talk and laughed along the way, so I felt hopeful that things would be OK. Even if Mrs. Graves didn't admit everything, maybe my mother would reconsider beating me. That thought made me smile, and I squeezed my mother's hand a little tighter.

"Come on, Shoshanna. Let's make the light."

We jogged across the street and went inside the building. We walked into the office and approached the secretary's desk.

"Hello. How may I help you?" the secretary asked warmly. She did not know the mission my mother was on. One that was certain to make her day, week, or even her year very memorable.

"I would like to speak with Mrs. Graves," my mother responded.

"Mrs. Graves is in class."

"Is it possible for her to briefly step out? She reprimanded Shoshanna yesterday, and I want to know what happened."

"Oh, OK. I'll call Mrs. Graves and see if she can step out of class to briefly meet with you." The secretary called Mrs. Graves over the intercom and explained the situation.

My mother and I took a couple of seats and waited. It wasn't long before Mrs. Graves walked into the office.

"Who's looking for me, Ms. Johnson?"

My mother rose to her feet.

"I am," she said. "I'm Mrs. Perry, Shoshanna's mother."

"Whose mother?"

"Shoshanna's."

"I don't have a student by that name." Her tone was sharp with impatience.

"Her!" my mother said as she stepped aside so Mrs. Graves could see me.

"*Oh*, her. Yes, I know that little girl. She did a very naughty thing yesterday. She shoved another student down during a fire drill."

"Did you see her shove the other student?"

"No, but she was standing right behind the girl when she fell down."

"Did you ask her what happened?"

"The situation was straightforward."

"What happened after you determined the situation was straightforward?"

"I did what any other teacher would do. I disciplined her."

"How did you discipline my child?" my mother asked through clenched teeth.

Staring at my mother, I noticed something Mrs. Graves and the secretary had not. She had sat her purse down and was slowly removing her gloves. *This is bad ... this is very bad,* I thought. I slowly stood up and began moving to the other side of the room. Whatever was about to happen, I wanted to be as far away from it as possible.

"I slapped her face and shoved her to the floor, where undisciplined children belong," Mrs. Graves said.

My mother's eyes widened as she put her hands over her mouth and gasped.

"I admit, spitting in her face may have been excessive, but I was just so furious."

"You mean to tell me that what she said is true? And you spit in her face?!"

"I don't know what she told you, but it happened just as I've said."

Everything seemed to move in slow motion, yet it all happened so fast. My mother's hands balled into fists, and before anyone could react, she reared back and punched Mrs. Graves in the face.

"Don't you ever put your hands on my child!"

Several office workers grabbed my mother and restrained her. Mrs. Graves scrambled to her feet.

"How dare you hit me! You are going to pay for this. Call the police. I want her arrested!"

The secretary called the police. When she hung up the receiver, my mother quickly grabbed the phone.

"That phone is for office use only, Mrs. Perry."

"I need to call my husband. I'll only be a minute," she said, and dialed the number to our house.

When my father answered, her words tumbled out in a rapid stream. "Hurry and come to the school. The police were called on me, and I might get arrested."

We stood outside in front of the school, waiting for my father. It wasn't long before I saw him running toward us. He stopped in front of my mother.

"What happened?"

"That teacher said she slapped Shoshanna."

"She admitted that to you?"

"Yes. She also admitted shoving her to the ground and spitting on her, so I knocked the shit out of her."

"Ethiah! That was not the best way to handle this," he said.

He looked at me. "Are you OK?" I nodded.

He turned his attention back to my mother. "Did anyone else hear her admit those things?"

"Yes. The secretary heard everything, and she still had the nerve to call the police on me!"

"Of course she called the police. You hit a teacher. Stay out here while I go speak with them."

My dad stooped down so that he was at my level. "Are you sure you're OK, Noonie?" he asked, using the nickname he called me.

"Yeah, I'm OK, Abba," I mumbled.

He gave me a hug before heading inside.

I heard the blare of sirens before three police cars stopped in front of the building. The officers went inside and weren't in there long before two of them came outside and handcuffed my mother.

"You are under arrest for assault," one officer told her.

My dad came outside and grabbed my hand before turning to the officer. "Like I told you in there, if you arrest my wife, I want the teacher arrested as well. She admitted to slapping my daughter and spitting on her. I fully intend to press charges against her and take legal action against the school district."

The officer placed my mother in the back of the car.

"This ain't right. I want that teacher arrested! Why am I the only one being arrested?" my mother protested.

My father, the other officers, and I went back inside the school. With his usual diplomacy—which I found very impressive—my father reiterated the shared culpability in the situation, and after hearing his reasoning, the school agreed not to press charges if my parents agreed not to press charges either. My father agreed, and the officers released my mother. The school had one additional stipulation: neither my mother nor her children could ever return to the school.

When I learned that the school had expelled me, I was furious. I was grateful my mother had stood up for me, but she had reacted to the situation the way she reacted to everything—impulsively, without regard for the consequences.

I heard Mrs. Graves had faced no consequences. My mother became a neighborhood hero for confronting a racist teacher. And me? Although I had done nothing wrong, the school expelled me anyway, leaving me to bear the consequences of everyone else's actions ... alone.

Chapter 5

> When we are no longer able to change a situation,
> we are challenged to change ourselves.
>
> —Viktor E. Frankl

It was finally summer break, which meant long, boring days at home. Although, following the incident at the school, I had already been home for weeks.

"What are you doing with that lighter?" I asked Cain, the oldest of my mother's six children.

Cain was much older, so he frequently babysat the younger siblings, including me. He and Betsy had a different father than the rest of us, something I believe he resented.

"I'm playing with it. Mind your own business." His tone was sharp.

Curiosity held me in place as I watched Cain flick the lighter over and over. It was one of those cheap plastic lighters with a metal roller wheel you had to press with your thumb to ignite. Once lit, you held down a lever to keep the flame alive.

Cain stared intently at the flickering flame, his eyes showing a strange intensity. He kept flicking the lighter, letting the flame dance, and then extinguishing it when the metal roller grew too hot for his thumb. Each time, his thumb jerked away from the burning metal, but he'd wait a few seconds and start again.

He flicked the lighter again, and this time, when the heat from the metal burned his thumb, he pressed the lighter to my bare leg.

I screamed as intense pain shot through me. "Aaaah!" Desperate for relief, I tried to wrestle his hand away, but his strength overpowered me. "Please stop!" I pleaded as the pain deepened.

The smell of burning flesh invaded my nostrils, and my vision blurred. He wrapped his free hand around my head and pressed it tightly over my mouth. His hand instantly silenced my screams. I felt the heat of his breath against my ear as he growled, "If you tell anyone, I'm going to kill you." The sound of his voice was pure evil.

I continued to squirm, and when he finally released me, I scrambled to get away. My knees buckled, and I began crawling toward the door. I didn't get far before he jerked me to my feet.

He stared at me with cold, dark eyes, his mouth twisted into a cruel grin. "What are you going to do, go crying to your daddy? He's not here, and if you try to tell Ema, I'll tell her you were playing and burned yourself."

"Let me go!"

"I'll let you go when I'm ready to let you go. Go put on some pants," he ordered.

"I can't. Pants will make my leg hurt worse."

"Do you want me to burn you again?" The cruelness in his tone was unsettling.

I limped to the closet and grabbed a pair of pants. I waited for Cain to look away and allow me to change privately, but he continued to stare. *He's going to watch me change?* I thought, as a wave of shame washed over me. My hands trembled as I slipped off my shorts. I dragged the pants over my legs, the fabric scraping against the burn. I winced in pain, and Cain laughed. The pain was intense, but I wanted to get out of that room as fast as I could, so I continued. I held my breath to block out the pain and carefully slid the pants up to my waist. I fastened the button and looked up at Cain.

"Now you can leave," he said.

I hurried out of the room with my leg throbbing and tears covering my face. As I stumbled down the hall, I heard Cain's voice behind me. "Remember what I said. You better not tell anybody."

My mother was downstairs entertaining friends, and despite my brother's warning, I wanted her to know what he'd done. Limping, I held on to the wall for support as I made my way into the room where my mother was. I leaned against her chair and coughed as the smoke filling the room burned my throat. I let out a soft moan, hoping to get her attention. The pounding music drowned out the sound, so I tried again.

"Ow, my leg hurts," I said near her ear.

Nothing.

I moaned again, this time louder. Still no response. So, finally, I reached out and tugged her arm.

"Ema," I said, my voice cracking.

She turned toward me, and instead of seeing a look of concern on her face, I saw her narrow her eyes and press her lips into a hard line. Was she angry?

"Why are you in here? Didn't I tell you to stay out of this room?" she asked, her voice sharp.

"I'm sorry," I said. "I just wanted to tell you something."

"Can't you see I'm busy? Go back upstairs!"

"I don't want to go back upstairs. My leg hurts."

"I said take your ass upstairs … now!" she said, jabbing her finger toward the door, her tone leaving no room for argument.

She didn't ask me what I had wanted to tell her or why my leg was hurting. How could she not see that I needed her? The sour taste of betrayal made me feel sick to my stomach. As I limped out of the room, I glanced over my shoulder. She had already turned her attention back to her guests, laughing as if I'd never been there. To her, my appearance was nothing more than an unwanted interruption that she quickly forgot.

The hallway felt longer than usual as I limped toward the bathroom. I pushed the door open and angrily rummaged through the cabinet, clinking bottles against each other. There was nothing to treat a burn—no ointment or disinfectant. Desperate for relief, I slowly removed my pants. The fabric stuck painfully to my skin, making me wince. I turned on the faucet in the tub, and cold water flowed out. I slid my leg under the stream. When the cold water hit the burn, I grimaced in pain. A blister was already forming, so I reached for the bar of Castile soap. I gently lathered the area around the wound, careful not to burst the blister. I rinsed away the suds and dabbed the area dry with a towel.

Instead of putting my pants back on, I wrapped the towel around my waist and tiptoed to my bedroom. The thought of encountering Cain sent a chill down my spine, so I crawled under my bed to hide. I curled into a ball on the floor of the dark space and wrapped my arms around myself in a tight hug. I cried until I fell asleep in the cold, lonely space.

There were many more instances of abuse involving Cain, like the times he dragged me out of bed in the middle of the night and took me to the coat closet beneath the stairs. While my innocence and self-worth were being stolen, I could hear the thumping sound of loud music and raucous laughter from a nearby room where my mother was partying with her friends.

After what would seem like an eternity, he would jerk me to my feet and send me back to my room, broken and battered. Cain's cruelty and my mother's indifference to it taught me a harsh lesson: I couldn't rely on anyone to protect me. If I wanted safety, if I wanted freedom, I would have to create it for myself—and that's exactly what I planned to do.

As I got older, I dreamed of a life beyond the city I grew up in. The world maps in the back of our family encyclopedias showed me how much there was to explore. Reading stories about successful Black women in *Jet* and *Ebony* magazines showed me that being successful was possible. I saw the world as a big place with a lot to offer, and I wanted to experience it. So, while my siblings dreamed of getting the latest toy or gadget, I dreamed of a life beyond the streets of Chicago. I dreamed of financial security and independence.

"Look at this car," I said, pointing to a glossy page in the magazine I was holding.

"That's nice," my brother Daniel said, barely looking up.

"I'm going to buy one someday," I said matter-of-factly.

"With what money?"

"With my money. I'm going to be rich someday."

Daniel shrugged and flipped through his own magazine.

"Check this out," he said, pointing to a picture of a race car set. "This is what I want."

"Wouldn't you rather save your money and buy a real car?"

"Nope. I just want this one."

"Well, I'm buying a house and an *actual* car," I said.

"That won't happen. You're just dreaming," he said, laughing.

For me, it wasn't a dream. I was going to make it happen. I read every book I could get my hands on, ranging from the dictionary (which helped me increase my vocabulary) to novels like *Jane Eyre* and *Little Women* about strong heroines that helped me find my inner strength. To learn strategic thinking and leadership, I read *The Prince* and *The Art of War*. I also read the Bible—the greatest how-to book ever written. I wanted to be prepared for anything and everything as I worked to build the life I wanted.

Chapter 6

Life isn't about finding yourself.
Life is about creating yourself.

—George Bernard Shaw

By the time I was a teenager, I was the child my mother expected to be responsible. I was supposed to make moral decisions and do the right thing. She never asked about my homework or school assignments because she just expected them to be done. My mother acknowledged my good grades, but she didn't overly celebrate them because she expected them. I was her independent, smart, and capable child.

My mother relied on me a lot, and truthfully, I embraced the extra responsibility. To me, it wasn't a burden—it was an opportunity. I saw each task as a chance to develop skills like communication, organization, and negotiation, skills I believed would shape me into the person I wanted to become. The tasks started off small, like asking me to cook dinner. With limited ingredients, I had to make something that would feed everyone.

Spaghetti quickly became my favorite go-to meal. It took little to make, and I enjoyed the process. The ground beef sizzled in the pan, its smell mingling with the sweet aroma of the sautéed onions. I'd stir in tomato paste, which transformed the mixture into a vibrant red hue. If we had mushrooms or bell peppers, I'd toss them in too, though they were a rare treat. Fresh garlic, however, was almost always on hand, and its bold flavor more than made up for the absence of other ingredients. A pinch of salt, a generous shake of oregano, and a dash of pepper brought the sauce to life. My favorite addition was my secret ingredient: a sprinkle of chili powder for an unexpected zing. Spaghetti was always a family favorite.

It wasn't long before my responsibilities grew to include tasks like reviewing bills to ensure they were accurate or figuring out and explaining to my mother why a bill was higher than usual.

"Shoshanna, why is the light bill so high?" she would ask.

"Probably because we used more electricity," I'd say, trying to sound reasonable.

"Do you want a pop in the mouth?"

"No."

"Then don't be smart."

"I wasn't being smart," I'd say, trying to hide my frustration that the threat of violence was always her reaction. "Logically, if the bill is higher, we must've used more electricity than last month."

"Don't guess. Go through all the bills for the last three months and figure out why it's suddenly higher. You can find them in the shoebox on my dresser."

And so, every month, I'd sift through all the bills, scrutinizing the numbers and delivering a report to my mother. It became routine, and though I didn't always enjoy it, I learned how to track patterns, catch discrepancies, and make sense of what the numbers meant.

When I was about fourteen, she handed me my biggest assignment yet. My mother had planned to spend the day running errands and paying bills, but an unexpected call from work had changed her plans. I was in my room enjoying a book when I heard her yell for me.

"Shoshanna!"

"Yes?"

No response.

Maybe she hadn't heard me, so I said it louder.

"Yes!"

Still no response.

Her silence was her way of saying, *I'm not going to yell for you again. Get up and come down here now, or else!*

I begrudgingly set my book aside and went to the kitchen, where I found her sitting at the table with stacks of papers in front of her and a distressed look on her face. I stood there, waiting.

She finally looked up. "Come over here and sit down."

I joined her at the table and saw that the piles of papers were stacks of bills. *Oh, good,* I thought, *she just needs me to do a bit of comparative analysis. That won't take long, and then I can head back to my room and continue reading my book.* The only thing was that the distressed look on her face didn't align with my theory.

"What's wrong?" I asked.

"All the bills for the house are due, and I have been called in to work, so I can't go pay them."

"Just pay them tomorrow."

"I have to work tomorrow too. Besides, they are due today."

"Why did you wait until the last minute to pay them?" Quickly realizing that was the wrong thing to say, I adjusted my tone and asked, "What do you want me to do?"

"I need you to take care of them for me."

"Take care of them? What do you mean, take care of them? I don't have any money, and I don't know how to pay bills."

"I'll give you the money, and you will figure it out."

"Figure it out? How?"

"I said you'll figure it out."

Her tone left no room for debate. So, rather than complain about spending my day running errands or ask why my older brother (who was also home) couldn't do it, I simply said, "OK."

Before she left, I used the few minutes I had left to ask every question I could think of to fully understand what was expected of me.

"How will I know how much to pay?"

"Pay the minimum amount due for each bill, unless you can work out a deal to pay less."

"What kind of deal?"

"Sometimes, if you explain you can't pay the minimum balance due, they'll allow you to pay less."

"How do I get them to do that?"

"Meet with a customer service representative and negotiate a payment plan."

"What bill should I pay first?"

"I don't care," she said, already moving toward the door. "Just make sure you take care of all of them before the offices close. Map out your bus route to hit each stop on time and stretch your bus fare."

"What should I do if they won't help me because I'm a kid?"

"Make them."

"Make them? How am I supposed to—"

"I have to go," she interrupted, cutting me off mid-sentence.

We'd had less than fifteen minutes of rushed conversation before she left me alone to figure it all out. She handed me a stack of bills, an envelope full of cash, a city map, and enough money for one bus transfer with two dollars remaining for lunch.

"What should I do if I have questions?"

"You'll figure it out. And don't screw up your bus route, because if you mess up, it will cost extra fare, and there won't be enough money for the bills. Also, make sure you understand the payment terms, and get them to take the least amount of money possible to prevent our utilities from being turned off. I have to go."

This was the first time that I realized how stretched things were for her. I had figured that, since she worked, she had been paying the bills, and we were fine. But her words—"Get them to take the least amount of money possible to prevent our utilities from being turned off"—gave me a different perspective. If I failed, we could lose electricity, or the phone, or water. This new perspective overshadowed any fear that I had because I knew I couldn't fail, so I was determined not to.

"OK," I said, "I got it."

She grabbed her car keys and headed out the door. Before she was out of shouting range, she looked over her shoulder and yelled, "Wear something nice! If you look like a professional, they will treat you like one." And then she was gone.

I sat at the table for the next hour, mapping out the most efficient route that would maximize my time and not cause me to go over my budget for the bus fare and my lunch. When I finished, I had just completed what would be the first of many strategic planning sessions in my life. I now knew the best order to travel, I'd rehearsed what I would say at each stop, I knew precisely how long each stop could take while still allowing me to remain on schedule, and most importantly, I had visibility to all the bills, so I knew the most I could commit to paying in each case without sacrificing other bills.

After my planning session, I went upstairs to put on the closest thing I had to professional-looking clothes. Because I was a teenager with few occasions to dress professionally, I had limited options. I pulled on a navy-blue pencil skirt and paired it with a black T-shirt and a cropped jacket. A pair of black flats finished the look. I counted and recounted the money and then tucked it and all the bills in my bag.

As I walked to the bus stop, my nerves started getting the better of me. I felt like everyone I passed was staring at me. It was like they somehow knew I had a bag full of cash, and they were waiting for the right moment to snatch it and run. My legs were shaking, and my heart was beating in my chest like a drum. *Why does she think I can do this? I'm just a kid, not a grown-up. I should be reading a book or playing outside with my friends.* It had all seemed so easy when I had been sitting at the kitchen table. But now, it was real, and if I messed up, the whole family would suffer. *Breathe ... You can do this*, I coached myself. *Just look straight ahead and keep walking.*

The pounding in my chest slowed and my legs moved easier. The bus stopped in front of me, and when the doors opened, I took a deep breath and climbed the stairs.

"Good morning," I said, greeting the driver as I carefully counted out the bills for my fare.

"Good morning."

"Are you having a good day?"

"So far, so good," he said with a nod.

I paid my fare, and he gave me my transfer.

"Here you go."

"Thank you." I secured my bag and turned to find a seat.

"Have a great day, ma'am," he called after me.

Ma'am? Did he think I was a grown-up? A confident smile spread across my face as I took my seat. Maybe I was ready for this after all.

My first stop was the rental office. I walked inside and handed the lady at the counter my payment slip, along with the correct number of bills.

"Would you like a receipt?" she asked.

"Yes, please."

I inspected the receipt she handed me, thanked her, and left. The transaction had gone easier than I'd expected. She hadn't even asked where my mother was or questioned why I was by myself. I couldn't help but smile. I was off to a strong start.

The next several interactions were going to be tricky because I did not have the full payment, which meant I'd need to negotiate payment arrangements. I stepped onto the bus and sat in front, close to the driver. I told him where I was going, and he confirmed the stop I needed to take and the direction I should walk to reach my destination. After having paid the rent, the weight of the cash in my bag felt considerably lighter, but I still clutched the bag tightly to my chest.

I got off the bus at the specified stop and walked toward the utility company. The minimum amount due was fifty dollars, but the most I could pay was thirty-five dollars. I felt butterflies in my stomach. *Is my mom right? Will they actually agree to a payment arrangement? What will I do if they say no? Or worse, what if they refuse to speak with me?*

I pushed the large, heavy doors open and stepped inside the lobby. I was looking for a check-in desk or a customer service sign when a well-dressed woman approached me.

"Hello. How may I help you?"

I looked at her matching two-piece suit and immediately wished that I'd had on something as nice.

"I'm here to pay a utility bill," I said.

"OK, right this way."

She led me to a bullpen with several desks separated by a small partition. We approached a desk with an empty chair beside it.

"This is Leslie. She will help you."

As the lady walked away, Leslie greeted me. "How may I help you?"

"Hi, Leslie. I'm here to pay a bill."

"Do you have a copy of the bill with you?"

"Yes, I do," I said, and I gave her the bill.

"It looks like you owe fifty dollars today."

"That's right, but I don't have that much to pay today. I hope I can pay something toward the balance today and make payment arrangements for the rest," I said.

"How much can you pay today?"

"What's the minimum I can pay to prevent the service from being turned off?"

She clicked on her keyboard. "If you pay thirty dollars today and agree to pay the remaining twenty dollars in two weeks, we will not disconnect the service."

I had enough money to pay that amount, but I was feeling empowered, so I made a counterproposal. "Thank you so much. It is very kind of you to help me. Is it possible for me to pay twenty dollars instead and pay the balance in two weeks?"

"I'm sorry, but we usually like to collect at least half the amount due."

"Oh, I understand," I said. "If the power is disconnected, what will it take to get it turned back on?"

"Look, I want to help you. Can you at least pay twenty-five dollars today?"

"Yes. I can pay twenty-five dollars today," I said enthusiastically.

"OK, pay twenty-five dollars today and the rest in two weeks, and we won't disconnect your service."

"Thank you so much, Leslie! I really appreciate your help."

I counted out the bills while she logged the details of our arrangement into her system. I handed the money to her, and in return, she handed me a receipt and a printout of the agreed payment terms.

As I stood to leave, she smiled and said, "Have a great day."

"You too, Leslie," I said, returning her smile.

Stepping onto the street, I felt ten feet tall. I'd done it! I'd negotiated better payment terms than expected and stayed within budget. My heart raced with excitement—the feeling of success was exhilarating. She'd treated me like every other customer who was there that day. She never asked my age or where my parents were, and she didn't treat me like a child. We interacted like two professionals conducting business, and it felt great! The rest of the day proceeded in the same manner: greet, discuss payment, agree on terms, exchange cash, and get a receipt.

By the time I walked in the door at home, I was both exhausted and energized. I had gone into the world and conducted business on my own, completing all the transactions correctly. I had receipts, detailed notes of each agreement, and the correct amount of cash left over. While waiting for my mother, I sat at the table and reviewed my notes. I was counting the remaining cash again when I heard the door open. Before my mother was fully inside, I began telling her about my day.

"Ema, I did it!"

She dropped her bag onto the table and slumped into a chair. Her face was heavy with exhaustion.

"Look," I said, "I have everything right here. And guess what? I even have money left over."

"That's good," she said, her tone flat.

The weariness in her voice stopped me, and I looked up at her face. "What's wrong?"

"I've had a long day, and I'm tired," she said with a sigh.

"Don't you want to hear about the bills?" The excitement in my voice faded into disappointment.

"Of course I do, but I already know you did everything perfectly."

"How do you know that?"

"Because you always do."

I knew her words had been meant as a compliment and that I should be happy. But, somehow, her comment made my accomplishment feel small. Maybe it wasn't as big of an accomplishment as I thought. As if sensing my disappointment, she moved her chair closer to mine and leaned toward me.

"I asked you to do this because I know you are the only one who can do it. No one else in this family can do what you did today. I knew you would do well, and I can't wait to hear all about it," she said.

Her words settled over me like a warm embrace, and I launched into a detailed explanation of my day. She listened attentively as I explained how much I'd paid at each stop and the payment terms I'd negotiated. I handed her the receipts, the remaining cash, and a stack of neatly organized printouts of the agreements with the names of the people I'd spoken with at each location, just in case any issues came up later.

When I finally finished my update, she reached across the table and squeezed my hand. "Good job. I knew you could do it."

From that day on, I was my mother's go-to person for taking care of important business. As time went on, she provided fewer and fewer instructions. Eventually, she started just leaving the stack of bills and money on my dresser. I did everything from paying bills to making bank deposits and withdrawals, and the more I did these things, the more I learned the language of business. To better interact with the people I met, I adjusted my mannerisms and speech to match theirs.

Instead of using "Mr." or "Ms." as children were expected to, I addressed them by their first names. To sound more mature, I started introducing myself as Shonna instead of Shoshanna. I learned how to make small talk and asked about their day or their family (if they had pictures on their desk) as I waited for them to complete my transaction. I was getting an immersive education on how to navigate the business world, and I was enjoying every minute.

Being the *chosen* one had benefits, like traveling around the city and conducting business like an adult, but it also had drawbacks. I was still a kid, but I had to act like an adult, which made relating to my siblings increasingly difficult. My mother grew to rely on me so much that she failed to groom anyone else to step in and take over. I always planned to leave home someday, but my mother didn't think I would. After all, no one left home. They might move out for a while, but inevitably, they would come back and either move in with her or somewhere nearby. But that wasn't my plan.

One day, while I was going over some tasks with my mother, I asked about her plans.

"Who's going to do this when I move out?"

"You're not moving out," she said, tilting her head slightly in confusion.

"Yes, I am. Eventually, I'm going to move out, and I'm never moving back." I didn't say those words to hurt my mother, but they were true.

"No, you are not!" Her sharp tone meant the conversation was over.

The conversation may have been over, but my plans weren't changing. I was leaving. I knew it, and deep down, I think she did, too.

Chapter 7

A bend in the road is not the end of the road …
unless you fail to make the turn.

—Helen Keller

I began preparing to join the military when I was seventeen years old. Military history had always fascinated me, and I especially loved studying war strategy. I watched documentaries and movies about World War II, captivated by the intricate details of military planning and the execution of various campaigns. I was most intrigued by the paratroopers of the 82nd Airborne Division. They were so extraordinary that I became obsessed with joining their ranks. I didn't know if it was possible for someone like me to join the 82nd Airborne. In the movies I'd watched, there were no women or people of color among the paratroopers, but that didn't mean there couldn't be.

I'd told my mother that I wanted to join the army and become a paratrooper, but she had never taken me seriously. She'd dismissed the idea, convinced it was just a childish obsession with the army uniform and the prestige of the 82nd Airborne. Becoming a paratrooper wasn't just about the uniform or the prestige. It was about becoming the person I wanted to be. The training would strengthen me and build the fortitude I needed to face whatever life threw my way. The military would also be my way out. It would provide me with room, board, and an income—everything I needed to start a life on my own. And once my time in the army was over, I would have learned valuable skills and would continue my education with military benefits. Joining the 82nd Airborne Division wasn't just a dream; it was the crucial first step toward creating the life I wanted.

Excited to move forward, I visited my local army recruiting office, and a recruiter greeted me.

"Hello. How may I help you?" he asked as he walked toward me.

"I would like to join the 82nd Airborne Division."

"How old are you?" he inquired with a laugh.

"I'm seventeen."

"Why do you want to join the 82nd Airborne Division?"

"Why wouldn't I? They are the best in the world," I said enthusiastically.

He laughed again, louder this time. "Well, it's not that simple. If you want to join the army, I can help you with that, but you can't go to the 82nd Airborne Division."

"Why not?"

"It is extremely difficult to get in, and most people get rejected. I'd guess less than 10 percent of the people who try actually get in. Plus, you're a girl."

He walked back to his desk and began flipping through papers.

"Excuse me … I have a few more questions," I said.

"What is it?" He did not mask his irritation.

"Are girls allowed to join the 82nd Airborne Division?"

He looked up from his papers. "Technically, yes, but very few soldiers actually get in, and none of them are little girls."

Ignoring his snide comment, I asked, "So are girls allowed in, then?"

"Yes, but I don't have time to waste on a little girl's fantasy."

I was losing patience, but I wanted answers, and I would make him do his job, so I persisted. "What do I have to do to get in?"

"Well … first, you have to actually join the army. From there, you can request to go to airborne school, but acceptance isn't guaranteed. And even if accepted, you're unlikely to actually graduate. And if you don't graduate airborne school, you will still be in the army, but you will not go to the 82nd Airborne Division."

I contemplated his words for a moment and then said, "OK, I'd like to sign up."

His eyes widened as if he couldn't quite believe what he'd just heard. Once he realized I was serious and noticed that I wasn't speaking or acting like a silly little girl, his tone changed. He began treating me courteously and with respect.

Over the next several hours, the sergeant explained the entire process to me, including the Armed Services Vocational Aptitude Battery (ASVAB), the process for the entrance physical exam, and the requirement for my mother's permission since I was only seventeen years old.

I filled out the paperwork, and he scheduled a time for me to take the ASVAB, a test that measures one's abilities and helps predict academic and occupational success in the military. Doing well on the exam was important because it would determine my job options. As I understood it, to be assigned to Fort Bragg (where the 82nd was headquartered), after successfully completing airborne school, I had to be accepted into a job category the 82nd needed. He also gave me the information I needed to schedule my physical exam. He told me that, after they received my scores from the ASVAB, we could talk about job options and explore the possibility of me going to airborne school and eventually to the 82nd Airborne Division.

I wrote down everything he said, including all the various dates, and I took a copy of the paperwork that my mother needed to sign. My heart raced with excitement. Not only were women allowed to be paratroopers in the 82nd Airborne Division, but there was also a genuine possibility that I would become one.

I had not discussed my military aspirations with my mother in a while, and I had not told her of my plans to visit a recruiting center. I didn't think it was necessary to tell her because I assumed it was my decision. Besides, I managed myself, so I didn't think I needed her permission. I had already told her of my plans to leave one day, so I didn't expect the news to surprise her. I could not have been more wrong!

When my mother got home, I met her at the door. "Guess what, Ema. I have the most exciting news."

"What is it?" she asked matter-of-factly.

"I visited an army recruiting station today, and I'm joining the army."

"You did what?"

In my excitement, I missed the sharp edge in her voice, so I kept talking. "Yep, and not only am I joining the army, but I'm also going to be a paratrooper with the 82nd Airborne Division. Well, at least, I plan to. I'm going to sign up for the army first and then take it from there, but joining the 82nd is my goal. I have all the information, and I also have some papers for you to sign. Can you believe it? I'm going to be a paratrooper."

"You're going to be a what?!"

"A paratrooper ... you know, the soldiers who jump out of airplanes into combat."

"You're not doing a damn thing. Who in the hell gave you permission to go to a recruiting station?"

Her response surprised me. *Who gave me permission? Why do I need permission to plan my future?* I took a deep breath and said, "I didn't know I needed permission to make decisions about my life. I've already filled out the papers, and I'm scheduled to take the test."

"*What test?*" she replied.

My mother was beyond angry. She faced me with her hands on her hips. I was certain she was going to hit me. I stood my ground anyway.

"The army entrance test. I take it in two weeks. After that, I take my physical and then fill out the rest of the paperwork."

"You are not taking a test, and you are *not* joining the army. *Go to your room now!*" she yelled.

When my mother encountered resistance, she resorted to threats and bullying to impose her will. She'd scream and maybe even hit me to get me to see things her way. Faced with those potential responses, there was no use for me to continue pleading my case, so I went to my room without saying another word. I didn't understand why she was so angry, but I fully intended to take that test and continue the process. There was nothing she could do to stop me ... or so I thought. That's when I remembered the paperwork that I needed her to sign. *Crap! She'll never sign that paperwork.*

The next morning, I called the recruiter and asked him what would happen if my mother refused to sign the paperwork giving me permission to join.

His response was short and clear. "You won't be able to enlist until after you turn eighteen."

It would be nearly a year before I'd turn eighteen, and I didn't want to wait that long. I had decided on my future, and I wanted to pursue it as soon as possible. I knew getting my mother to agree to sign the forms would be difficult, but I believed it was possible. All I needed to do was present a sound and logical case, and she would hopefully come around.

The next day, my father called and asked me to stop by his office. I always enjoyed visiting him at work, so I agreed. When I walked into the building, I took the stairs up to his office and found my dad sitting at his desk, looking over some papers.

"Hey, Abba," I said with a smile.

"Hey, Noon," he responded. "Come have a seat."

I sat next to his desk, my curiosity piqued. "Whatcha doing?" I asked, always interested in whatever he was working on.

"I'm just closing a sale," he replied.

My dad worked in sales, spending his days in a small office selling encyclopedias, the kind with red leather covers and glossy pages. He was good at it, often ranking as the top salesperson in the area.

He glanced at me, his tone light, almost amused. "So what's this I hear about you joining the army?"

"You heard?" My voice was full of energy. "I'm really excited, but I don't think Ema is going to sign the papers."

"Why do you want to join the army?" he asked, his tone steady.

"It's something I've always wanted to do. Plus, it's a way for me to start life on my own."

"Have you thought about joining the army but not jumping out of airplanes?"

"No, because that's what I want to do," I said, confused by his question.

He let out an exasperated sigh and set down the papers he was holding. "Look, Noon, being Black in the military is tough. And being a Black woman will make it even tougher. You're smart, and there are plenty of things you can do here in Chicago."

"Like what?" I felt disappointed that he wasn't being more supportive. He was a veteran himself, so I thought he would understand better than anyone.

"For starters, you can stay home a little longer and help your ema."

The wheels in my mind clicked into place. *Now I get it*, I thought. *She told him to convince me not to go.* The realization felt like a physical blow. Hurt quickly replaced the eagerness I'd felt in sharing my excitement with my dad. The person I'd expected to support me had chosen her side instead. He didn't care about my future any more than she did.

I soon discovered that my mother had made a plan of her own. She'd enlisted the help of my father and several others to talk to me. Their mission was to discourage me from joining the military and convince me that staying home was a much better alternative. They used guilt, fear, and several other tactics to help me see the error in my chosen path. In each case, I patiently listened as they explained that the military was no place for a female, jumping out of planes was too dangerous, and I was abandoning my mother when she needed me. My personal favorite was that I could be sent to war to fight for a country that had enslaved my people.

Meanwhile, continuing with my plan, I went to the courthouse and got a copy of my parents' divorce certificate, which I needed to verify that my mother was my legal guardian and could sign the papers. To expedite the process, I filled out the forms in advance, so the only thing she had to do was sign them. I even found a notary who was willing to visit our home to notarize her signature. I tried to make it as easy as possible for her because I believed that if I presented an excellent case and made it easy, she'd have no choice but to give in and sign the papers.

During the days leading up to me presenting my case, I did everything she asked me to do with a smile. She seemed pleased, which led me to believe that I'd made progress toward getting her to soften her stance and change her mind. However, I was unaware that she'd taken the fact that I hadn't brought up the army to mean that *her* plan had worked, and I had abandoned my plan to leave. Our differing perspectives collided in a big way when I approached her with the packet of papers.

One evening after work, she was relaxing on the couch when I entered the room, my face beaming with anticipation. "Hey, Ema, do you have a minute?"

She glanced up at me. "What do you need?"

"Remember those papers that I told you I need you to sign? I have them here. I've already filled them out to save you the trouble, and I also got a copy of your divorce from Abba, so you don't have to worry about that either. The papers need to be notarized, so I contacted a lady that my recruiter recommended, who will come to the house."

She jumped off the couch, and without warning, she was right in my face. The first thing she exploded over was the fact that I had taken it upon myself to get a copy of the divorce certificate. I hadn't realized that she'd thought the terms of their divorce—which I was well aware of—were some sort of secret. My dad and she had divorced many years ago. In fact, he had remarried and had another family. In my mind, getting a copy of the divorce certificate was just another thing I needed to do to move things along.

"You got what?" she yelled. "You had better not have a copy of our divorce documents. That is personal information that has *nothing* to do with you."

I knew the idea of me leaving hadn't thrilled her, but her reaction was more over-the-top than I'd expected. In a moment of temporary insanity, I stepped back, creating some space between us, and replied, "Personal business? Not only is it not personal business, it's public record, and I have every right to have a copy since I'm in it."

"You give it to me right now," she said furiously. "And you better have not read it."

"Why are you so mad?"

"Watch your tone before I slap you across your mouth."

"My tone? I know that you and Abba got divorced. I was there when he left us in that cold house with no electricity and no food, drinking water from the toilet," I said as my anger exploded.

"Do *not* talk disrespectfully about your abba."

"I'm not trying to. I just want you to sign the papers so I can get out of here."

"I'm not signing shit, so get out of my face and go to your room!"

"Ema, I really need you to sign the papers."

"*No.* And I said go to your room."

I should have let it go and just gone to my room to figure out a different plan, but I didn't do that. Instead, I defiantly lifted my chin, looked at her, and said, "I read it, and when were you going to tell me I'm a bastard?" As soon as the words left my mouth, I knew it was a low blow.

She stared at me in amazement, the fight in her gone.

"You are not a bastard, Shoshanna," she said. Her voice was barely above a whisper.

I pressed on. "Yes, I am. By definition, a bastard is a child born out of wedlock. And you and Abba didn't get married until after I was born."

"We were married in the eyes of God, and that's all that matters."

"It isn't all that matters to me." I was grasping at straws, attempting to use guilt to get my way.

"I don't owe you an explanation," she said.

"I believe you do, and if you will not give me one, at least sign the papers so I can leave."

"No," she said.

My plan had failed. I was seventeen, I was not enrolled in school, and I was not able to join the army. I called the recruiter again and asked if there was any other way that I could join without my mother's permission. He told me there wasn't, and that I would just have to wait. He and I worked backward from my eighteenth birthday and figured out the date when I could resume the process. After that, we parted ways and agreed to stay in touch as the date got closer. I wasn't happy, but at least I had a plan.

With nothing to do until I turned eighteen, I went to the local community college and, thanks to financial aid, I signed up for a full semester of classes. I figured that going to school would be a good way to keep busy while I waited. While I was at home, I balanced school with continuing to take care of the household errands.

Two months before turning eighteen, I resumed the recruitment process and decided not to tell my mother. I was afraid that if she found out, she would stop it. I took the ASVAB and met with an army counselor to review my test scores and discuss my job options. The counselor reviewed my scores and explained the jobs that I had tested well enough for. Afterward, we discussed the next steps.

"Based on the information we've discussed, what do you think you'd like to do in the army?" he asked.

"I want to go to the 82nd Airborne Division."

"You what?"

"I want to go to the 82nd Airborne Division. Didn't my recruiter tell you?"

"No, he didn't. Did he promise you that you would go to the 82nd? If so, don't believe him. Recruiters exaggerate all the time."

"No, he didn't promise that I would go. He said it was difficult to get in, but that it was possible."

"He is right. It is difficult to get into the 82nd, but for you, it's impossible. Like I said, recruiters exaggerate all the time. Let's focus on selecting a job for you, and then I will tell you where you will probably go."

What was with people? They were quick to tell me what I couldn't do, yet no one spoke with facts.

"OK," I said. "What job qualifies me for airborne school and then the 82nd?"

"I told you that you can't go to the 82nd," he said with a hint of irritation in his voice.

"Why?"

"For starters, you're a girl."

"Are girls allowed in the 82nd?"

"Yes, they are, but less than 1 percent of the paratroopers in the 82nd are females."

"How did the ones that are in there get in?" I asked.

"They applied for airborne school and were accepted."

"OK, then I want to do that. Pick a job for me that will allow me to go to airborne school. I don't want a potential promise to go to airborne school at a future date; I want it documented on my enlistment paperwork."

"Well, before all of that, you need a job. So, I ask you again, what do you want to do?"

"Sir, I don't care what I do, as long as it allows me to go to airborne school and it's a job that the 82nd needs. Can you help me with that?"

He sat for a moment in quiet reflection, looking off into the distance. Finally, he turned toward me with a hint of nostalgia in his eyes and said, "You remind me of my daughter ... overly ambitious. Yes, I can help you with that," he said with a resigned sigh.

A huge grin spread across my face.

We reviewed the roles, and he determined that my best chance of getting into the 82nd would be to enlist as a unit supply specialist. They were in need throughout the army, but especially at Fort Bragg, where the 82nd was located. We completed the paperwork, which took me to Fort Jackson, South Carolina, for basic training; immediately followed by unit supply school in Fort Lee, Virginia; and finally, to Fort Benning, Georgia, for airborne school. All I had to do was complete my physical exam and wait until November.

My mother found out that I was still pursuing the military when the doctor's office called with lab results that said I was anemic. Because I was still a minor, the nurse discussed the results with my mother, who immediately wanted to know why I had gone to the doctor. The nurse didn't elaborate and suggested that my mother speak directly with me or with the attending physician.

When I got home, my mother confronted me. "Shoshanna, why did you go to the doctor?" Her tone carried no trace of concern, only anger.

"How do you know I went to the doctor?" I asked, stalling for time.

"Don't play with me," she demanded.

I tried to be vague because I didn't want things to fall apart when I was so close. "I wasn't feeling well, so I went in for a check-up," I said.

"Not feeling well how?" The intensity in her voice increased.

"I don't know. Maybe a cold or something."

Because she'd assumed that I had gone to the doctor because I was pregnant, she'd already made an appointment for me to see another doctor the next day.

"Why do I need to go to another doctor? I already went."

"Because I want answers, and you won't give them to me."

"I told you I wasn't feeling well. But I'm OK now, so why are you making me go to the doctor again?"

"You're going to see an ob-gyn," she said firmly.

"A baby doctor? Why do I need to see a baby doctor?"

"Because I want to know if you're pregnant."

"What?!"

"I said I want to know if you are pregnant."

"Pregnant? Where is this coming from? Why would you think I'm having sex? I don't even have a boyfriend."

"You and the people at that doctor's office are being dodgy, and I have the right to know what's going on with you."

"Nothing is going on with me. I needed iron supplements, that's all."

"The only time a woman needs iron supplements is when she's pregnant, so you're going."

Her insinuation that I was pregnant bothered me more than her insistence on another doctor's visit. I was her most responsible child. I had never given her any trouble. No boys, drinking, or drugs. I'd never smoked cigarettes, and I didn't even curse. So why was she suddenly microparenting me?

I was so angry that the next day I skipped the appointment. When she called the doctor's office for the results of the examination, and they told her I had been a no-show, she was furious.

"Why in the hell didn't you go to your appointment, Shoshanna?"

"I told you I didn't need to go."

She grabbed my arm with an intensity that made me gasp. "Do you think I'm playing with you?"

"Ema, I'm not pregnant. The army wouldn't let me join if I was. I leave for basic training in a few weeks." And that's how she found out I had joined the army.

She released my arm.

"I'm sorry," I whispered.

She turned on her heel to leave the room. She had only gone a few steps before she turned back to me, the hurt in her eyes clear. Without saying a word, she walked away. I didn't think I had done anything wrong, but the overwhelming feeling of grief that filled my chest indicated otherwise.

Over the next few weeks, we barely spoke. I avoided discussing any service details with her, except for telling her about my departure date.

On November 16, 1988, one day before my birthday, I left home. My mother and I parted ways agreeably, but not in the way I had hoped. We hadn't reconciled our differences. There was no going-away party, and no birthday celebration. We shared a quick hug before I walked out the door, and I celebrated my birthday alone, sitting in the military inception center.

I had some regrets about how I'd left things with my mother, but I didn't regret leaving. The circumstances may not have been ideal, but all I wanted was to be free.

Chapter 8

Freedom (n.): To ask nothing. To expect nothing.
To depend on nothing.

—Ayn Rand

The first few weeks of basic training felt like a whirlwind. I barely had time to process one task before being thrown into the next. There were vaccinations, stacks of paperwork, and being issued my gear: socks, boots, a dress uniform, and the green camouflage fatigues that would become my second skin for nearly the next decade. I took a physical fitness test, which only reinforced my disdain for long-distance running, but to my surprise, I excelled at marksmanship, discovering I was a natural with a rifle in my hands.

The best part of basic training was the responsibility that came with it. Because I'd had some college education, I joined the army as a private first class, which frequently allowed me to be a leader among my peers. Like the time when I was selected to be a squad leader, tasked with making sure the ten or so people in my squad were always prepared, in the right place, and ready to train. It was an honor, and I was proud the drill sergeant had chosen me for the role. At times, the extra responsibility reminded me of the tasks I used to manage back home; but now, it felt different. I was finally on my own—accomplished, free, but admittedly overwhelmed. Those moments always brought a smile to my face as I thought, *I've been training for this for most of my life.*

After several weeks had passed, much to my surprise, I still wasn't homesick. Over time, things got better between my mother and me, and she was no longer angry over the way I'd left. We exchanged letters, I called home periodically, and once, she even sent me a care package. It was filled with toiletries, a book to read, and some of my favorite snacks (most of which were confiscated). The drill sergeants especially enjoyed eating my Lay's Flamin' Hot potato chips.

"Thanks, PFC Perry," one of them said as he walked past my bunk, licking the red powder from his fingers.

I had been in the military for about six weeks when the Christmas holiday arrived. The drill instructors encouraged every recruit to go home so they wouldn't be stuck babysitting troops in the barracks. I bought a train ticket home and planned to spend the two-week break in Chicago.

When I got home, everything felt different. I hadn't been gone long, but I had changed, and so had the dynamics of the house. My room belonged to someone else. The few belongings I'd left behind—posters and other personal touches—had been removed, as if to signal that I no longer lived there. I was expected to sleep on the couch or share a bed with one of my sisters. I hadn't expected my room to stay untouched forever, but the finality of it all hit harder than I'd expected. I felt like a visitor.

I was thrilled to see my sister Miriam. The *only* regret I had about leaving home was leaving her behind. Four years younger than me, she wasn't just my sister; she was my best friend. Growing up, we were two peas in a pod, inseparable and unwavering in our loyalty to each other. Anything I had, half was hers. And in return, she gave me her full support, no matter what. Like the time when I didn't want to wear glasses, she made sure I passed the eye exam.

"Come this way and have a seat in that chair," the optometrist had said to me.

"Can my sister come in with me?"

"Sure. Sister, have a seat right over there," he said, motioning to Miriam.

He dimmed the lights and directed my attention to the vision chart projected on the wall. It displayed rows of capital E's pointing in various directions, starting with large ones at the top and shrinking to barely visible ones at the bottom.

"I'm going to highlight a row," he explained. "I want you to tell me the direction the letters are pointing—up, down, left, or right—OK?"

"OK," I said nervously.

The first few rows were easy. "Up, up, left, down, right," I said, rattling off the answers with confidence. But the doctor moved quickly, and soon I couldn't make out the letters at all. Squinting at the blurred shapes, I hesitated.

"Which direction is the shape pointing?" he asked, waiting for my reply.

I glanced at Miriam, sitting across from me, and noticed that her eyes were darting upward.

"Up," I said tentatively.

"That's correct."

I smiled, relieved.

"And this one?" the doctor asked, pointing to another blurry line.

I looked at Miriam again. This time, she shifted her gaze to the left, then right, right again, and up.

I rattled off the sequence.

"Right again," he said.

The doctor continued down the chart, and with a quick glance at Miriam, I guessed correctly each time. The doctor stepped out, and I heard my mother's raised voice through the door.

"What do you mean she doesn't need glasses?!" she yelled.

"She tested a perfect twenty-twenty and even read several lines on the twenty-fifteen scale," the doctor replied calmly.

"That's impossible! Test her again," she demanded.

"I have other patients, Mrs. Perry. Your daughter doesn't need glasses, so I can't write her a prescription."

My mother was furious, but inside the exam room, Miriam and I were doubled over in laughter. We huddled together, hands covering our mouths, trying not to burst out hysterically as the doctor continued to helplessly defend himself.

She and I created a secret language that only we understood. It was a way for us to communicate without anyone else—especially our mother—catching on. The bond between Miriam and me was unbreakable, something my mother couldn't understand and didn't always appreciate. Such as the time when I missed curfew and stayed out all night, and Miriam taped a note to the outside of my bedroom door:

Shoshanna, I tried to stay up and wait for you, but I'm falling asleep. Ema fell asleep before your curfew, so no matter what time you come in, I'm going to tell her that you were home by 10:00 p.m. OK? Love you. Hope you had fun. Wake me up when you get home.

Love,
Miriam

Unfortunately, my mother found the note before I did. When I walked into the house, I heard my mother yelling at Miriam.

"You were just going to lie for her?" she screamed.

Miriam stood in the hallway, staring at the floor, her hands trembling.

"Answer me!"

"Yes," Miriam whispered, her voice cracking.

"You're so damn loyal to *her* that you're just saying to hell with me?" my mother asked, pointing her finger toward me.

"What's going on?" I asked, moving to stand next to Miriam.

"She's a liar, that's what's going on!" my mother shrieked.

My mother grounded Miriam for two weeks—no watching TV, no going outside. She was only allowed to leave her room to eat and use the bathroom.

Once we were upstairs, Miriam explained what had happened. Tears were streaming down her face.

"Thank you," I said, pulling her into a hug.

"I'm sorry you didn't get the note in time," she cried.

"It's OK," I reassured her. "I'll keep you company during your punishment."

"You will?" she asked, her voice full of hope.

"Yep. And we're going to make it fun," I said, squeezing her more tightly.

During those two weeks, we made our plan to escape together. I would join the army, and she would join the marines. We dreamed of leaving and starting new lives side by side. Our plans changed when I left first.

Without me, Miriam no longer had anyone to protect her. She didn't have anyone to remind her to dream big or to give her a nudge when she needed to be brave. My loyal, faithful sister— who had always been there for me—was left to fend for herself in the very environment I had fought so hard to escape. I knew I'd abandoned her, and the guilt cut deep, a wound that I knew not even time would fully heal.

Despite that, when I came home, my sister was excited to see me. We picked up right where we'd left off … as two peas in a pod. I told her all about the army and how hard the training was, and she filled me in on everything that had happened since I'd left, like the time when our mother had asked our younger sister to deposit five hundred dollars into the ATM, but she'd accidentally entered fifty instead. It had taken the bank several days to fix the mistake.

The first night I was home, we stayed up all night talking, laughing, and reminiscing. I had really missed my sister.

My mother seemed happy that I was home too. She also seemed determined to remind me that I was still a child.

One day, when I got back from visiting friends, my mother called me into the kitchen. "Shoshanna, bust those suds." (Which meant for me to wash the dishes.)

I looked over at the sink, which was overflowing with dirty dishes. Some still had food on them, and there were several pots with baked-on food that appeared to have been there for days, not hours. I hadn't used any of the dishes that were in the sink, so I didn't understand why she was asking me to wash them. And, in fact, she wasn't *asking* me to wash them; she was *telling* me to wash them.

Confused, I asked, "Why do I have to do the dishes? I didn't use any of them."

My mother didn't say a word; she just reared back and slapped me across my face harder than I had ever been hit before. It felt like she had broken my jaw. I stared at her in disbelief as tears began streaming down my cheeks. I didn't say a word. I just turned and began washing the dishes. It took me several hours to finish them, but I didn't leave the kitchen until I was done. Not only were the dishes done, so was I. I knew without a doubt that I no longer belonged there.

The next morning, I changed my return ticket to leave that evening. Miriam was sad that I was leaving so soon, but she understood why.

The remaining months of basic training and unit supply school went by quickly. I pushed myself physically and mentally. I met people from all over the country, and I quickly realized that not everyone had grown up like I had. There was Private Holden, who had grown up on a farm in Texas and had helped deliver baby calves. There was also Private Davis, whose family was so close that both her parents and all her siblings traveled to South Carolina to see her off to basic training. Private First Class Ford also stood out with her stories of summers spent vacationing in Europe, and her family's homes in California and New York. I couldn't understand why someone from such a wealthy background would join the army, but she said it was because she wanted to make it on her own. Although the extravagant care packages she received *every* week said otherwise.

I had conversations with White people, which was new. Other than during a brief period living in Georgia, I had never spent much time around White people, apart from teachers or the people I'd met when I was conducting business for my mother. I also met and became friends with Mexicans, whom I had never encountered before joining the military. I realized that the world I'd grown up in was a very small representation of the country I lived in.

Every time I left one city and went to the next, I made more friends and learned more. I arrived at Fort Benning for the basic airborne course about five months after joining the army.

On my first day of training, I was in awe of everything. I was among some of the most elite soldiers in the world, and I felt honored to be there. The first thing I noticed was that there were black hats instead of drill sergeants. The black hats were an elite class of trainers who would help transition us from being legs (non-airborne soldiers) to airborne soldiers ready to be part of an elite fighting force. The second thing I noticed was that all branches of service went to Fort Benning for airborne school, so I was in a class with soldiers, sailors, marines, and even Navy SEALs. As I looked around the formation, I saw that the recruiter had been right: there were very few women. That fact made me feel even more honored to be standing there. I quickly learned, though, that being a woman didn't set me apart. Aside from having separate barracks, we were treated no differently than the men.

Everything moved at a fast pace. We ran everywhere we went, and we had a sense of purpose in all things. The black hats explained that, if we were lucky, we would be at Fort Benning for three weeks: ground week, followed by tower week, and finally jump week.

Upon arrival, we were given an army physical fitness test—consisting of a timed two-mile run, push-ups, and sit-ups—which was the first cut. If we didn't pass the fitness test, we were out. For those who made the cut, ground week continued with intensive training that consisted of running ... a lot of running.

We learned the basic components of a parachute, we practiced exiting an aircraft using a mock door, and we jumped off a thirty-four-foot tower while attached to a cable. From the ground, the tower didn't look very tall, but the first time I stood at the top, I felt my knees buckle and my lunch fought to stay down. The black hat hooked a cable to my pack and shoved me toward the edge of the platform. I closed my eyes, sucked in a breath, and flung my body forward. I immediately felt myself sailing through the air, smoothly gliding along the cable. I opened my eyes and saw an instructor waiting for me at the other end. As he unhooked me from the cable, adrenaline surged through me, I looked at him and said, "I want to do that again, Sergeant Airborne."

The end of ground week was the second cut, and we lost about a third of the class. This level of training was unlike anything I had ever experienced in my life. Most days, after the morning run, I would duck off to find a patch of grass to eject whatever was left in my stomach from the night before. The training was as much mental as it was physical. We had to truly believe that we were capable of doing the things asked of us if we even hoped to have a prayer of surviving each day. We had five marines in the class, and much to my astonishment, they all left the program after ground week. I was still there, though. I had survived the first week and was ready for more.

Tower week came next. During tower week, we had to qualify on the swing ladder trainer, complete several mass exits from the 34-foot tower, and demonstrate parachute canopy confidence and control when dropped from the Ungawa Tower—a 250-foot tower used to practice steering and landing. The tower was an imposing steel structure with four outstretched arms.

When it was my turn, I stood beneath one of the arms, my heart racing as the instructor secured my harness and clipped me into a mock parachute. With a sudden tug, the cable began pulling me off the ground. My stomach tightened as I was slowly lifted higher and higher, the earth shrinking below me. I fixed my gaze on the horizon, trying to steady my nerves.

At 250 feet, a sharp jerk signaled that I had reached the top. A loud clunk echoed through the air, and before I could process the sound, the parachute released. The canopy floated above me as I began to glide, carefully steering just as I'd been taught. My heart raced.

In what felt like an instant, my feet touched the ground. I had conquered the tower and was one step closer to becoming a paratrooper. As I removed my harness, pride swelled in my chest, the kind of pride that reminded me why I was here and how far I was willing to go to accomplish my goals.

We also continued the rigorous physical training routine that week, which included lots of running! The end of tower week was the third cut, and we lost more students.

Finally, it was jump week. During jump week, we had to successfully complete five jumps from an aircraft at 1,250 feet. The night before the first jump, people displayed a variety of emotions. Some were talkative and described every aspect of what they thought the jump would be like. Some had nervous energy and were questioning whether they would actually do it. Some actually decided not to go through with it and quit the program. I was eerily peaceful. I wasn't afraid, and I didn't feel the need to play out the details of what I expected. Instead, I mentally revisited the things I had learned during the first two weeks to ensure I wouldn't forget anything.

The morning of my first jump was a special day for me. It meant that I had made it through the first two weeks and was only five jumps away from becoming a paratrooper. We went through the prejump training, donned our parachutes, and headed for the aircraft. There it was ... a beautiful C-130 Hercules. It was a large aircraft with two sets of propellers. It was army green in color and had an American flag painted on the tail. My first thought was, *Wow ... that's badass!*

I boarded the aircraft through the rear door, and with the weight of the parachute and reserve, I could barely walk. I moved in more of a penguin waddle instead of a graceful stride. At that point, I had only flown twice in my life. I focused my eyes on the back of the person in front of me and kept moving forward. I didn't think; I just walked. Before long, I was finally in the aircraft and was sitting in a netted seat, squished against other soldiers. There was no turning back. I was doing it.

Once the doors closed and we took off, the noise of the engines was the only thing I could hear. The rest of the aircraft was mostly quiet. Some people dozed off, some prayed, and others (like me) just sat and waited.

We weren't in the air for long before the jump masters—the people in charge of the jump—began yelling commands. "Get ready!"

Upon hearing this, every jumper on the aircraft echoed the jump master's command. "Get ready!"

The next command was, "Outboard personnel, stand up!" which was immediately followed by, "Inboard personnel, stand up!"

After that, every jumper in the aircraft was on their feet.

The jump master's next command was, "Hook up!"

And we all attached our static lines to the anchor line cables.

He then yelled, "Check static lines!"

This was done to ensure everyone's static lines were connected properly and free from damage.

The next command we heard was, "Check equipment!" which was followed by each jumper checking the equipment of the jumper behind them before turning around and allowing the next jumper to inspect their gear.

Everything was happening so fast.

The next thing we heard was, "Sound off for equipment check!" followed by a series of OKs from each jumper. The command sounded up the line, starting at the back, with the person at the front sounding off with, "All OK, jump master!"

After the equipment check, the jump master looked out the door several times to coordinate the drop zone location with the flight crew. As we approached the drop zone, the jump master began issuing his final commands, all of which were echoed by every jumper on the plane.

"Thirty seconds!"

The roar of the C-130 Hercules engine was deafening. I looked around to see if anyone looked afraid. I was met with nothing but blank stares looking straight ahead in nervous anticipation. No one moved, no one made a sound. Only the noise of the wind and yells of the jump master filled my ears.

"Stand in the door!"

Shit ... this is really happening. Is it too late to turn back? What the hell am I thinking? Of course, it was too late to turn back. And why would I want to? Quitting now would mean they had been right—the recruiters, my mother, and every other naysayer who'd thought I was crazy to believe that I could do this. *They can't be right. I can do this; I must do this!* My hands were shaking, my throat was dry, and it suddenly felt like it was over one hundred degrees inside the plane. Maybe it was.

"Go!"

It's time. This is actually happening. The soldiers in front of me began shuffling forward. I briefly wondered if my feet would actually move when the shuffling finally reached me. *What if I stop at the door? No, I won't! Don't think, just keep moving. Don't think, just keep moving. Don't think, just keep moving.* As I chanted in my head (or, at least, I think it was in my head), I looked ahead and saw the door. Before I knew it, it was my turn.

With every ounce of courage that I could summon, I handed my static line to the jump master, turned, and placed my hands on the outside of the aircraft door. I did it in the same way I had done when we'd practiced exiting the aircraft during training over the prior weeks.

With a vigorous thrust, I flung myself forward into the great blue sky and began counting. *One one-thousand ... two one-thousand ... three one-thousand ...* Swoosh! There it was, the most amazing sight I had ever seen: a beautiful, round silk canopy floating above me. I was soaring in the sky, and the view was like nothing I could have ever imagined. It was peaceful up there, calming.

I felt tears prick my eyes, and I realized that I was crying. I wasn't crying out of fear; I wasn't afraid. I was crying because all the stress and pain that had preceded that moment had been worth it. My hard work had meant something. In that moment, I was flying 1,200 feet above the earth; in that moment, I had conquered my fears; in that moment, I had triumphed over doubt; in that moment, I had proved the naysayers wrong; in that moment, I had proved to myself that I could do anything. Most of all, I was crying because, in that moment, I was free!

I completed four more jumps that week, and at the end of the week, I was awarded the coveted silver airborne wings. One month later, I made my sixth jump at Fort Bragg, North Carolina, onto the Normandy drop zone from a C-130 aircraft, as a paratrooper with the 82nd Airborne Division.

Chapter 9

Strength does not come from physical capacity.
It comes from an indomitable will.

—Mahatma Gandhi

The day I donned my battle dress uniform for the first time with airborne wings on my chest and a double-A patch on my left shoulder was a day that forever transformed me. As a paratrooper, I was confident, strong, and brave. The words "I can't" ceased to be part of my vernacular, and I internalized the belief that I could do anything. I stood taller, I spoke more assuredly, and I fully embraced my standing among the most elite group of fighting men and women in the world. The outward symbols of the double-A patch and burgundy beret told everyone I encountered that I was a badass! No one treated me like a kid or questioned why I was there. I'd earned the right to be there—no, I'd earned the *honor* of being there.

I loved everything about my time at Fort Bragg, North Carolina. I was assigned to the 82nd Finance Battalion, where I worked as a unit supply specialist. I was entrusted with the responsibility of overseeing millions of dollars of equipment and weaponry. Everything I learned was introduced quickly and required immediate application. I learned discipline, process, accountability, and most importantly, I learned what it meant to be a leader.

A leader isn't simply the person in charge. They are responsible for the well-being and care of other human beings ... their fellow soldiers. Being a leader means being confident, courageous, and bold while also being humble and service-minded, putting the needs of others above your own ambitions. During my time at Fort Bragg, I met many men and women whom I admired and respected. Men and women at whose command I would have walked through fire if the mission called for it.

Many great things in my life happened while I was at Fort Bragg. I learned to shoot and became an expert marksman, and I finally got a driver's license. (By the way, learning to drive in a US Army-issued Humvee is pretty amazing.) I learned how to lead others with honor and respect, and I turned twenty-one and had my first drink ... legally, anyway. There were many more firsts and milestones, but the one I am most proud of is that, while at Fort Bragg, I earned a new identity: Private First Class Perry, US Army paratrooper.

As part of my training and onboarding, I attended a unit armorer course where I learned how to disassemble, reassemble, and maintain several military weapons, including a .50 caliber machine gun, M203 grenade launcher, M16 rifle, and Beretta M9. I was learning to shoot and maintain some pretty awesome military firepower.

I was the only female soldier in the class, which meant there was no shortage of offers of help or invitations to lunch. When I was stationed in the 82nd Airborne Division, I believe there were roughly seventeen thousand paratroopers in the division, less than 3 percent of whom were women, so being the only female soldier in a class wasn't anything unusual. None of the invitations interested me, and I remained focused on the course content.

That was the case until I met Carlos. Carlos was of Mexican descent, he had a stoic demeanor, and he looked perpetually pissed off. He never engaged with any of the other soldiers in the class. He arrived early every day, disassembled and reassembled each weapon with ease, ate lunch alone, took his breaks alone, and unceremoniously left as soon as we were released for the day. There was something about him that intrigued me. For starters, I'd never met a first-generation Mexican. He had an exotic look about him, and the fact that he was the only person in the class (apart from the teacher) who hadn't hit on me also intrigued me.

One day, during one of our breaks, I went up to Carlos and introduced myself. He didn't seem particularly interested, but he was polite. Up close, he seemed different. His voice was low, and he looked at the ground. He wasn't a pissed-off loner; he was just shy. His voice may have been soft, but when he looked up, his eyes were hard and unwelcoming. Nevertheless, always a sucker for a tortured soul, I persevered and invited him to eat lunch with me. He accepted my invitation.

As we chatted over lunch, I got to know Carlos. I learned that, though originally from Chihuahua, Mexico, he and his family lived in a small town in Texas called Pecos. He told me all about Pecos and how it had one high school, a grocery store, and a single traffic signal.

"Only one traffic signal in the whole town?" I asked in disbelief.

"Yes, there's only one, and it hasn't been there long."

Being from Chicago, I couldn't imagine a city that small.

"Does that even count as a city?" I asked sarcastically.

"Yes, it's a city," he said, rolling his eyes.

"I bet you had to dodge tumbleweeds on your way to school," I joked.

He smiled and laughed as he gave me a friendly shove, muttering what I'm sure was a curse word in Spanish.

We continued to eat lunch together every day for the rest of the class, and we continued to see each other after the course ended. Within a few weeks, we were officially dating. Hanging out with Carlos was fun, but I quickly realized that he had a terrible temper. Carlos drove a silver Audi, and his car was the nicest car I had ever ridden in. It had all the bells and whistles: a booming radio, a sunroof, and power everything. Carlos was very proud of his car, and he took great care of it.

One night, when we were out riding around, he cracked the driver's side window to let in some fresh air. When he attempted to roll the window back up, it didn't move. Carlos pressed the button over and over, but the glass didn't move. I quietly watched him as he attempted to fix the window. He pulled over and turned the engine off, hoping that restarting the car would fix the issue. Unfortunately, it did not. After several minutes of failed troubleshooting, he began screaming angrily, both in English and in Spanish. I remember being confused by his behavior and wondering how screaming would help matters, but before I could ask why he was screaming, he began furiously kicking the door as hard as he could. As I looked on in horror, he continued to kick the door while shouting obscenities, which only made matters worse. The previously half-opened window was now fully opened as his kicking had caused the glass to fall the rest of the way down the door shaft.

For the first time since meeting him, I was afraid of what Carlos might do. I had never seen him react so violently to something so seemingly trivial, and it scared the hell out of me. I remember thinking, *What if I say something that he doesn't like? Will he react that way with me, too?* I was in the middle of nowhere with a maniac who was physically and verbally assaulting his own car in two languages!

Once it appeared that his tirade was over, I softly asked him to take me back to my barracks. He looked at the window one last time, muttered, "Fuck it," and then drove toward the barracks I lived in. I didn't know what to say, and he didn't seem interested in talking, so we rode in silence as the cold wind rushed through the open window.

I strongly considered discontinuing any contact with Carlos. However, when he turned up at my barracks several days later to let me know that he'd gotten the window fixed and invited me to an off-barracks weekend, for some reason, I agreed. I rationalized to myself that Carlos' behavior from a few nights ago had been episodic, a one-time incident. I told myself that the broken window had ruined what had otherwise been a fun evening, and that the cost that would be incurred to fix the broken window must have been stressful. I decided to ignore the glaring red flags and look the other way, and Carlos and I continued dating.

We had been dating for several months when, one day, I noticed a pattern of feeling sick. I wasn't sick all the time; I would wake up feeling nauseous, but the queasiness would usually subside by midday. I was also exhausted all the time. I enjoyed a good nap as much as anyone else, but it seemed that all I wanted to do was sleep. I tried several over-the-counter medicines and home remedies to get rid of the bug I had, but nothing worked.

After a couple of weeks of feeling sick with no improvement, I started to think it could be something worse. What if it was some sort of plague? I wasn't sure if plagues were still a thing, but I was very concerned that the sick feeling hadn't gone away or improved at all after a few weeks. I had tried everything, including the most reliable home remedy for any cold: a teaspoon of fresh garlic soaked in honey. Not only did that make the nausea worse, but the taste of garlic also tortured my taste buds for several days. Deciding that medical intervention was needed, I went to the doctor.

"Hi, PFC Perry. What brings you in today?" the doctor asked.

"I don't know, really. I think I must have caught a nasty bug or some kind of plague that I can't shake. Is there a flu or something going around?"

"No, I don't think so," he said. "But that doesn't matter. We'll figure out what's going on and get you fixed right up. Let's start with some vitals and go from there."

The nurse who was assisting the doctor took my weight, temperature, and blood pressure. Everything was normal.

When the doctor returned, he asked me a few more questions. "When did your symptoms begin? Are they present all the time, or just sometimes? Have you ever had these symptoms before? When was your last menstrual period?"

I responded, "About two weeks ago. No, I feel sick mostly in the morning, but sometimes at night too. I don't think I've had these symptoms before, but maybe when I had a cold or something. Hmm ... my last menstrual period. Wait, let me think. What day is it? I'm not sure when it was, but I'm certain that it's due any day now."

"No problem," he said. "We'll draw some blood, run a few more tests, and I'll call you as soon as I get the results. In the meantime, drink lots of fluids, and rest as much as you are able."

"OK, but what do you think it is?" I asked.

"I'm not sure yet," he said. "It could be a stubborn bug or a touch of anemia. Whatever it is, we'll know in a few days."

I left the doctor's office convinced that my symptoms were caused by anemia. I had suffered from anemia previously, and the constant fatigue made sense. The nausea was new, but maybe that was a symptom of anemia I just hadn't experienced before. I hadn't taken my iron supplements for a very long time, so it made sense that the anemia would return. This was good news because anemia was easy to address. Restart the iron supplements and eat more green, leafy vegetables, and I'd be as good as new. My fear of having an incurable plague subsided, and I made a mental note to begin taking my iron supplements again to get a head start on feeling better.

A few days later, I was working in my office when the phone rang.

"Hello. PFC Perry speaking. How may I help you?"

"Hi, PFC Perry. This is Doctor Sanders, and I have the results from your blood work."

"Oh, great. Is it anemia, like you thought?"

"No, it isn't anemia. You're pregnant."

Pregnant? Did I hear him right?

"Are you there?" he asked.

Nothing.

"Hello? PFC Perry, are you there?"

"Um, yes, I'm here. What did you say?"

"I said you are pregnant."

The room began to spin, and I suddenly needed to sit. I flopped in the chair that was beneath me, and I closed my eyes to stop the spinning. I took several deep breaths before I spoke again.

Once I'd somewhat regained my composure, I said, "I can't be pregnant."

"Well, you are, PFC Perry, and we need to begin your prenatal care right away."

"My what?"

"Your prenatal care, to ensure the baby has a healthy environment to grow in. Please stop by the clinic as soon as possible to pick up a prescription for prenatal vitamins."

He said a lot of other words, but I didn't hear any of them. My mind was busy processing the fact that I had a human being growing inside of me. Why hadn't I considered that as a reason for my sickness? Probably because becoming a mother at this point in my life wasn't part of my plan. Maybe because I was naive enough to think that unprotected sex wouldn't result in a baby.

This was all too much to process, so I interrupted the doctor's instructions and said, "I have to go."

I hung up the phone and sat at my desk with my head in my hands for what seemed like several hours. I wasn't sad or unhappy, per se. I was just shocked. I'd always wanted to be a mother eventually, but in my version of motherhood, I was happily married, in my mid-thirties, and working as a successful professional of some sort. Being a mother at twenty years old was not part of my plan. But that's the thing about plans; they don't always work out the way you envision, and only the most adaptive of people are able to create positive outcomes despite the changes. Was I one of those people? That was yet to be determined, but I had more pressing questions to deal with.

How would Carlos react? Would he stand by me and support me, or would he abandon me and leave me to raise our child on my own? What would I tell my mother? Things hadn't gone well the last time I had seen her, but in the months that followed, she tried to mend our relationship. Though she never apologized for slapping me, she acknowledged that I was an adult and was free to make my own decision. We had started speaking periodically and had managed to reach a good place. Would this news change that? Would she think that I was a failure and try to make me move back home? What about my military career? Could I be a paratrooper and a mother at the same time? I had a lot of questions, and I was terrified of what the answers would be.

The first question that would need to be immediately answered was whether I was in this alone. I had to tell Carlos that I was pregnant, and his response was what I feared the most. Carlos and I had never talked about marriage, primarily because we hadn't been dating long enough to think about being together forever. His temper notwithstanding, I believed that Carlos was a good man at his core. And from what I knew of him, he was responsible. I knew from listening to him talk about his family, especially his parents, that he took the idea of family very seriously. In fact, I admired how close his family was. They cared for each other and looked out for one another, and I desperately hoped that his sense of family and responsibility would apply to me too. I was still processing the information myself, and I knew it was a lot to take in, so I didn't have any expectations as to how Carlos would react or what he would say. I just prayed for the best.

I met up with Carlos for dinner to share the unexpected news.

"Hey, I have something to tell you," I began, my voice shaky.

"What's up?" he replied casually, continuing to eat.

"Remember when I wasn't feeling well? Well, I got a call from the doctor today."

"And?"

"And ... I'm pregnant."

Carlos froze mid-bite. "You're pregnant?" he asked, his full attention now focused on me.

"Yes, and before you ask, you—"

Before I could finish, he stood up and moved around the table. The action was so swift that it caught me off guard. He slid into the seat next to me and grabbed my hand.

"It's going to be fine. Everything is going to be OK," he said solemnly.

"You're not mad?" I asked hesitantly, my voice caught in my throat.

"No. I always figured I'd have kids someday, so why not now, and why not with you?" he said with an assuredness that surprised me. "I'm going to do the right thing. I will be there for my family."

His family? Was I now considered part of his family?

The reassurance that I wouldn't have to go through the journey alone, and the sense of belonging, filled my heart with joy. Carlos seemed nervous, but he wasn't angry. And for the first time since hearing the news, I exhaled and allowed myself to breathe.

Neither of us wanted to think about telling our parents. How would they respond? Would they see us as reckless, jumping into something so life-altering when we barely knew each other? Would they abandon us, or worse, demand an abortion? The thought of facing this journey without their support was scary. But, for now, none of that mattered. We sat in silence, hand in hand, allowing the life-changing news to settle over us. We both were scared, but at the same time, we felt calm. We also felt joy. And, surprisingly, we felt peace.

Carlos decided to tell his mother first. Mainly because I was too chicken to call my mother, and he was kind enough to give me more time to ponder what I would say to her. Carlos called his mother, and through the receiver, I could hear a lot of yelling in Spanish. I didn't know what she was saying, but the sounds of an angry mother yelling at her child was a universal language that I understood all too well. When the call ended, I asked Carlos what his mother had said.

He summarized the entire conversation in one sentence. "She said, 'You are going to marry that girl. You aren't going to drop your pants all over the place making babies.'"

"What?!" I exclaimed. "Married? We can't get married; we never talked about that."

"No, we never talked about it, but it makes sense. I want my child to have my last name, and I want to be involved in raising it," he said.

"Being involved in the baby's life doesn't mean that you and I have to get married," I countered.

"No, it doesn't, but it's the right thing to do, for our child and us as parents."

I thought about what he'd said, and he was right. The options were to either bring a child into the world out of wedlock and try to work out some sort of co-parenting arrangement between two active-duty soldiers or get married and raise our child together as a team in a loving, happy home. I wasn't ready to be married, and I had no idea how to be a wife. Remembering how I'd felt knowing that my parents hadn't cared enough to get married before I had been brought into the world tipped the scales, and I agreed to marry Carlos. My only condition was that it needed to happen before the baby was born. I would marry him and attempt to give our baby a happy family. But if it didn't work out that way, I could always take my child and leave.

Being engaged made calling my mother somewhat easier. I called her the next day and led my announcements with the engagement. She asked a lot of questions about Carlos: where he was from, what his ethnicity was, and why I was suddenly getting married. I told her that he was originally from Mexico but that his family lived in a small town in Texas.

"You're marrying a Mexican?" she asked. "Does he even speak English?"

"Yes, he speaks English very well. He grew up in Texas. He speaks Spanish, too, though," I explained.

"Do you think his family will accept you?"

"I don't know, but I hope so. I haven't met them yet, but he talks a lot about them, and they seem nice. There's something else too," I said.

"What?" she asked.

"I'm pregnant." I held my breath as I waited for her to respond. I didn't know if she would be happy for me, but I hoped that she would at least be supportive.

My hope was realized as she exclaimed, "My baby is having a baby! Congratulations! If this is what you want, I am happy for you."

I was very relieved. She asked questions about how I was feeling and what I planned to do about my military career. She also inquired about Carlos's religion, and she wanted to know when she would meet him. She was not happy that I was marrying a Mexican, or that he didn't share our Jewish faith. Those were by far her biggest concerns. She wanted her grandchild to be raised in the customs and traditions that I had been raised in, and she knew being married to someone of a different faith would make that difficult. I explained to her that Carlos was Catholic but that he really didn't practice his religion. I told her that he never went to church, talked about religion, or tried in any way to influence my beliefs.

"Does he eat pork around you?" she asked.

"Yes, he does, but he doesn't try to get me to eat it," I explained.

"Is he going to bring swine into your house?" she continued.

"I hope not, but we haven't discussed that yet," I responded.

"Do you talk to him about your faith, and will he celebrate the holy days?"

"No, we don't really talk about religion. He knows that I don't eat pork, but I haven't talked to him about the holy days yet."

"I can't believe you're marrying a *gentile*," she hissed, elongating every syllable to emphasize her disdain.

"Ema!" I exclaimed.

"Well, you are," she snapped.

Despite her concerns, she told me that she loved me, and she asked me what she could do to support me. She also began telling me many tried-and-true old wives' tales to follow. "Don't cross your legs." "Eating spicy food is bad for the baby." "Don't raise your arms over your head ..." She enthusiastically continued her list of dos and don'ts, and I studiously jotted down as many as I could.

I didn't want my choices and decisions to be burdensome for my mother, so I told her that I was fine and didn't need anything, but I promised to let her know if that changed. I made it clear that I had no intention of moving back home, and that I had no expectation of her raising my child. I explained that becoming a mother meant that my military career would look different, but it didn't mean that it was over.

My mother took the news of me being engaged and pregnant better than I had hoped, and I was very grateful for that. I wanted my mother's advice and guidance throughout this journey, and I didn't want a rift between us to prevent her from being involved in the pregnancy and birth of her newest grandchild.

With the business of telling our parents behind us, Carlos and I began discussing next steps. In order to save money, we decided that we would continue to live in our respective barracks on base for as long as we could. This decision worked out well, and when I was about six months pregnant, we had saved enough money to move into a nice apartment to get ready for the arrival of our son.

In full disclosure, I had no idea what the sex of the baby was, but I began referring to the baby as "he" and "Joshua" from the very beginning because I was convinced that the child I was carrying was a boy. Joshua was a name that I'd selected for my eventual son when I was around eleven years old because, in the Bible, he was a great leader who succeeded Moses in leading the Israelite people. He was a man of strength and great courage, and he had an unwavering faith in God—all attributes I wanted for my son. So, when I learned I was pregnant, I assumed I was having a son, and I began calling him Joshua.

Everyone in my battalion was excited for Carlos and me. They threw us a baby shower and supplied everything we needed to get started as new parents. My company commander purchased a crib, one of the sergeants purchased a car seat, someone else bought bed linens and diapers, and everyone else contributed enough items to fill two nurseries. The most special gift was a collective gift from the entire battalion. One of my fellow soldiers, Specialist Chambers, had asked everyone in the battalion to contribute a swatch of fabric from something they owned. People contributed fabric swatches from college T-shirts and sweatshirts with their favorite sports teams' logos. They contributed hats that represented something from their hometown or favorite hobby, patches from jackets, and a number of other items that held special significance to them. She then stitched all the pieces of fabric together to create the most beautiful tapestry that became Joshua's first baby blanket. The blanket was a beautiful collage of colors and patterns, each with a special significance. That gift was so much more than a baby blanket; it was a one-of-a-kind heirloom from my military brothers and sisters who had honored my child and grafted him into our 82nd Airborne Division family.

Chapter 10

My pregnancy was pretty uneventful. I didn't have prolonged morning sickness, I had no heartburn, my weight was as it should be, and I don't recall craving any weird foods. My checkups were normal, and as my due date approached, my doctor explained the signs that would indicate I was in active labor. I learned about the phenomenon called Braxton-Hicks contractions, what to do when my water broke, and what I should expect if a cesarean section became necessary.

Before the baby was born, Carlos and I had an important piece of business to tend to: we had to get married. I didn't expect a wedding ceremony filled with family and friends, and I didn't want anything fancy. I was six months pregnant, and I didn't feel much like a blushing bride, so we decided we would go to a justice of the peace. Since we hadn't planned for a specific date, we went to Dillon, South Carolina, to get married. In Dillon, you could apply for a marriage license on any day of the week and get married twenty-four hours later.

On Friday, January 12, 1990, Carlos and I drove an hour south on I-95 to Dillon. When we arrived at the makeshift chapel, we applied for a marriage license and stayed overnight in a hotel to satisfy the twenty-four-hour waiting period.

The next day, we presented ourselves to the justice of the peace, paid the fee, and waited in the waiting room until it was our turn to be married. Finally, an older lady who was playing the roles of receptionist, waiting room attendant, and (in some cases) witness, called our names and indicated that we were next. We waited in a small hallway until we were escorted inside the room where we would exchange our vows and become husband and wife. Saying the words "I do" proved to be a lot harder than I'd expected.

As I listened to the justice of the peace recite the marriage vows for Carlos to agree to, I realized that being someone's wife was actually a big deal. Carlos and I were from different ethnic backgrounds, which meant we saw gender roles very differently. We held different religious beliefs, neither of us had met the other's family, and I'm not certain that we were even in love. Sure, we loved each other, but I don't think we were *together-forever* in love.

As a whirlwind of thoughts flooded my brain, I began to feel lightheaded. I could no longer hear the justice of the peace, or anything else happening in the room, when out of nowhere, my subconscious began trying to get my attention. *Do I think this is a big deal? Well, yeah.* My subconscious prodded, *Shoshanna, did you hear me? Do you need me to repeat it for you?* Why was my subconscious asking me questions? What was I supposed to have heard? My subconscious again asked, *Shoshanna, do you?*

I shook my head, trying to make sense of this annoying internal dialogue, when I realized that it hadn't been my subconscious asking me questions. The justice of the peace was asking me to repeat my vows.

As my confusion cleared, I looked at the justice of the peace and asked sheepishly, "Do I what?"

He sighed in exasperation and repeated, "Do you take Carlos to be your lawful husband, to live together in holy matrimony, to love him, to honor him, to comfort him, and to keep him in sickness and in health, forsaking all others, for as long as you both shall live?"

I stared at him, attempting to process what he was asking me to commit to. No one had told me that I would have to commit to anything for as long as I lived. That didn't sound like an agreement with an exit clause; it sounded pretty permanent. If everyone who got married committed to these same things, why were there so many divorces? Had my parents committed to love, honor, and keep each other for as long as they lived?

Suddenly, this felt very heavy, and I wanted to say, "No, I don't promise those things at all. I just want to be married so that our child has a family."

I didn't say that, though. Instead, in a barely audible whisper, I said, "I do."

Being married didn't feel any different. I was the same person as before, only now I was referred to as someone's wife. The marriage began nicely as Carlos and I prepared for the arrival of our child. We had moved into our new apartment, and the nursery was ready. The only thing left for us to do was wait for the baby to arrive.

The closer I got to the due date, the more exhausted I felt, so when I wasn't at work, I slept. One afternoon, I was sleeping on the sofa when I was startled awake by a sharp pain in my abdomen. I lay there as still as possible to see if the pain would happen again. Five minutes, ten minutes, nothing. So I dozed off again. Before long, I was once again awakened by the discomfort. I remembered that the doctor had said that I would know I was in labor when the contractions were consistent, slowly increased in frequency, and gradually increased in intensity. Despite the ever-increasing pain, I didn't think that I was in labor because my water hadn't broken. Besides, the baby wasn't due for another four days. Nevertheless, I decided to begin timing the contractions. According to my data, the pain occurred about every twelve minutes and lasted only a few seconds. It was also reasonably tolerable. *This isn't too bad*, I thought, *so it can't be labor.* I lay there for several hours timing the pain, and eventually, it was occurring consistently every five minutes. Each contraction lasted around thirty seconds, and every round was slightly more intense than the last. The pattern seemed consistent with labor, so I called Carlos to get his opinion on what I should do.

"Carlos, can you come here for a minute?"

Carlos came downstairs. "What's up?"

"I'm trying to figure out whether or not I'm in labor."

"Are you having contractions?" he asked.

"I think so."

"How far apart are they?"

"About five minutes, maybe four," I answered.

"*Five* minutes?! Didn't the doctor say for us to go to the hospital when they were ten minutes apart?"

"Yes, but I wanted to be extra sure."

Carlos began panicking and running around the house at full speed, grabbing the things we'd packed to take to the hospital. "We have to go to the hospital now," he said.

"OK, let me run up and take a quick shower."

"A *shower*?! You don't have time to take a shower. You're getting ready to have a baby!" he yelled.

"I'm OK. I'll be quick," I called as I climbed the stairs.

When I returned, Carlos was frantically pacing around the living room. He looked up as I entered the room. "Can we go now?"

"Yes, we can go now," I said.

"How are the contractions now?" he asked.

"They're about the same, but they are lasting a bit longer now," I responded.

Carlos and I arrived at the hospital and got checked in. After a quick examination, the doctor confirmed that I was, in fact, in labor. My water still hadn't broken, but the contractions were steady.

In order to move things along, the doctor suggested that Carlos and I walk around. It was nice outside, so we decided to walk around outside so that we could get some fresh air. After walking around the hospital campus for a few minutes, Carlos suggested that we walk to the bank to deposit a check that he'd forgotten to deposit. I wasn't too uncomfortable, and the bank was just under two miles away, which didn't seem far, so I agreed.

We walked slowly and made it to the bank without incident. As Carlos stood in line waiting for his turn, I realized that the contractions were becoming far more intense, and I wondered whether I'd be able to walk back. We didn't have our car with us, so I really didn't have a choice. As Carlos approached the teller to begin his transaction, I leaned over to him and asked him to please hurry up.

The teller looked at me and asked, "Ma'am, are you OK?"

"Yes," I said, "I'm in labor, but it's OK because the doctor told me to walk around to move things along."

"You're in labor?"

"Yes."

"And you walked here from Womack Hospital?" she asked.

"Yes."

"Oh, my goodness. I don't think the doctor meant for you to walk this far. When they tell you to walk around, they usually intend for you to stay inside the hospital," the teller explained.

As I listened to the teller, the worst contraction that I had experienced thus far hit me. It felt like my insides were being split in two, and I yelled out loud. At this, every person inside the bank looked at Carlos as if he was the most horrible person in the world.

A lady approached us and asked, "Why did you make her walk this far?"

Before Carlos could answer, another contraction hit, and my knees buckled.

"I can't walk back." I grimaced as another wave of pain hit.

Carlos stared at me with a panicked look on his face, likely wondering what the heck we were going to do. I didn't want my son to be born in a bank lobby, but I could barely move, let alone walk two miles.

A man who was waiting in line approached us and said, "Please let me drive you back to the hospital."

"Yes, please!" I exclaimed before Carlos could respond.

Carlos and the kind gentleman carried me to the man's car, and once I was tucked inside, he quickly drove us back to the hospital. Carlos grabbed a wheelchair and wheeled me back to the maternity floor.

When the nurse saw us, she ran over and asked, "Where have you two been?"

I moaned and said, "We walked to the bank to move things along, like the doctor asked."

"The bank? He didn't ask you to walk to the bank. What were you thinking?" She gave Carlos a disapproving stare as she took the wheelchair from him and pushed me to my room.

From there, everything went pretty quickly. The labor pains intensified to the point where they were unbearable. The doctor confirmed that I was fully dilated and instructed the nurse to move me into the labor and delivery room. Once I was in position, the doctor instructed me to push the next time a contraction started.

"I can't!" I cried.

"Yes, you can," Carlos said in my ear.

I pushed as hard as I could. I did this over and over until I finally heard the doctor's voice exclaim over the sounds of a crying baby, "Congratulations! It's a girl."

Did I hear him correctly? We have a girl? Huh, imagine that ... I guess her name won't be Joshua, then.

They wrapped the baby in a blanket, and the nurse asked, "Would you like to hold your daughter?"

My daughter ... Wow, I'm a mother, I thought as I took the tiny baby into my arms and stared at the most perfect little face I'd ever seen.

I didn't get to hold her very long before she was whisked away to be cleaned up and have several newborn tests administered.

I smiled at Carlos, who had the biggest grin imaginable on his face, and I said, "You didn't faint."

He smiled back and said, "You're damn right I didn't."

My smile widened a bit more before, feeling exhausted, I dozed off.

I woke up to a room full of people. Many of my friends and coworkers had come to meet the baby, and the nurse was moving around the room filling trays with diapers, baby wipes, and other supplies that I would need. Carlos held our daughter while everyone looked on and commented on how beautiful she was.

One of the ladies, the commander's wife, turned to me and said, "You did good. She is perfect."

Another commented, "I'm sure you had terrible heartburn, because she has a head full of hair."

Someone else asked, "How much did she weigh?"

And so went the questions. I answered them as I beamed with pride at my daughter.

Finally, the company commander looked at me and asked, "What is her name?"

I had not thought of a single name for a girl because I had been certain that I was having a boy.

"I don't know, sir. We haven't decided on a name for her yet," I replied.

"You haven't picked out a name?" someone asked in disbelief.

"Not yet," I said, embarrassed.

The conversation in the room quickly turned to baby name suggestions.

"What about Julia?" someone suggested.

"She doesn't look like a Julia. She looks like an Elizabeth," another person replied.

"What makes her look like an Elizabeth?" the person responded.

Someone else offered Linda, another person suggested Lisa, and still another person offered Mary. Fortunately, it was time for the nurse to teach me how to feed my new baby, so everyone was asked to leave. I was grateful for the visit, but I was exhausted and a bit overwhelmed at the same time.

After everyone had left, the nurse, Carlos, and I were the only ones who remained in the room.

As the nurse gave me instructions on how to nurse my daughter, I looked at Carlos and asked, "What are we going to name her? I never selected any girl names because I thought we were having a boy. I can't believe that I called her Joshua for nine months!"

Carlos replied, "Let me name her."

I considered his request, which made sense because I had no idea what her name should be. However, I was very hesitant to give Carlos complete control over naming our daughter, so I came up with a compromise.

"How about you select three names that you would like for our daughter, and I will pick two names from your list to be her first and middle names? Please don't pick anything crazy. Keep in mind that she will have to grow up with the name you select, and I don't want her to be made fun of or picked on because she has an unusual name."

Growing up on the South Side of Chicago with the name Shoshanna, I was all too familiar with how mean kids could be if you were too different.

"I'm not going to pick anything crazy," he said. "I'm going to pick names that are tied to her Mexican heritage," he continued.

"Her last name will tie to her Mexican heritage. Just pick something nice," I said.

Carlos turned to the nurse and asked, "How long do we have before we have to tell you what we've decided for her name?"

The nurse replied, "I need to know in two days so we can have her name recorded on her birth certificate and order her Social Security card."

"OK, we'll have a name in two days," Carlos said.

"For now," the nurse replied, "we'll just call her Girl Fuentes."

I tried to think of a few backup names, just in case I didn't like any of the names that Carlos chose, but I couldn't come up with anything that felt right.

Whenever I would ask Carlos what he had come up with so far, he would simply reply, "I'll tell you at the end of the two days."

The deadline had finally arrived. We were taking Girl Fuentes home the next day, so it was officially time to give her a name.

Looking quite satisfied, Carlos said to me, "I have my picks."

"OK, let's hear them."

"OK, but don't interrupt until I tell you all three. I'll list them starting with my favorite."

"OK. Whatcha got?"

"My number one choice that I like the best is Belinda."

Surely, I hadn't heard him correctly. I looked at his face, waiting for him to burst into laughter, but he didn't.

He smiled with pride at his choice. "Belinda Fuentes!" he exclaimed.

"*OK*, what are the other two options?"

"My second choice," he continued, "is Mary. Every Mexican girl has Mary somewhere in her name."

Not too bad ... I might be able to work with Mary, I thought. "So what's your final choice?" I asked, almost afraid to hear his response.

"Well, technically, I could only think of two names that I like, so I decided for the third choice I would select the name of the most beautiful actress on TV."

"An actress? What actress?" I asked in disbelief.

"You know who my favorite actress is!" he exclaimed.

"No, I don't. Who is it?"

"What show do we watch almost every night?" he asked with a smile on his face.

"Oh, the show *A Different World*," I responded.

"And who is my favorite actress from that show?" he asked with a grin.

"Are you talking about Jasmine Guy?" I asked tentatively.

"Yep, you guessed it. My third choice is Jasmine. And remember, you have to pick two names from my list," he added, just in case I had forgotten the agreement.

"OK, I will pick two names from your list." I had no idea how I would make any of the three names work, but I was certain that our daughter would not be named Belinda. While the name itself was fine, it felt more appropriate for an older woman, not a baby girl born in 1990.

"Which two names are you going to pick?" he asked.

I got out of the twin-size hospital bed that I had been lying in and moved in the direction of the door. I was headed to the nurses' station to inform them that we had decided on a name for Girl Fuentes.

When I reached the door, I looked over my shoulder, smiled at Carlos, and said, "You'll find out the two names I picked when you sign her birth certificate tomorrow." With that, I headed to the nurses' station to name our daughter.

The next morning, I was being discharged, which meant that it was time for Carlos and me to take our daughter home and begin caring for her on our own. The notion of being responsible for a newborn infant was a terrifying thought. At the hospital, we had nurses and aides who showed us what to do and answered the dozens of questions I had each day. At home, it would be just us, two people who knew nothing about caring for a newborn. I didn't even have one of those parenting self-help books filled with tips and suggestions for new parents. I had no idea what was normal or when to be concerned. As I thought about it, I made a mental note to visit a bookstore as soon as I could to pick up some new parenting reference materials.

The nurse met with Carlos and me to review the discharge instructions and schedule our first follow-up appointment. She also provided several numbers that we could call if we had questions or concerns after we took our daughter home. The last piece of paper she handed over was the baby's birth certificate for us to review. She asked us to look over all the information to make sure it was accurate. If it was all correct, we were each instructed to sign where indicated.

I took the piece of paper, gave it a once-over, and then affixed my signature. I handed the birth certificate to Carlos who immediately looked at the name printed at the top. It read *Jasmine Marie Fuentes.* I knew he had chosen Mary, but I figured since Marie was a close-cousin variation, the adjustment would be OK.

Carlos smiled, hugged me, and whispered, "It's perfect." He then signed his daughter's birth certificate.

We left the hospital and headed straight home to get Jasmine settled in.

Over the next few weeks, I began to feel more confident feeding, bathing, and taking care of her on my own while Carlos worked during the day. When Carlos got home, he would take over baby duty while I cooked dinner. Jasmine was a happy baby, and we were a happy little family. Carlos and I may have had different ethnicities, upbringings, and religious beliefs, but what we had in common was a strong desire to be the best parents we could possibly be to our beautiful baby girl.

We were very fortunate that Jasmine began sleeping through the night almost immediately. I would get up once or twice to feed her, but for the most part, when she went to sleep, she was out for the count.

I would call my mother three or four times a day, especially during the first few weeks, with endless questions: Should the baby sleep on her stomach or back? Should I bathe her every day, or is that too much for a newborn? Do I apply ointment every time I change her diaper, or only if her bottom is red? Each time, she would reassure me that I was doing a great job before providing some very helpful advice. On one such occasion, I called my mother, crying hysterically. When she answered the phone and heard me sobbing on the other line, she immediately panicked.

"What's wrong, Shoshanna? Did something happen to Jasmine?"

I spoke through waves of sobs and said, "No, she's OK, but she *hates* me."

My mom softened her voice and asked, "Why do you think she hates you? You're her mother; she loves you."

"Because she has been crying nonstop for hours, and I have tried everything to soothe her. I walked with her, I fed her, I checked her diaper, I rocked her, but nothing has helped, and she just won't stop crying!" Maybe it was postpartum depression, or maybe I was just feeling very overwhelmed, but whatever the reason, I had abandoned my usual calm demeanor and was having a full-scale meltdown.

My mother continued to speak in a very soothing voice, like only a mother can. She told me to lay Jasmine down and make a warm bath for her. As I prepared the bath for Jasmine, my mother stayed on the line and offered comforting words to help me calm down. Jasmine screamed throughout the entire bath, and afterward, my mother talked me through swaddling her while she continued to shriek. Once Jasmine was clean, dry, and swaddled, my mother told me to sit on the sofa and softly rub her back while humming. I think the humming was more for me, because it helped calm and relax me as I slowly rocked. After about ten minutes of rubbing and humming, Jasmine let out a big burp before drifting off to sleep. I carried her upstairs and laid her in her crib. I grabbed a few pillows and lay down on the floor next to her bed, in case the crying started again. The room was filled with nothing but silence. I drifted off as well, and we both slept soundly for several hours.

The next time I spoke to my mom, I asked her what had been wrong with Jasmine. I was terrified that it might have been something I had done. She told me I hadn't done anything wrong, and that Jasmine had been suffering from something called colic, which was very common in babies. I was relieved that I hadn't done anything to cause my daughter discomfort, and I was very thankful for my mother.

Chapter 11

Strength and growth come only through
continuous effort and struggle.

—Napoleon Hill

After a month of maternity leave, I enrolled Jasmine in day care so I could return to work. It was hard leaving her with strangers, but that was part of life as a military parent. Carlos and I both were in the 82nd Airborne Division, so we were constantly preparing for drills, jumps, and potential deployments. We took shifts being with Jasmine while we each performed our military duties.

We had not yet experienced a situation where we were both called into duty at the same time, but that was always a very real possibility. Because of this, we had to arrange short- and long-term care for Jasmine in the event that duty called us both away. We had legal documents drawn up that designated an immediate care provider who would stay with Jasmine until her long-term care provider arrived. We signed powers of attorney, set up bank accounts for the caregivers to access, and created a file that contained important documents such as Jasmine's birth certificate, Social Security card, vaccination records, etc. This process was required for all dual-military couples, to ensure they could fulfill their military responsibilities without worrying about the well-being of their dependent children. It was the sort of thing you did to ensure you were well prepared, but you hoped that you would never have to activate your plans.

Carlos was in a field artillery unit, so he was called away much more frequently than I was. It wasn't unusual for our home phone to ring at 1:00 a.m. with a voice on the other end informing Carlos where he was to report in less than an hour. Carlos kept his gear packed and ready to go at all times. With each call, he would spring out of bed, grab his gear, and head out into the night, prepared for whatever duty requirements awaited him. In every instance, he returned home, informed me that it had just been a drill, climbed back into bed, and went to sleep. Sometimes, they would don parachutes, board an aircraft, and fly around for several hours before jumping onto a drop zone back at Fort Bragg. There were also instances when they hiked to a site in the middle of nowhere to practice drills. The thing that was always consistent was that each time, within twenty-four hours, he would return home, and life would proceed as normal.

On August 7, 1990, the phone rang as it had many times before. After listening to the reporting instructions, Carlos began his usual routine. He stumbled out of bed, kissed me goodbye, and told me that he'd be home soon. Then he walked down the hall to kiss Jasmine goodbye before grabbing his gear and heading out the door.

I rolled over and went back to sleep, desperate for my last couple of hours of sleep before I would be forced to get up and start the day.

When my alarm clock finally rang, I looked over and noticed that Carlos wasn't home yet. I was disappointed, but I wasn't concerned because it wasn't unusual for him to have to stay after a drill to clean equipment. We only had one vehicle, and it was with Carlos, so I had no way to take Jasmine to day care or get to work myself. I called my friend Trina who lived nearby, and I explained the situation to her. I asked her if she would drive me to drop Jasmine off at day care and then take me to work. She agreed.

By the time I'd showered, dressed, and packed Jasmine's bag, the doorbell rang. We loaded the car and dropped Jasmine off at day care before proceeding to the 82nd Finance Battalion where I worked. Trina asked if I needed a ride home, but I politely declined, assuring her that Carlos would be home in time to pick me up. I thanked her for the ride, waved goodbye, and went inside the building.

When I walked inside, everyone was buzzing, talking about some sort of invasion that had occurred overnight.

I walked up to one of the other soldiers and asked what everyone was talking about.

"Haven't you heard?!" he exclaimed. "Iraq invaded Kuwait, and the US along with other allies are getting involved."

"Getting involved? Involved how?" I asked.

"They are sending troops to Kuwait and Saudi Arabia. The rumor is that soldiers from the division went last night," he continued.

"Really? Which soldiers do you think went?"

"I don't know, but surely the infantry, armor units, and artillery will be among the first to go."

"My husband is in the artillery battalion," I replied. "When he gets home, I'll ask him if he's heard anything."

"Where is he now?" the soldier asked.

"His unit was called in early this morning around one o'clock, and he hadn't returned home yet when I left this morning."

"Maybe he is already on his way over there," he said in a matter-of-fact tone.

"No chance, it was just a drill. Besides, he told me he would be home soon," I replied with a little too much edge in my voice. I softened my tone to mask the tension that was building in the pit of my stomach.

"He has our only car, so I'm sure he'll be here to pick me up at five o'clock. When he gets here, I'll ask him if the rumors are true."

"Whatever you say," the soldier replied.

I turned and walked into the office I shared with three other soldiers and began my work for the day.

As the end of the day approached, I called home to check in with Carlos to make sure he would be leaving soon to pick me up. I assumed that he had gone home and gone straight to bed. It was 4:00 p.m., so surely he was awake by now, but in case he wasn't, a phone call would help nudge him along. I dialed the number to our house and waited for him to pick up. The phone rang several times before the answering machine clicked on. "You've reached the Fuentes residence. Please leave your name and—" I hung up before the announcement finished. Maybe he'd gotten home later than I'd thought and had turned the ringer off.

I waited half an hour before trying him again. I continued to pack my things and made small talk while I waited with the few people who were still there. I dialed the number to the house again, listened as the line rang, and just as before, the answering machine clicked on.

"Darn it," I muttered as I hung up the phone.

I decided to try him at his unit. If a conflict had actually happened and the US was sending troops, he might still be at work helping his unit prepare to deploy. I dialed the number to the CQ desk at the 2nd Battalion, 319th Field Artillery Regiment.

The phone rang several times before the person on duty finally answered. "Good afternoon. 2-319. How may I help you?"

"Hi. May I speak with Specialist Fuentes?" I asked.

"Specialist Fuentes isn't here."

"Do you know when he left?"

"No," the voice on the other end replied.

"Have you seen him within the last hour?"

"No."

"OK, thanks for your help." I hung up the phone, satisfied that Carlos was either passed out at home (which wouldn't be like him), or he was on his way to pick me up. It was more likely that he was on his way, so I waited.

Five o'clock became six o'clock, and then six thirty. Carlos hadn't shown up, and I wasn't able to reach him at home. Meanwhile, I had to pick Jasmine up from day care in thirty minutes before late fees would begin accumulating.

Carlos was never late for anything, so I started to get worried. Why hadn't he called to let me know what was going on? I hoped and prayed that he was just asleep at home, but I knew deep down that was not likely the case because oversleeping was not something that Carlos did … ever!

My mind shifted to figuring out how to get to the day care and then home. Everyone in the office had already left, so there was no one there for me to ask for a ride. I phoned Trina and asked if she could pick me up.

While I waited for Trina to arrive, I called the day care and told them I was running late. They appreciated the call and said that Jasmine would be packed and ready to go when I got there. I arrived at the day care twenty minutes late and expected to pay the dollar-per-minute late fee. When the director saw my frenzied state, she took pity on me and was gracious enough to waive the late fee.

As Trina pulled away from the day care, I sat in the passenger seat of her car with my hands trembling and my heart racing. *What if he isn't home? He has to be home. Where else could he be? Why haven't I heard from him?* As my thoughts continued to swirl, I felt sick to my stomach. "Please be there, please be there, please be there," I muttered to myself.

When we pulled up to the house, the first thing I noticed was that the car was not in the driveway. My heart sank, and I genuinely began to panic as my mind continued to race. *Where is he? Surely, he hasn't been shipped off to some foreign country without so much as a goodbye. What if everyone was right, and he was one of the soldiers who had been shipped to Saudi Arabia or Kuwait? This can't be happening.*

I jumped out of the car and ran into the house. I searched every room for any sign that Carlos had been home, but everything was just as I'd left it that morning. I began to cry. As I walked down the stairs to go back to the car to get Jasmine, I saw that Trina had come inside. She sat on the sofa with Jasmine and her daughter, Latisha, lying next to her.

I looked at her through my tears and said, "I think he's gone off to war."

She looked at me compassionately and said, "My husband called me earlier and told me he's being deployed. He couldn't tell me where he was going, and we were only able to talk for a few minutes. He doesn't know when he'll be able to call me again, but he promised to call me as soon as he was able."

I stared at her in disbelief and asked, "Why didn't you tell me?"

"I didn't tell you when I picked you up because you were already very upset, and I didn't know for sure that Fluey was gone too." Fluey was a nickname that people used for Carlos because they had a hard time pronouncing Fuentes.

As I listened to her tell me the details of the conversation she'd had with her husband, who was assigned to an infantry unit near Carlos's, the reality of what was happening began to sink in. He was gone, and I did not know what I was going to do. I didn't know how to be a single parent to a four-month-old infant. Correction: I didn't know how to be an active-duty single parent to a four-month-old infant. I didn't even have a driver's license. I had a military-issued license to drive military vehicles, but I didn't have a civilian driver's license. Growing up in Chicago, I'd taken the bus or the L everywhere I went, so all I needed was a dollar and a transfer to go anywhere in the city. I never took driver's education, and my parents never taught me how to drive. Why hadn't I asked Carlos to teach me to drive?

As I continued to cry, I realized I didn't even know where he'd left the car, so even if I could figure out how to get my driver's license, I didn't have a vehicle to drive. I composed myself and turned my attention back to Trina.

"Thank you for helping me today. I really appreciate it. And I'm sorry that your husband has been deployed. What are you going to do?" I asked.

"I'll stay here until he calls me again. If he is going to be gone for a long time, Latisha and I will move back to Virginia to be closer to my family," she said.

"That sounds like a good plan," I said.

We chatted for a little longer before she gathered her daughter and headed for the door. "What time do you want me to pick you up tomorrow?" she asked.

"You're giving me a ride tomorrow too?"

"Yes. We don't know what's going on, and we have to stick together. I'll drive you around as long as you need me to, and if you find out where Fluey left the car, maybe we can figure out how to get you a driver's license."

I was so grateful that I began to cry again. She gave me a hug and then left.

After she left, I tried to go about my normal routine, except nothing was normal. Being in the house alone, not knowing where my husband was, was not normal. Not knowing when he was coming home was not normal. Not knowing if I would ever see him again was not normal. There were so many things that I hadn't said when he'd left that morning. Why hadn't I gotten up with him to see him off?

Tears began to run down my face again, and as I cried, the harshest reality of all hit me: there was a strong possibility that I could get deployed too! As the thought of me being deployed overwhelmed my brain, I sobbed uncontrollably and held my daughter against my chest.

I sat holding Jasmine, crying for hours, only taking a break to feed her or change positions. The silence in the house was deafening, and I desperately needed a distraction, so I turned on the television. As I clicked through the channels, searching for a mindless sitcom, the phone rang. I jumped up and ran to the kitchen.

"Hello!" I answered.

"Hey, it's me."

It was Carlos! Thank God, it was Carlos. "Oh my God, I'm so happy to hear from you!" I shouted. "Where are you?"

"Look, I only have a few minutes to talk, so listen. I left the car in the parking lot behind my unit, and the keys are at the CQ desk. I left my wallet and my wedding ring in the glove compartment," he explained.

"What are you saying? Why are you telling me this?"

He ignored my questions and continued his instructions. "Have someone take you to get the car so you can get back and forth. And please call my mom and let her know what's going on."

"What is going on?" I asked.

"I can't tell you anything, but just watch the news," he said.

"Carlos, are you leaving me? What am I going to do without you?" I asked softly.

"You're going to take care of my daughter until I get home."

I began to cry.

"Don't cry. You're going to be fine," he urged.

"When are you coming home?" I asked as I continued to cry.

"I don't know, Shonna," was his somber reply. "Look, there's a shitload of angry soldiers waiting to use the phone, so I have to go. I'll call you again or write to you whenever I can. Kiss my baby for me and go get the car tomorrow. I love you."

Click.

"I love you too," I whispered as the line went dead. I couldn't bring myself to hang up the phone, so I just held it to my ear until I heard the noise of a rapid dial tone.

I put the phone on the cradle and turned the television to the news.

It was several weeks before I spoke to Carlos again.

Once the not-so-secret secret operation was officially made public, everything began moving at a hundred miles per hour. The division was on high alert, and every paratrooper who hadn't been part of the initial deployment was preparing to head to Saudi Arabia or was assigned guard duty to protect the base and the military equipment housed there. I fell into the latter category.

My unit was tasked with guarding one of the many motor pools. I was paired with another soldier, and we were assigned the evening shift from 6:00 p.m. until 6:00 a.m. We spent the long twelve-hour shifts pacing and watching for anything that was out of the ordinary.

Getting to and from the base wasn't ideal, but it wasn't as complicated as I'd thought it would be. Trina dropped me off every evening, and my duty partner gave me a ride home after our shift ended. I didn't like having to depend on other people. All my life, I'd strived to be independent. But in this situation, I didn't have a choice. And while I didn't like feeling helpless, I was grateful for the people who were willing to help me.

Things got complicated when Trina told me she was moving back to Virginia in two weeks. Her leaving meant that I would no longer have a ride to get around, or anyone to watch Jasmine when I was on evening duty. As I thought about my situation, it occurred to me that I owned a car, and technically, I had a driver's license. My military-issued driver's license did not extend to privately owned vehicles. Despite this, I decided I would use my own car to get around, and if I was stopped, I would feign ignorance, suggesting that I wasn't aware that I wasn't permitted to drive a private vehicle. What officer would penalize me for driving to perform my military duties when the country was at war? While this seemed like a solid plan, there was no need to make my life any more complicated than it already was. I needed to take the driving test and get my actual license as soon as I could.

When I reported for duty that evening, I asked the other soldiers if any of their wives would be interested in providing overnight babysitting services. Everyone in the battalion knew my husband had been deployed, so several people stepped up and offered to check with their wives to see if they would watch Jasmine when I was on night duty.

The next day, one of the sergeants informed me that his wife had agreed to watch Jasmine. I thanked him and asked him how much she was going to charge me. He just smiled and said, "You'll have to take that up with her."

I was relieved and filled with gratitude that I had reliable childcare, but I was also concerned about the cost. I didn't expect her to watch Jasmine for free, but even with Carlos's paycheck still coming in, I only had a little money to pay for both a babysitter and Jasmine's spot at the day care. I needed the childcare, so I agreed and decided that I would figure out how to make it work.

"What is your wife's name?" I asked.

"Melissa, and she's looking forward to meeting you both," he replied.

"I'm looking forward to meeting her too. When can she start?"

"She can start as soon as you like. Here is our number. Give her a call, and the two of you can work out the details." He scribbled his home number on a torn piece of paper and handed it to me.

I grabbed the slip of paper and said, "Thank you, Sergeant Riley. I really appreciate your help. Melissa's too."

He smiled, nodded, and walked away.

Melissa began watching Jasmine the following week. The first time that I dropped her off, I arrived early so that I would have time to go over everything with Melissa. When I arrived, she greeted me at the door with a huge smile.

"Specialist Fuentes, I'm so happy to meet you. And this little bundle of cuteness must be Jasmine," she said.

"It's nice to meet you as well," I replied.

She scooped Jasmine up in her arms, looked at her, and smiled. "You and I are going to get along just fine," she said, using a baby-talk tone.

I was happy that she also had a child who was about Jasmine's age, because Jasmine enjoyed being around other kids. That also meant that I didn't have to pack a bag of toys to help keep Jasmine entertained while she was there.

After Melissa and I discussed Jasmine's eating and sleeping routines, I said, "Sergeant Riley said that I should ask you how much this will cost."

She laughed and said, "He did, did he?"

"Yes. And how often would you like to be paid? I get paid monthly, but I could probably pay you every two weeks if monthly is too long," I added.

"Well, let's just call this one mother helping another," she said.

I looked at her in complete amazement. "You don't want me to pay you?" I asked.

"No, that won't be necessary. You just go do your duty so our troops can come on home. Just consider this me doing my part."

My eyes filled with tears.

She was kind enough to look away and pretend not to notice. "Now go on and get out of here before you're late. Jasmine is in excellent hands."

I gave her a big hug that was probably a bit too long, but I was extremely grateful.

Prior to Trina moving, I was able to get my driver's license, although I narrowly passed the driving test. I believe the instructor was far more lenient on me than normal, which I appreciated.

The first time I drove on my own was the day after I got my license, when I went to take Jasmine to day care. Fortunately, this was one of the rare days when I had morning duty, and I was grateful that I didn't have to deal with being a new*ish* driver trying to navigate an unfamiliar vehicle at night.

As I walked to the vehicle with Jasmine in my arms, I said a silent prayer, thanking God for this kind blessing. I loaded Jasmine into her car seat, buckled myself in, and started the car. *So far, so good.* I put my foot on the brake, shifted into reverse, tapped the accelerator, and backed out of the driveway way too fast. I immediately jammed on the brake and took a few deep breaths before trying again. "You can do this," I muttered to myself. This time, I eased off the brake, and the car slowly rolled backward. This was better.

Once I was fully out of the driveway, I shifted the car into drive and pressed the accelerator softly. The sensitivity of the pedal was far greater in the car than it was in the Humvee. I had to step on the pedal in the Humvee quite hard before it would even budge, but this vehicle only required the slightest touch.

I approached the exit to my neighborhood and said another silent prayer before entering traffic. I gripped the steering wheel tightly and stayed in the far-right lane. As cars zipped past me, I sped up so that I was at least driving the speed limit.

After driving a few miles, I noticed a burning smell. *Oh, crap. What now?* I didn't want to be late, so I continued to drive, deciding that I would see what it was when I got to the day care. A few cars honked at me and yelled something as they drove by, but I couldn't tell what they were saying.

I had less than a mile to go before I reached the day care when I stopped at a red light.

A guy in the car next to me rolled down his window and yelled, "Your tires are smoking!"

"What? I can't hear you," I said.

"Your tires are smoking. Pull over!" he yelled.

"I can't pull over. I have to drop my daughter off!" I yelled back.

"Then check your parking brake."

"My what?"

"Your parking brake!"

The light turned green, and I stepped on the pedal to continue my journey. Whatever he had been yelling seemed important, but I had no idea what he'd been talking about. I pulled into the day care's parking lot a few minutes later and saw the same car from the red light pull in as well. Was he following me? Why was he following me? I grabbed Jasmine as quickly as I could and headed for the door. The rancid smell of burning rubber permeated the air around my car. What the heck had I done?

Once I was inside, I checked Jasmine in and got her settled. When I went outside, the guy was leaning on his car. He didn't appear to be threatening, but I still thought it was odd that he had followed me and was waiting outside.

Once I got within earshot, he said, "I think you were driving with your parking brake on."

I looked at him with a confused expression. "What?"

"You were driving with your parking brake on," he repeated.

"How do you know?" I asked.

"For starters, your tires are smoking. May I take a look?"

I nodded, and the guy started walking toward my car. I think he sensed my nervousness, so he moved slowly, with his hands raised, as if to say, *I just want to help.*

He opened the driver's side door and said, "Yep, you sure were. Why didn't you release the brake before you started driving?" he asked.

"I didn't know I had to. My friend parked the car yesterday, so she must have turned it on," I replied.

"Well, let me show you how it works, so you will know next time." He showed me how to engage and release the parking brake several times. He explained to me what it was for and when to use it.

I thanked him before getting in the car and heading to work. With the parking brake released, the car drove a lot more smoothly and was easier to navigate.

As I drove to work, I chuckled to myself, thinking about all the cars that had honked at me and the drivers who had yelled as they'd passed. "They must have thought I was an idiot," I said out loud, and then for the first time in a long while, I laughed.

As the war efforts went on, there were many times when I was very angry that I hadn't been selected to go to Saudi Arabia. Fighting for my country was the very thing I had signed up for. Desert Storm was my chance to be one of those soldiers I had watched in the movies fighting for America and her allies. Although no one ever said it, and I doubt it could officially be true, I believe that someone didn't think it was necessary to deploy a new mother of a four-month-old baby, especially when her husband had already deployed with the first wave of soldiers. When I asked why I hadn't been deployed, they told me there were already enough supply specialists over there. Maybe that was true, but deep down, I couldn't shake the question: *Why not me?*

Carlos had been deployed for almost a year. It is said that stress ages you, and I found that to be true. At just twenty-one, I felt much older. My back ached like I was twice my age, dark circles settled stubbornly under my eyes, and even my laughter was weighed down by exhaustion. During my time as a single parent, I navigated considerable challenges and had many new experiences. I learned how to be a soldier, mother, and single parent all at the same time. I navigated the ever-present fear of not knowing whether I would see Carlos again. I learned to function on four hours of sleep, sometimes less. I experienced my daughter teething and the intermittent fevers that accompanied it. I navigated ear-splitting tantrums, which Jasmine had perfected by the time she was six months old. I listened to her utter her first word, which was "Da-da," even though she hadn't seen her da-da in several months. I dealt with chronic tonsillitis that eventually resulted in me having an emergency tonsillectomy.

Most importantly, I learned that I didn't have to do everything on my own. When I found out that I would be confined to bed after my tonsillectomy, I considered postponing the surgery despite the pain because I didn't have anyone to help with Jasmine. Instead, I picked up the phone and called Trina, who was living in Virginia at the time. Without hesitation, she traveled back to North Carolina to care for both me and Jasmine while I recovered. That experience taught me the value of humbly asking for help and accepting it with gratitude when it was offered.

Chapter 12

> There is always some madness in love.
> But there is also always some reason in madness.
>
> —Friedrich Nietzsche

Carlos returned home two weeks before Jasmine's first birthday. I dressed her in a pink dress with white ruffles, matching tights, and a pink bow in her hair. Jasmine had been born with a full head of hair, and now, at almost a year old, it had grown long enough for bows to clip in easily.

"Are you ready to go see your dad, Jasmine?" I asked, holding her up to the mirror.

"Da-da," she babbled.

"Yes, we're going to see Da-da," I said, smiling back at her reflection.

For myself, I chose a simple outfit—jeans and a button-down blouse. Jasmine was the star of the show today, so I opted for comfort over glamour. Once we were ready, I fastened her in her car seat and drove to the base. The parking lot was already packed, and hundreds of people crowded against the fence, eagerly waiting for the planes to arrive.

As I anxiously waited for the plane carrying Carlos and the other soldiers back to Fort Bragg, I considered the fact that I didn't know what to expect when he returned home. I had been a single parent for eight months and had established new routines, systems, and processes to manage our home. Would Carlos embrace those new systems, or would he insist on taking over as head of the house with all decisions defaulting to him? Would I be OK with sharing decision-making responsibility, especially when those decisions pertained to Jasmine? I had more parenting experience, and I knew what was best for her. But she was his daughter too.

I also wondered how the war might have changed him. Would he be the same person he had been before he'd left? Or, like me, had he been altered by an unexpected life event filled with unprecedented change? Had the war left him feeling heroic, or damaged? Proud, or angry? I had heard of something called post-traumatic stress disorder, or PTSD, that affected soldiers who went to war, but I didn't know anything about it. Would he suffer from that? Despite my many questions, I was certain of one thing: I was glad that he was home. And that was the only thing that mattered.

The plane finally landed, and as soldiers streamed out, met by overjoyed loved ones, I spotted Carlos. He looked much older than I remembered. His once-smooth face now had lines that made him look tired, as though he hadn't slept for months. His eyes carried a heaviness that hadn't been there before, and the youthful energy I remembered had been replaced by the weary composure of someone who had seen and endured too much. The smile on his face wasn't one of joy. It seemed sad.

I ran over to him, carrying Jasmine, and threw my free arm around his neck. "Welcome home. We are so happy to see you. Would you like to hold your mini-me?" I asked.

The more Jasmine aged, the more she looked like a tiny, female version of her father. Carlos turned toward her, and his entire demeanor changed. His face lit up as the biggest smile stretched across it. He grabbed Jasmine in his arms and held her tightly. I couldn't quite tell, but it looked as if he was crying. As he held on to her, she didn't fight the hug or try to wiggle out of his embrace. She simply laid her head on his shoulder and her tiny arms hugged him back.

Carlos seemed happy to be home, but in many ways, he acted like a guest, so I tried my best to make him feel comfortable. As for Jasmine, she did something every day that fascinated him and made him smile. Whether it was saying, "Da-da," pulling herself up and standing, or feeding herself with meticulous care, everything she did impressed him. It was heartwarming to watch him experience the firsts that I had seen our daughter do many times. The highlight was when she took her first steps. Like a true Daddy's girl, she saved that special first for her father to see. I was happy that Carlos was there to experience it, especially since he had missed so many others. And, of course, her first steps were to walk to him.

Another first that Carlos was home to experience was Jasmine's first birthday. I couldn't believe our little girl was turning one. The past year weighed heavily on Carlos and me, so I was thankful to have something wonderful to celebrate. This was our first big celebration as a family, and I wanted it to be special. I planned to invite Jasmine's playmates from day care, Melissa and her family, and a few of our friends. Trina was back in town, so she and Latisha would definitely be invited. As I discussed my ideas with Carlos, he vetoed them all. No cookout in the park because he had a new aversion to open spaces. A party at the house was out because he had a new aversion to being surrounded by a lot of people. Going to see the latest Disney movie was a nonstarter because he had a new aversion to loud noises, as well as being in a dark room with limited exits. I was beginning to get a glimpse into some of the ways the war had changed him. After exhausting every possible idea, we chose Jasmine's favorite place—Chuck E. Cheese—to celebrate her birthday. We kept things small; it was just the three of us. It was intimate for Carlos yet still celebratory for Jasmine. And it was perfect. She had both of her parents with her, she had a table full of presents, and she was surrounded by the Chuck E. Cheese characters playing instruments and serenading her. Our little family was back together, and we were all very happy.

As the weeks and months passed, the euphoria of Carlos being home faded. Too much had changed. We couldn't go back to the way things had been before, no matter how hard we tried. He was different. I was different. He had returned from a year in war with distrust and exhaustion in his eyes, his spirit hardened by what he'd witnessed and endured. Meanwhile, I had spent the year raising our daughter alone, learning to rely on others and embrace the strength of community. While he saw the world through the eyes of a soldier—guarded, defensive, and scarred—I was opening myself up to the idea of trust, and learning to let people in. Those differences didn't just exist, they clashed ... hard.

He wanted to play a more active role in Jasmine's parenting, while I was determined to maintain the routines and schedules I'd worked so hard to establish. I'd say no, only for him to override me and say yes. I argued that he was spoiling her, and he thought I was being too strict. When we weren't arguing about child-rearing, we argued about bills, household responsibilities, and even what to watch on television. Carlos had developed a taste for gory crime shows and violent movies—things I didn't want to watch and certainly didn't want Jasmine exposed to. So, yeah, we argued about that too.

Before long, all we ever did was argue. The arguments were frequent and intense. There was no longer any friendship or companionship, just constant friction. The situation continued to devolve until it was no longer a marriage. We were two people living under the same roof, who had forgotten what it meant to be a husband and wife—our time apart had created a division that slowly eroded our marriage. A marriage that, in many ways, never had the opportunity to fully bloom.

Carlos began spending less and less time at home, until one day I noticed him packing a duffel bag in the bedroom.

"What are you doing?"

"What does it look like? I'm packing."

"I can see that you're packing, but why are you packing?"

"Because I'm going to stay somewhere else for a while."

"Somewhere else? Where?"

He didn't answer. Instead, he slung the bag over his shoulder and started walking toward the door.

"You can't take the car. I need it to get around!" I exclaimed.

"I'm not taking the car," he said, still heading for the door.

Before he left, he stopped in the living room and kissed Jasmine on the top of her head. "I'll see you soon, *mija*," he said to his daughter.

And then he was gone.

I stood there, frozen for a moment, before walking over to the window. I watched him climb into a pickup truck. As the truck drove away, a strange feeling washed over me: relief. I was actually relieved that he had left, which meant the arguing would finally stop.

Carlos regularly dropped by the house to visit Jasmine, and occasionally, I took her to see him. Outside of those brief interactions, we had very little contact. After several weeks, the relief I had initially felt when he'd left was replaced with loneliness and anger.

During one of his visits, I decided to tell him how I felt.

"Carlos, I'm angry," I said, watching him bounce Jasmine on his knee.

"Why are you angry?"

"Because after a year of being gone, you're home, but at the same time, you're not."

"That's because you only want to do things your way."

"That's not true. I just want some balance. And to be honest, when you left, I was relieved because all we did was argue. But now, I just feel hurt and lonely." Tears slid down my cheeks.

He set Jasmine down and moved closer to me. "I'm sorry," he whispered. "I know the past year has been tough on you too. How about we start over?"

We had a long discussion that ended with us agreeing to give things another try.

He moved back home, and it wasn't long before the tension and strain returned.

I walked into the living room where Carlos and Jasmine were watching TV. I looked at the screen and saw a police officer slamming a man to the ground, with a barefoot woman in the background holding a cigarette and screaming.

"What the hell is this?" I snapped. "How many times do I have to tell you she can't watch this crap?"

"She's my daughter, and she can watch whatever the hell I want her to watch."

"Change the channel. Now!"

"No!"

I marched over to the TV, yanked the plug from the wall, and took Jasmine into another room.

We'd forgotten how to communicate or even be civil to each other. There were fleeting moments of intimacy, but they were the exception, not the norm. After months of miserable bickering, I concluded that the marriage could not be saved, and I started thinking about divorce.

Before I had a chance to discuss the future of our marriage with Carlos, I received some life-changing news. I was pregnant with our second child. My cycle was two weeks late, so I purchased a home pregnancy test, peed on the white stick, and waited. The thought of being pregnant brought out mixed feelings. I knew I wanted a second child, hopefully a son, but things were not good between Carlos and me. I wondered if bringing another child into this environment was the right thing to do. The possibility of being a single parent again was daunting enough with one child, let alone two. Jasmine was only a year old. How would I be able to take care of two small children if I ended up on my own?

As I waited for the results, I reflected on how happy we had been when I was pregnant the first time. Sure, the circumstances were different, and a lot had happened since then, but having another child might be just what we needed to reset our marriage and start again. Regardless of the emotions, if the test was positive, I was having this baby, no matter what. An abortion was absolutely out of the question. Despite the circumstances, if I were pregnant, I knew this child was a blessing, a gift from God.

After the allotted time had passed, I picked up the test. If the end of the stick had turned blue, I was pregnant. If it was white, I was not. I nervously looked at the end of the stick and was met with a dark-blue hue. There was no mistaking the result. I was definitely pregnant.

I told Carlos I was pregnant. Much to my surprise, he was happy about the news of us having a second child. I thought he would be upset or would look at it as a way of me trying to get him to stay home. His reaction was the complete opposite. He smiled, gave me a hug, and said, "Maybe we'll have a boy this time."

With the news of us having our second child confirmed by a visit to the doctor, things got better between us. He went to all my doctor's appointments with me, and we prepared the nursery together. We had some of Jasmine's things, but she was still using most of them, so we shopped together for the things the new baby would need.

Carlos and I didn't pick out any baby names in advance, but we both were excitedly hoping for a son. I refused to make the same mistake I'd made with my first pregnancy, so I referred to the infant as *the baby* for the entirety of my pregnancy. Deep down, I really hoped for a boy, but I didn't want to jinx it. I would only say "the baby" until I officially knew the gender, which wouldn't happen until I gave birth.

One of the most exciting things about being pregnant the second time was that I knew what to expect. The most challenging thing about this pregnancy was being pregnant in the South during the summer. The baby was due in mid-July, and it was unbearably hot that year. By the time I was in my final trimester, I was miserable and uncomfortable most of the time.

Overall, things went well, so I continued to work throughout my pregnancy. In fact, I found out I was pregnant a few days after I took part in an airborne operation. That meant that I had been pregnant during the jump, and my unborn child had had their first airborne jump before they were born. Thankfully, the baby wasn't hurt, and I now had a cool fact to share with my child when they were older.

We celebrated Jasmine's second birthday and told her that one of her presents was that she would get to be a big sister. I wondered how Jasmine would react to a baby sister or brother. By two years old, she was quite spoiled, and I wondered if she would adapt well to no longer being the sole focus of our attention. I had read a few parenting books that encouraged including the older sibling in activities that pertained to the baby, employing them as a helper of sorts. Those books also cautioned that the older child might regress and resume behaviors they had outgrown, such as wanting to return to a bottle or wetting the bed. Jasmine was still in diapers, so I wasn't worried about her wetting the bed. She had been off bottles for quite some time, at her own choosing. There were already signs of tension when some of her old things were put in the new nursery.

One day, I was putting sheets on the baby's bed, which was Jasmine's old crib.

She stood in front of the crib with her hands on her hips and shouted, "*Mine!*"

I scooped her up and said to her in a gentle voice, "Jasmine, we agreed you are giving your old bed to the new baby. You have a big-girl bed, so you don't need this baby bed anymore."

She turned toward the bed and shouted, "*Mine!*"

I sat her on the floor and knelt in front of her. "Jasmine, you are a big sister now, and sharing is important. You don't need this bed anymore, so we are going to let the new baby use it, OK?"

She defiantly shouted, "No!" before falling onto the floor, kicking and screaming in a boisterous tantrum.

Jasmine was a bossy little girl, so I decided giving her small tasks to help me would go a long way in helping her embrace her new sibling. No matter what, I knew that she'd be a great big sister.

On the evening of July 6, 1992, I was home with Jasmine while Carlos was on all-night CQ duty. It was Carlos's birthday, and I thought it was terrible that he had to work all night.

When I asked him what he wanted for his birthday, he replied, "A son."

As he walked out the door, I smiled and asked him, "Do you want me to go into labor to get you out of duty tonight?"

In typical Carlos fashion, he replied, "Hell yeah."

"I'll see what I can do," I said.

Of course, I didn't actually believe that I would go into labor that evening because the baby wasn't due for another three weeks. The saying, "Be careful what you wish for," rang true for me that evening.

Later that night, I had finished the dinner dishes, put Jasmine to bed, and settled under the covers, hoping for some relaxation before I dozed off. As I clicked the channels on the television while looking for a mindless comedy, I suddenly felt a sharp pain in my side. I sat up and piled a few pillows under my back. It wasn't unusual for the baby to lay funny and cause a bit of discomfort. Usually, it was in the form of the baby laying on my bladder, causing frequent trips to the bathroom. There was discomfort but never pain. After getting into a more comfortable position, I resumed channel surfing.

A few minutes later, it happened again. This was definitely unusual. Maybe it had something to do with dinner. I tried repositioning myself once more, hoping that would do the trick. I felt myself tensing up, so I took a few deep breaths and tried to relax. Getting stressed out would only make things worse.

I sat motionless for about ten minutes. The pain hadn't happened again, so I assumed it was over. *Good ... now I can relax and get some sleep*, I thought. Abandoning the idea of watching television, I snuggled down under the covers.

Just as I dozed off, another stab of pain kicked in. "What the hell?!" I exclaimed. "I can't possibly be in labor." The pains weren't occurring in any discernible pattern, so I didn't think they were labor pains. They also felt different than I remembered, so I thought something might be wrong.

I didn't want to panic unnecessarily, so I timed the pains for a while to see if they fit the pattern for labor pains: regular intervals that increased in intensity and frequency. The pains were pretty intense, but the frequency was sporadic. This felt like labor, but I wasn't sure, so I called Carlos and told him what was happening. He immediately left work and drove home.

When Carlos arrived, we timed the pain intervals for about an hour before he decided it was time for me to go to the hospital.

"I'm not sure that I'm in labor; it might just be indigestion from something I ate," I said.

"It doesn't matter. The pain isn't going away, so you need to get checked out," he said.

"What if we drive all the way to the hospital and it's nothing?" I pleaded.

"Then I'll bring you back home and tuck you in. Stop fussing, woman, and get ready to go."

I grabbed my purse and headed for the car. The more I moved around, the more it hurt.

Once I was in the car with my seat belt fastened, Carlos began driving toward the hospital. As he turned onto the freeway, I let out a moan. He must have taken my discomfort as a sign that he needed to drive faster. He punched the accelerator to the floor as he said, "I'm about to break the sound barrier."

"Wait, no!"

But it was too late. He was already flying through traffic. I held my breath and gripped my seat belt tightly as Carlos weaved in and out of traffic at a frantic, and undoubtedly unsafe, pace.

Less than five minutes into him "breaking the sound barrier," blue lights flashed behind us and a siren blared.

"Oh no, you're being pulled over!" I exclaimed.

"Damn it," he muttered.

I wondered for a brief second whether he would actually pull over before I felt the car slow down. Carlos pulled over to the shoulder of the road and waited for the officer to approach the vehicle.

"Surely they will see that I'm in labor and let us go," I said.

"Maybe they'll even escort us to the hospital," he offered.

The officer walked up to the driver's door and tapped on the glass. Carlos made a dramatic show of rolling down his window, no doubt so the officer would see that he was irritated.

"Do you know why I stopped you?" the officer asked.

"Probably because I was speeding," Carlos replied.

"Yes, you were going forty miles over the speed limit," the officer continued.

"Damn right, I was speeding. I'm taking my wife to the hospital!" Carlos shouted defiantly.

"Officer, I'm in labor," I chimed in, hoping to calm things down and maybe elicit the officer's help.

The officer peered inside the car, looked at me, and then looked back at Carlos before asking for his license and registration. Carlos handed the officer the requested documents.

"Wait right here," the officer said before walking back to his car.

We waited for what seemed like an eternity for him to return, and when he finally did, he handed Carlos a speeding ticket. He was explaining that the ticket required a mandatory court appearance when Carlos interrupted him.

"What? You're giving me a fucking ticket? I told you my wife is in labor."

"Watch your tone, sir," the officer warned.

"Fuck that. My wife is over here in pain, and you're writing us a bullshit ticket!" Carlos continued ranting.

The officer glanced inside the car again and said, "Don't miss your court date, and watch your speed." Thankfully, he ignored Carlos' shouting and walked away.

Once the officer drove past us, Carlos reentered traffic and resumed our trip to the hospital. I was nearly in tears from the pain, but I was also furious with Carlos because his speeding had not only delayed us getting to the hospital, but we also had a speeding ticket we couldn't afford to deal with. We continued the drive to the hospital in silence, with Carlos driving mostly at a reasonable speed.

When we arrived at the hospital, I was checked in and examined, and the doctor confirmed that I was, in fact, in early labor.

"Early labor? Did I do something wrong?" I asked, concerned.

The doctor reassured me that early labor was common, and that I was far enough along for him to safely deliver the baby. The doctor gave the nurses some instructions before turning to me and saying, "I guess the little guy is ready to be born, so we're going to help him out."

I smiled when he left the room, and I considered his word choice: "little guy." Was that his way of telling me it was a boy, or was it just a generic phrase he used? Either way, I prayed for a healthy, happy baby, because in the end, that's all that really mattered.

After several hours of checking and rechecking, I was not dilating as expected, so the doctor broke my water to help move things along.

Several more hours later, I still had not reached full dilation. The doctor came in to check on my progress, and I noticed a worried look on his face.

"What is it?" I asked. "Is everything OK?"

"The baby is in fetal distress and its heart rate is fluctuating, so we need to deliver it now. You can't have a vaginal delivery because the umbilical cord is wrapped around the baby's neck, so we need to do an emergency cesarean section right away." He then turned to the nurse and began shouting orders. "Prep the operating room. Notify the NICU in case the baby needs special treatment. Call the anesthesiologist and tell him that we don't have time for general anesthesia, so we will be doing the C-section by epidural."

As I listened to the doctor shout orders, I began to pray. *Please, God, let my baby be OK. Please let it be heathy and strong. Please, God, let everything be OK.*

The nurse came over and began explaining the procedure to me.

"What did he mean when he said that he is going to do the procedure by epidural?" I asked.

"We will put a needle in your back that will numb you, and then the doctor will surgically remove the baby," she explained.

"Numb me? Does that mean I'll be awake during the surgery?" I asked.

"Yes, you'll be awake, but you'll be groggy, and you shouldn't feel anything," she explained.

"I don't want that," I cried. "I don't want to be awake when they cut me open."

The doctor interjected. "We don't have time for full anesthesia, plus it's risky, so we're going to do an epidural."

I began sobbing hysterically. "I don't want this ... I'm scared."

The doctor ignored my cries and told me that I didn't have a choice.

Carlos, who had been sitting in the corner observing everything, stood and looked the doctor right in the face, and said, "My wife is afraid, and she doesn't want to be awake during the surgery, so put her to sleep and deliver my baby now!"

The doctor stared at Carlos briefly before turning to the nurse and directing her to prep me for general anesthesia. In that moment, I could not have been more grateful for my husband. He saw that I was terrified, and he took charge of the situation.

As the nurse started an IV, the anesthesiologist approached my bed and softly explained, "I'm going to put a mask over your mouth and nose. I want you to take a few deep breaths, and when I tell you, begin counting backward from one hundred. Can you do that?"

"Yes, I can do that," I replied.

As he placed the mask over my nose and mouth, I heard a peculiar sound. I thought to myself, *What is that noise? Wait, is that music? Music in the operating room? Is that possible, or has the anesthesia already kicked in, and I'm just imagining music?* No, music was definitely playing. I strained my hearing in an effort to identify what was playing. It was a soothing melody sung by a 1960s-style, Frank Sinatra-type crooner. I could just barely make out the words, but what I could hear sounded lovely.

> Oh, my love, my darling
> I've hungered for your touch
> A long, lonely time
> Time goes by so slowly
> And time can do so much
> Are you still mine?
> I need your love
> I need your love
> God speed your love to me

Fully relaxed by the soothing melody, I closed my eyes and took a few breaths as the anesthesiologist had instructed. The air smelled funny, but I did my best to breathe in without coughing. After a few breaths, I heard him say, "OK, start counting backward from one hundred."

"One hundred ..."

I started feeling heavy.

"Ninety-nine ..."

I couldn't keep my eyes open.

"Ninety- ..."

I didn't make it past ninety-nine before I was out.

Sometime later, when I woke up in the recovery room, the first person I saw was Carlos, with a big smile on his face. "Welcome back," he said.

"Is the baby OK? What did we have?" I muttered groggily.

Carlos smiled even bigger than before, saying, "The baby is just fine. Ten fingers, ten toes, and I didn't send him back."

"We had a boy?" I asked.

"Yep, and I'm going to buy him a football as soon as I leave here," Carlos said proudly.

I felt a stab of pain in my stomach as I chuckled. "Ouch ... don't make me laugh. That hurt. Where is he?"

"They are getting him cleaned up and checking him out."

"Is he really OK?" I asked tentatively.

"My boy is perfect!" he exclaimed. "And you know what? His birthday is the day after his dad's."

Just then, the nurse rounded the corner carrying the most handsome little boy I'd ever seen. He wasn't as big and plump as Jasmine had been, but he shared the same full head of hair. *I guess that heartburn thing is a myth*, I briefly thought.

I felt tears sting my eyes as I reached for my son. As I held him, I looked down at his handsome little face and softly said, "Hello, Joshua," before the tears broke free and began running down my cheeks. My heart was overflowing with so much love and joy that the only response that felt appropriate was to cry.

I looked up at Carlos and said, "I already have a name for him. His name is Joshua. I haven't decided on a middle name, though, so you can pick his middle name if you'd like."

"I'd like to name him after my dad. How about Jose for his middle name?" Carlos asked.

"I like Jose," I said with a smile. I looked at the nurse and said, "Meet our son, Joshua Jose Fuentes."

The nurse looked at our son and said warmly, "Hello, Joshua," before turning to leave.

That's when I remembered the music, so I called out to the nurse. "Excuse me," I said.

The nurse returned to my bedside. "Yes, Mrs. Fuentes, do you need something?" she asked.

"This is going to sound strange, but I'm certain that I heard music in the operating room."

"Music?" Carlos asked, curious.

I continued. "I'm wondering if you could ask the doctor what the song was. I liked it, and since it was playing when my son was born, I'd like to know what it was," I said.

"I don't know about music," the nurse replied, "but I will ask the doctor if there was music and will let him know that you'd like to know what it was."

"Thank you very much. I appreciate that."

The nurse left the room, leaving Carlos, Joshua, and me— *our little family*—alone.

The nurse returned about an hour later. "You were right," she said.

"I knew I heard music!" I exclaimed.

"You sure did," she said.

"What was the song?" I asked eagerly.

"Your son was born to the song 'Unchained Melody' by an old group called The Righteous Brothers," she continued.

"The Righteous Brothers," I said, putting extra emphasis on the name. "I really like that," I said, smiling.

Carlos and I were overjoyed by Joshua's arrival. July 7, 1992, was one of the happiest days of our lives. Mom and baby were both healthy, and our special little family had been restored.

Chapter 13

> It is during our darkest moments
> that we must focus to see the light.
>
> —Aristotle Onassis

Shortly after Joshua was born, as Carlos and I were trying to mend our broken family, I received a call from my mother. Her voice lacked its usual cheerful tone, eager for updates about her grandchildren. Instead, it was distant and strange.

"Shoshanna, I need you to do something," she said.

I tensed. "What do you need me to do?" I asked cautiously.

"I'm sending Rebecca to live with you."

I blinked, gripping the phone more tightly. Rebecca, the youngest of my mother's six children, and I had never been particularly close. The age gap between us was wide enough that she felt more like a relative than a sister. And now, suddenly, she was supposed to live with me?

"To live with me? Why on earth would she come live with me?"

"She's four months pregnant, and I can't deal with it," my mother said, her voice flat, as if discussing a minor inconvenience. "You're on your own, and being around family will be good for her."

"She *is* around family," I protested. "Besides, I have two kids of my own to take care of. I can't handle a teenager."

"She can help you with your kids, and it'll be good for her to be around you."

I gritted my teeth. "No, Ema. This is too much."

"You don't have a choice," she said, her tone signaling that the discussion was over. "I already bought her ticket. She'll be there in a few days."

After she hung up, I stood there, furious with myself for not pushing back harder. But it wouldn't have mattered, my mother hadn't asked. She had decided. And I had no choice. Two days later, my sister would arrive.

I told Carlos about my mother's decision, and he was just as upset as I was. He questioned why we had to take responsibility for someone else's child, and he pointed out the financial strain it would create, something I hadn't even considered.

When Rebecca arrived, I tried to make the best of the situation. I cleared out the spare room for her and made sure she had the basics. The following week, I enrolled her in school and scheduled a doctor's appointment.

From the very beginning, things were a disaster. She and Carlos argued constantly, and I was stuck in the middle.

"Move this typewriter for me," Rebecca said to Carlos, with an edge to her tone.

"No. Move it yourself," he shot back.

"I can't, I'm pregnant. I'm not supposed to lift anything."

"So? That's not my problem."

"I don't need you to move it anyway, you dirty Mexican."

Carlos jumped up from the couch and got in her face.

"Who the fuck are you talking to?"

"You!"

I quickly laid Joshua down on the couch and jumped between them.

"Carlos, get out of her face! She's pregnant!"

"Yeah, get out of my face, Mexican," Rebecca sneered.

"Shut up, Rebecca!" I snapped. "Go to your room. I'll bring you the damn typewriter."

Carlos turned and stormed toward the front door.

"Carlos!" I called after him, but he didn't stop. He got in the car and drove off.

The tension between them was constant, and each one expected me to take their side.

After Rebecca had the baby, things got worse. She started skipping school, smoking marijuana, and getting into shouting matches with me.

My sister stayed with us for just over a year, and the arrangement ended in complete disaster, leaving irrevocable damage to my marriage. One day, without warning, my mother showed up at my house and declared that she was taking Rebecca and her baby home.

"You and Carlos have been mistreating them," she accused.

I stared at her, dumbfounded. "Mistreating them? They're not being mistreated," I said.

"I asked you to take care of my baby, and you have the nerve to mistreat her?"

"You didn't *ask* me to do anything!" I snapped. "You forced me to take her, and she's acted like a spoiled brat the entire time.

And now you show up to *rescue* her?" My voice was sharp with anger.

My mother's expression grew dark. "You'd better watch your tone."

"No! I have been the one taking care of her and your grandson for over a year because you couldn't handle it."

"Watch it, Shoshanna!" she warned again.

I exhaled sharply, shaking my head. "You know what? Go ahead, take them. I have my own family to worry about."

The next day, she took Rebecca and her baby back to Chicago.

My mother's hypocrisy cut deep. Where was her outrage when I was being abused by Cain? I was hurt. I was furious. And I was done. I didn't speak to my mother for more than a year.

Even after Rebecca was gone, the damage remained. The strain between Carlos and me only deepened. We barely spoke, and when we did, our words were filled with resentment. He constantly brought up the disaster with my sister, blaming her presence for the cracks in our marriage. But I saw things differently. I blamed him for not being more supportive when I needed him the most. The distance between us grew, and neither of us seemed willing—or able—to move beyond it.

The last day that Carlos and I lived together, I was asleep on the couch after an overnight CQ duty. Carlos was in the bedroom getting ready for work when he woke me up and said, "Hey, I need to borrow your uniform because I don't have a starched one to wear today."

Carlos and I wore the same size in our battle dress uniforms, and since we had the same last name, rank, and patch, it was not uncommon for us to wear each other's uniforms. However, on this day, I refused to let him wear mine.

"No, you can't wear my uniform. I only have one pressed set, and if you wear it, I won't have one to wear tomorrow," I snapped.

"You can wear the one you wore today. It doesn't even have any wrinkles," he said, annoyed.

"I said no. Leave it alone, and wear one of your own," I demanded.

As I lay on the sofa, half asleep and half watching Joshua (who was crawling on the floor), I heard a strange sound coming from the bedroom. It sounded like paper being shredded, but why would Carlos be shredding paper? I heard the noise again and again, so I got up to see what it was.

When I entered the room, I saw Carlos using a box cutter to shred my military fatigues. Not just the one I'd refused to let him wear ... he was shredding all of them!

I looked at him in horror and yelled, "What the hell are you doing?!"

Carlos moved quickly toward me, and I realized that he aimed to hit me. He had never hit me before, so the action caught me by surprise. I turned my head in an attempt to dodge the blow, but I was a half second too slow, and his fist connected with the side of my head. I fell to the floor as he ran out of the house. I scrambled to my feet and felt a warm, wet sensation on the side of my head. I was bleeding. He had hit me, and I was bleeding.

Joshua must have felt the tension, because he was in the living room screaming at the top of his lungs. Fortunately, Jasmine was at day care, so I only had one child to manage. I picked Joshua up with one hand and held a towel to my head with the other hand in an effort to stop the bleeding. As I pressed the towel to my head, I realized that not only was I bleeding but I was also stranded at home without a vehicle. I picked up the phone and dialed the number to my unit.

When the desk sergeant answered, I asked to speak with one of the sergeants I worked with. I explained to him what had happened and asked if he could give me a ride to the doctor. He told me that he would be at the house in less than fifteen minutes, and he hung up the phone.

As I sat and waited for him to show up, I rocked Joshua on my knee and reflected on my parents' marriage. On many occasions, I had witnessed their heated arguments escalate to physical violence. They would fight and destroy each other's things before reconciling and making up. It was a vicious cycle that I had witnessed many times. I didn't want to live that way. I wasn't interested in whatever explanation Carlos might offer. There was nothing he could say to justify hitting me. He had threatened to hit me many times, but he had never actually followed through. This was a new dynamic in our marriage that I refused to accept.

As I sat there in my thoughts, the sound of the doorbell ringing brought me back to the present moment. I grabbed my purse and Joshua's diaper bag and headed for the door.

When I opened the door, the sergeant saw the blood on my face and stared at me in horror. "Where is he? I'm going to kick his ass!" he exclaimed.

"He went to work, but I don't need you to kick his ass. I need you to take me to the day care to drop Joshua off, and then I need you to take me to the courthouse," I replied.

"I'll take you to the day care, but then you need to go to the doctor. I think you need stitches."

"The doctor can wait!" I said. "I'm filing for a restraining order before I chicken out or change my mind. I will not live with a man who puts his hands on me," I said, fighting back tears.

The sergeant looked at me with compassion and said, "I understand. Where is the day care?"

When we arrived at the day care, I handed Joshua's diaper bag to the sergeant and asked him to take Joshua inside for me. I didn't want anyone to see the blood and ask questions, or worse, call social services.

He took Joshua inside, and within minutes, he was back in the car, and we were headed toward the courthouse.

We rode in silence for a while, and then the sergeant glanced at me and asked in a soft voice, "What are you going to do?"

My face was wet with tears, so I looked down at my feet and said somberly, "I don't know."

When we arrived at the courthouse, I asked him to wait for me while I went inside.

I approached the desk clerk, who looked at me and immediately exclaimed, "Oh my God, what happened to you?!"

"My husband happened to me. He hit me, and I would like to report it and file a restraining order."

"I understand that you would like a restraining order, but you're bleeding. You should get medical help first. Do you have anyone who can take you to the doctor? You might need stiches."

"I have someone waiting in the car for me, and I'll go to the doctor as soon as I have the restraining order, so please help me." My response was said in a tone that made it clear that I was not going anywhere until I had what I had come for.

The clerk gathered some basic information before escorting me to a separate area. I sat in a small waiting room that looked very different from the rest of the courthouse. It looked more like an office than a government building, and I was grateful for the privacy.

After a few moments, a gentleman walked in and introduced himself as the judge's clerk. He asked me to explain what had happened. After I finished explaining everything, he told me that he would hand-deliver my restraining order request to the judge, and it would be signed immediately. He explained that the restraining order meant that Carlos could not go to the house, day care, my job, or anywhere near the children or me—effective immediately. Because Carlos was a soldier, the civilian police could not get involved, so the clerk strongly recommended that I report the incident to the military as well. He went on to say that, if Carlos violated the restraining order, the civilian police would have the authority to arrest him, regardless of his military status.

He briefly left the room and returned with a signed restraining order with the judge's signature. He walked me to the main entrance of the building, looked at the blood-soaked towel, and told me to go straight to the doctor.

Before leaving, he said, "The restraining order will be delivered to his company commander to ensure he's aware and enforces it."

"OK," I replied.

He looked at me, his eyes heavy with sadness. "You've done the right thing. Good luck."

I walked back to the car feeling somewhat protected. I knew the restraining order was only a piece of paper that wouldn't provide physical protection, but it meant that the law was on my side and that I had taken a stand. I thought about the promise I had made to my younger self: I *will not* be a victim.

I climbed into the car and told the sergeant that I was all set. I apologized for taking so much of his day, but he wouldn't hear it.

"We're on the same team, and I've got your back," he said.

I was so grateful for his support. He drove back to the base and took me to the medical facility near our unit.

I went inside, and they immediately put me in a room. I wasn't in there five minutes before the doctor came in.

"Specialist Fuentes?"

"Yes, sir."

"Do you want to tell me what happened to you?" he asked.

"Yes, sir. My husband hit me," I responded.

"When did this happen?"

"This morning."

"What took you so long to come get looked at?" he asked.

I explained to him everything that had happened that morning: the fight, calling for help, dropping Joshua off at day care, going to the courthouse, and getting the restraining order. I told him everything. He asked me my husband's name and the unit he was in, and I told him that too.

He made a quick note in the chart he was holding and then said, "We're going to get you all cleaned up. You need a couple of stitches, but you shouldn't have any scarring." As he stitched me up, he said, "I'm obligated to report what you've told me to your husband's commander."

"I know."

"Are you OK with that?" he asked.

"Yes, I am. Are you going to call him before I leave?"

"I can if you want me to, but why?"

"Because he took the only vehicle we have, and I need to be able to take my children back and forth to day care and get to work myself," I explained.

"Oh, OK. I'll call as soon as I'm done here."

The doctor finished stitching me up, applied a bandage, and then left the room. He returned a few minutes later and advised that he had spoken with the first sergeant, who was very upset. He said that they were ordering Carlos to move into the barracks immediately, and that I could pick up the car as soon as I was able. The keys to the car and the house would be waiting for me at the CQ desk. The last thing the doctor said was that if Carlos even so much as called me, I was to let the first sergeant know, and he would deal with it.

Running on pure adrenaline, but completely exhausted, I thanked the doctor, asked the sergeant who was with me to drop me off at the car, and then I went home. For the next several hours, I toggled between sleeping and crying until it was time to go pick up the kids.

Chapter 14

No man is an island, entire of itself;
every man is a piece of the continent.

—John Donne

Not too long after Carlos and I separated, the military moved me to a new duty station at Fort Monroe in Hampton, Virginia. I made very little money, and without child support from Carlos, I could barely make ends meet. As the kids got older, the things they needed were more expensive. The cost of day care was rising, and Jasmine would start kindergarten soon, which would bring extra expenses and time commitments. Carlos and I didn't have any communication, and he refused to provide any financial support for the children. Because the army had reassigned Carlos to a unit overseas, the Soldiers' and Sailors' Civil Relief Act protected him against any legal proceedings, so I was not able to petition him for a divorce or child support. His location was immaterial, though, because I couldn't afford a lawyer. I wasn't even able to pay all the bills and keep the kids consistently fed. To further complicate matters, I was still a soldier in the military, so I had other duties and responsibilities that created stress in my life.

Despite this, in many ways, life at Fort Monroe was easier for me. There were no airborne operations, no multiday trips to the field, no early-morning physical training, and no overnight CQ or guard duty. Being stationed in Virginia was like having a civilian job that I went to from 8:00 a.m. to 5:00 p.m. every day. While on the surface that would have seemed amazing, it wasn't the version of the military I'd joined, and it wasn't the version of the military that I wanted to be in. Up to that point, I had spent my entire military career as a member of the 82nd Airborne Division. Being a paratrooper was the reason I'd joined the military in the first place, and apart from a few brief stays at various leadership schools, I hadn't experienced anything else. I'd never considered what military service outside the 82nd would look like, and in many ways, I resented being in Virginia.

I had been a member of one of the most elite fighting forces in the world, and now I was surrounded by ... what? By people who weren't that. I looked down on the other soldiers and my civilian colleagues because I felt like they were playing army. In return, they thought I was an arrogant, rude, obnoxious asshole. I didn't care, though, because they weren't my tribe. The men and women of the 82nd Airborne were my people, and that was where I belonged. Needless to say, I didn't have any friends. I attempted to justify my bad behavior by believing that this situation, this place, was beneath me and that I was meant for something greater. The reality was that they were right. I was an arrogant, obnoxious asshole, so it's no surprise that I felt alone and very much like a failure. The person that I had become wasn't the kind of soldier

I'd set out to be. I wasn't the kind of mother I wanted to be. And I sure as hell wasn't the kind of human being I planned to be.

After a while, the loneliness and isolation started getting to me. I began struggling with what I believe was depression. I didn't have thoughts of inflicting harm to myself or anything like that, but I was deeply sad all the time, and I struggled to find a reason to be happy. It was hard for me to look at my children every day and know that I was failing them. I was all alone in the world, without support from anyone. The father of my children refused to help me. My family couldn't help me. And I had been such a jerk to the people around me that I didn't have any friends who were willing to help me. There wasn't a whole lot that I could do about the first two, but I decided I could be less of an asshole and could try to make some friends.

I began going to events and interacting with the people I worked with. There were visits to their homes, and I met their families. It quickly became clear that, despite my earlier behavior and prejudice toward them, these were good people. We had more in common than we had differences. Many of the female soldiers that I met were also single parents. They offered advice and helpful tips, like where to find the best deals on groceries and where to go for the cheapest gas. We also exchanged babysitting services. Things weren't perfect, but it felt nice to no longer be alone.

I lived on the military base in a small home that was next door to a cottage-style house where an older gentleman lived with his dog. On nice days, he worked outside in his garden, and as soon as the neighborhood kids saw him outside, they ran over to pet his dog.

One day, I saw him outside, so I went over to introduce myself. "Hi, I'm Shonna. My kids are Jasmine and Joshua. They come over from time to time to pet your dog," I said.

"Hi, I'm Joe," he replied.

"My kids really like your dog. They keep asking me if they can get a dog, which they can't, so I'm glad they have your dog to visit," I said.

"The kids like that old dog, and he loves being petted," he said as he glanced over at the dog. "I'd like to believe they enjoy my funny stories, but nope, it's the dog," he said with a smile.

I smiled back and began asking him about his garden.

Joe was very nice, and he was easy to talk to. Like the children, I began visiting with Joe whenever I saw him outside. He told me about the various flowers in his garden, and I told him about the things happening in my life. Apart from helpful advice, I didn't expect anything from him. It was just nice to have someone to talk to. Someone who was willing to listen without judgment or criticism. Someone who was friendly and kind. And that's exactly how Joe was.

One evening, when I was visiting Joe, we began discussing religion. I told him I was Jewish. I waited for the line of questions I was usually met with when I told someone I was Jewish. The narrative usually went something like, "You're Black, so how are you Jewish? Is one of your parents Jewish? Did your parents convert to Judaism? What were you before you converted to Judaism? What temple do you go to? Is your family from Ethiopia?" And on and on the questions would go.

But not with Joe. When I told Joe I was Jewish, he simply smiled and said, "That's nice. Having a relationship with God is important."

I liked Joe even more! I never minded sharing my story with people. Sharing on my own was nice; being interrogated to prove my Jewishness wasn't. Talking to Joe felt easy, so I decided to share my story, even though he hadn't asked.

I told Joe that I didn't know a lot about how I came to be Jewish because I had been an infant when my family had moved to Israel. I've learned most of what I know from my older siblings, my aunt, and family friends.

"As I understand it," I began, "the year I was born, my parents embarked on a spiritual journey that led them to sell everything they owned and move the entire family to Dimona, a small town located in southern Israel, about twenty-two miles west of the Dead Sea."

I explained that while living in Israel my parents had fully embraced the teachings and lifestyle of the Jewish faith. I told Joe how the teachings of the Torah became the sole basis for how my family lived. My parents spoke fluent Hebrew, and they were very devoted to their faith. We studied the Torah, observed the Sabbath, and avoided anything that didn't align with our beliefs and teachings. We also observed holy days such as Passover and Yom Kippur, and my mom kept a kosher kitchen. Yet, despite all of this, my parents did not consider themselves to be Jewish.

When we moved back to the United States, my mother informed my school that under no circumstances could my brother and I eat—or even be in proximity of—pork. Dietary restrictions were extremely uncommon, so when my teachers learned I couldn't eat pork, they pulled me aside to ask why. I didn't know how to respond, so I asked my mother. I told her that my teachers wanted to know what religion I followed that forbade me to eat pork. My mother's response was, "We don't have a religion; we have a way of life given to us by God." When I went back to school and shared this with my teachers, they made no effort to mask their laughter.

I paused my story and glanced up at Joe. He was listening intently with a compassionate look on his face. His kindness inspired me to continue.

After the response I'd received from my teachers, I never discussed the subject of religion again. When someone asked why I didn't eat pork, I told them I was allergic to it. As I got older, I began to realize that the views, beliefs, and teachings my family followed were identical to those of the Jewish community.

I approached my mother one day and asked her why we tell people that we don't have a religion when, in fact, we are Jews. She exploded and began yelling that we aren't Jews, because we follow a way of life that was given to us by God. I challenged her assertion by pointing out that the Jews also follow a way of life given to them by God, and what's more, we follow the same way of life. My mother told me that I was being disrespectful, and she sent me to my room.

I didn't understand why she was angry, but from that day forward whenever anyone asked why I didn't eat pork, I told them it was because I was Jewish. It was easier to explain being Jewish, I told Joe, than to explain not having any religion. If you didn't have a religion, you were called a heathen, but if you had the *wrong* religion, you were just confused.

I paused in contemplative thought before continuing.

The first time I officially declared myself a member of the Jewish community, I told Joe, was when I'd joined the military and was asked what religion I wanted them to put on my dog tags. I remember pondering my choices. Atheist ... pass. Christian ... nope. Muslim ... close, but no. I chose Jewish because, in my heart, that's what I was, and had been my entire life. So I entered the military as *Shoshanna Perry, Chicago, Illinois, Jewish.*

Joe smiled and gave a nod of approval. I went on to explain to him how, when we were young, my brothers and sisters and I spent most weekends reading the Bible and being quizzed by our mother on the stories we'd been assigned to read. "Who were Abraham's sons?" she would ask. "Why was Hannah crying in the temple?" "Who was Uriah?" "Who were Jacob's twelve sons?" "How did the Israelites end up in Egypt?" My mother would spend hours quizzing us, and woe to us if we got any of the questions wrong.

"Do you know these stories?" I asked Joe.

He smiled at me and said, "Yes, all of them."

I was very impressed! Joe knew a lot about the Bible, which made our visits even more pleasant. We traded stories and talked about our favorite Bible stories. He hadn't told me what his religion was, but I was pretty sure he wasn't Jewish because most of the Bible stories he told me were from books I wasn't familiar with.

During one of our visits, he asked if Jasmine would be starting school in the fall. "Isn't she five years old?" he asked.

"Yes," I said, "I can't believe she's starting kindergarten already."

"Where are you going to send her to school?" he asked.

"I don't know yet. I have looked into sending her to the local school, but to be honest, I would love to send her to the Catholic school across the street," I replied.

"You're Jewish, so why do you want to send your daughter to a Catholic school?"

"That's a good question," I responded. "It's because I'm Jewish that I want to send her to a Catholic school."

He stared at me curiously as I continued.

"Everything I believe about religion and my faith has been driven by what my parents told me to believe. Even now, if I have a question about the Bible, I ask my mother. Judaism is the right religion for me, and I love it, but I don't feel like I ever had a choice."

He nodded as I continued.

"The kids' father is Catholic, so I believe they should also learn about the practices and rituals of his religion, because that's also part of who they are, and I want them to have a choice. Teaching them the laws and customs of Judaism is not a problem for me, but I don't know anything about being Catholic, so I can't teach them that. If they attend Catholic school, they will learn about Catholicism and then be able to choose the religion that's right for them," I explained.

"So you want your children to be Catholic?" he asked.

"No, not at all. I want them to learn about Catholicism and then decide to be good little Jews, like their mother. I just want them to choose it, rather than me choosing it for them."

He chuckled and said, "Then that settles it. You should send Jasmine to Saint Mary when she starts school."

"That would be great, except I've looked into it, and I can't afford to send her to Saint Mary," I replied. "Besides, that school is for rich people," I added.

"I'm certain that there are a lot of children who attend that school whose families aren't rich, but why don't you apply for a scholarship?" he asked.

I considered what he'd said before responding. "Even with a scholarship, I don't think I can afford to send her there. I casually looked into it once, and I think they only offer partial scholarships, which don't cover the costs of her books and uniforms. I'm doing OK, but I can barely make ends meet, so I just can't afford private school," I said.

"Let's talk to them. Can you meet me at the school tomorrow?"

"Joe, I'm really not asking you to get involved in this or to do anything. We're just talking; that's all. I tell you what ... maybe I'll visit that church across the street and talk to the preacher.

"Do Catholics call them preachers?" I wondered out loud before continuing. "I'll ask the preacher if there are classes I can take to learn about being Catholic, so I can teach my kids."

"They call them priests," he said.

"Oh, priests ... thanks."

"That sounds like a good plan," he said. "But will you meet me at the school tomorrow, anyway? What do you have to lose other than an hour of your time?"

Joe had been very kind to me, and I appreciated his friendship. So, while I didn't think there was even the slimmest chance that it would work out for Jasmine to attend Saint Mary, I agreed to meet him. After all, he was right. What did I have to lose?

The next day, after taking the kids to day care and checking in with work, I headed to the school as I had agreed to do. As I walked into the building, I realized I didn't even know who I was supposed to meet. I looked around for Joe, but I didn't see him, so I walked into the office.

"Hello. I'm not sure who I'm supposed to meet, but I think my neighbor Joe set up a meeting," I said to the lady sitting behind the desk.

"Are you Mrs. Fuentes?" she asked.

"Yes, I am."

"Great. Sister Mary Rose is expecting you. Have a seat, and she will be with you shortly," she advised.

"OK, thank you," I replied. Where was Joe? I was going to meet with the principal any minute, and he was late. What was I going to say to her if he didn't show up?

I had never met a nun before, so I wanted to ask the secretary what the proper greeting protocol was. Should I bow or something? Was I allowed to shake her hand? Should I call her Sister Mary Rose, or was that too personal for a first meeting? As my mind raced with questions, there was still no sign of Joe. I wondered if he had changed his mind.

"Excuse me, ma'am," I said to the secretary. "My neighbor arranged this meeting, and he isn't here, so maybe I should come back another time."

Just as the words left my mouth, the door to the office opened. I turned around and saw the tiniest lady dressed in a habit. She couldn't have been over five feet tall, but her presence was *much* larger. I was in such awe of her that I didn't immediately notice the man who accompanied her. He was wearing religious garments as well, so I figured he must have been their priest. *Wait, he looks familiar.* I stared at him briefly before my brain clicked into gear. *That's Joe! Why is that Joe? Why is my neighbor dressed like that? Oh my God, my neighbor is a priest! A priest at this very school!* That meant that he was also the priest at the church I planned to visit to ask about a Catholic class. How was it that I didn't know that? I'd never asked where he worked because I'd assumed he was retired. I felt like a complete idiot!

Joe smiled at me and said, "Hi, Shonna. This is Sister Mary Rose. She's the principal of Saint Mary."

I looked at her and smiled. I tentatively extended my hand toward her as I asked, "What should I call you?"

She shook my hand and replied, "Sister Mary Rose, please."

I turned to Joe and asked, "And what should I call you?"

He grinned and said, "You can continue to call me Joe, or Father Joe, if you wish."

The meeting with Sister Mary Rose and Father Joe went very well. They both agreed that it was the responsibility of the Catholic Church to educate Catholic children, and they offered Jasmine a full scholarship. I couldn't believe what was happening.

Before classes began, the secretary whom I had met earlier contacted other parents to request donations of uniforms that their children had outgrown for Jasmine to use. Other parents donated money to help cover the cost of her books.

Emotions overcame me as I was overjoyed and extremely grateful for the outpouring of kindness I was receiving. These people didn't know me or my daughter, yet they opened their hearts and their wallets to help us. They didn't ask for anything in return, and there were no strings attached. Many of them asked to remain anonymous, indicating that seeing Jasmine well prepared for school was thanks enough. In all my life, I had never experienced such selfless kindness from total strangers. My heart was full of a special warmth and love that I didn't understand.

I was experiencing a level of kindness that I had never offered to anyone. The question that plagued me was, why? Why were so many people helping me, a total stranger who had nothing to offer in return?

What I didn't know then (that I know now) is that what I was experiencing was the love of Christ. The people who helped me, including Father Joe and Sister Mary Rose, were answering God's call to love your neighbor as yourself. They expected nothing in return because God's grace was free to them and, as instruments of God's will, they had extended grace and kindness to me. They had blessed me with the opportunity to witness a pure and wonderful expression of the Christian faith.

Jasmine began school in the fall as a student at Saint Mary Star of the Sea Catholic School. I took her and Joshua to Mass every Sunday so that I could learn what she was learning in class. I wanted to make sure that she wasn't being taught an ideology that completely conflicted with my understanding of God's Word.

What I experienced in that church was the complete opposite. I didn't experience conflict; I experienced peace. I experienced a peace that I couldn't explain and that I didn't understand. When I was in Mass, I was happy. I felt a sense of family. Everyone was nice to me. They checked on me before and after Mass to see if I had any questions. No one treated me like an outsider, even though I wasn't Catholic and did not desire to become Catholic. No one stared at me when I stood a beat too late after everyone else, or when I didn't know any of the prayers. They didn't judge me when I made the sign of the cross wrong, or when I failed to make it at all. They were kind to me during a time in my life when kindness was what I needed most. I had never gone to church while growing up, but if this was what church was like, I understood why other people did.

Without child support, my financial situation got worse, so I took a second job. I worked for the military during the day and in the electronics area of a department store in the mall at night. I worked all the time, so I didn't get to spend much time with my children. We were barely getting by, but at least we were making it. I relied on the friends who were fellow soldiers or the wives of soldiers to watch my children in the evenings while I worked.

I hated leaving my kids every night, but I was thankful to have a support system. When I picked the children up, I always offered to pay the person who had been watching them. Fortunately, my offers were always met with, "That's unnecessary." Or "Don't worry about it. We have to look out for each other." I was so grateful because, in reality, I only offered to pay because it was the right thing to do. If anyone had actually accepted my offer, I wouldn't have had any cash to give them. The best I would have been able to give was a promise to pay them as soon as I got paid, which wouldn't have been possible because I had far more expenses than I had income. In fact, I usually spent most of my income before it even arrived. I spent the money I had paying bills like rent, utilities, and food, so there was rarely anything left over for unexpected expenses. Some weeks, the money ran out, and there just wasn't enough food, so I was always grateful when I picked the children up and they had already eaten. I was always offered food when I picked the kids up, but I would politely decline because I didn't want to feel like a charity case. Besides, it didn't matter to me whether I ate. As long as the kids didn't go to bed hungry, I was thankful.

Chapter 15

With a new day comes new strength
and new thoughts.

—Eleanor Roosevelt

One summer, the kids had gone to visit their grandparents in Texas, so I was on my own. Without the kids around to give me purpose, my days grew darker and darker, and it was a fight every day for me to find a reason to get out of bed. I was sick and tired of being sick and tired, and I had no reason to hope that things would get better. After work every evening, I would go home, take a sleeping pill or two, and try to sleep until it was time for me to go to one of my jobs again. If it was a weekday, I'd go to my military job and the department store. If it was a weekend day, I only had the department store to contend with. Either way, almost every day of the week, I had a job to go to. When I wasn't working, I had no desire to interact with civilization. The only thing I wanted to do was close myself off from the rest of the world and sleep. I was thankful for the work, but I was physically and mentally exhausted all the time.

One evening after work, I was feeling overwhelmingly tired and sad. During my shift, I tried to smile and be friendly to the customers, all while counting down the hours until I could head home. At the end of our shift, Jeannie, an older woman who worked with me, asked me to give her a ride home. Since her apartment wasn't too far out of my way, I agreed to give her a lift. I figured that it would only be a brief detour before I could go home and climb into bed. The next day was Sunday, and I didn't have to work at either job. I was planning to spend my entire day off sleeping—no food, no television, no visitors—just a long, deep sleep. I had been hoping to temporarily escape my painful reality and forget about my problems. I was too stressed to find sleep on my own, but I thought a sleeping pill would allow me to sleep until it was time for me to face the world again. And then I thought, *Well, one pill won't do the trick, so maybe I can take most of what is in the bottle to achieve my goal.* All I wanted was some peace.

When we arrived at Jeannie's apartment, I didn't bother parking. I pulled up to the front of her building and waited for her to get out.

Instead of getting out, she looked at me and said, in her thick Southern accent, "I'm scared. Come up with me."

"You're scared? Scared of what?" I asked.

"I watched a scary movie last night. Come on up. You ain't got nothing else to do tonight," she said.

"Jeannie, I'm exhausted, and I want to go home and go to bed," I protested.

Despite my protests, she would not be denied. "Just come check it out with me real fast. Once I see it's OK, you can go on home," she pleaded.

I agreed to go in with her, and I parked the car. I made no effort to hide my annoyance, but I followed her up the stairs to her apartment anyway.

We went inside, and she made an exaggerated display of checking every room. She checked under the bed, under the sofa, and even underneath the counters. She checked every closet and painstakingly checked them again.

"Jeannie, are you done? Clearly, no one is in here!" I said.

"Be patient," she said. "I just wanna make sure nobody's in here. Why don't you go sit on my bed while I finish looking, and as soon as I'm done, I'll come get you and you can leave."

While Jeannie's statement sounded like a request, I knew better than to argue with her. If I said no, she would just badger me until I gave in. So, too tired to resist, I complied. I went into her bedroom and sat on the edge of her bed.

Her bedroom was a small room that was sparsely furnished. There was a bed, one nightstand with a lamp on top, and a small television that sat on a makeshift TV stand. It was simple, but I supposed it was just enough for one person.

I hadn't noticed, but at some point during her search of the apartment, she had lit a candle that was on the nightstand beside her bed. The candle was tall and white, and it had a bright orange-and-blue flame that flickered, even though there was no discernible breeze in the room. As I looked at the candle, I thought about how it would take hours, maybe even days, for a candle that tall to burn down. I also wondered why she had a candle on her nightstand when she could easily just turn on the lamp if she needed light.

I continued to sit on the bed and stared at the flame. For some reason, it was mesmerizing. I had been staring at the flame for so long without blinking that my eyes began to burn. I was so fascinated by it that I didn't want to look away, so instead, I briefly closed my eyes to reset my vision.

At some point, I must have lain down unconsciously, because the next thing I knew, I was dreaming—at least, I think I was dreaming. My eyes were closed, and there was a movie playing in my mind. The scenes flickering across my subconscious felt more like a trance than a dream. The best way to describe it is that it seemed as if I was watching a movie where I was the leading character. I was both outside and inside the dream at the same time.

Whatever it was, I found myself in a vaguely familiar scene where I was riding a bike. There was someone with me, a figure dressed in bright white who was gliding along beside me. I never saw his feet, but based on his movement, I knew he was gliding, or maybe floating, but not walking. He was wearing a spotless white garment, maybe a robe, but much like the flame from the candle, the brightness illuminating his garment was too bright for me to look at directly. I attempted once to look at him, but the light was too strong, so I quickly looked away. I turned my head in the direction that the bike was traveling and looked straight ahead. I did not attempt to look at him again.

As I rode the bike, I traveled along a single road that took me to different scenes from my life. Some scenes were from my childhood, while others were more recent. The thing that every scene had in common was that they were all from moments in my life when I had faced incredible challenges. Each scene was a painful memory that I had forgotten, chosen to bury away deep in the recesses of my mind, or just didn't want to think about. My thoughts raced. *Why am I here? Why is my mind taking me on such a painful journey? How the heck can I wake myself up to end this?* None of my questions were answered, and the scenes continued to come: my brother burning my leg, and me feeling all alone when my mother failed to help me; being humiliated and getting kicked out of school; living in an empty house after my father left us during a winter blizzard without food, water, heat, or electricity; the pain of my mother not supporting me when I joined the military.

As I rode the bike, my companion and I stopped at each scene, and I watched it play out. As I watched myself navigate those familiar moments, I looked so alone, but for some reason, I hadn't felt lonely. I knew I had been afraid, but from the perspective of this dream, I didn't look afraid; I looked determined.

I didn't get to watch each scene for long. After a few moments, my travel companion—the figure in white—would gently nudge me, indicating it was time to move along. I had many questions, but it felt inappropriate to ask, so I continued as directed.

The desire to wake myself from the dream quickly faded, and I no longer felt anxious. I wasn't afraid at any point during the journey, because I felt like I was traveling with a friend. A friend I had never met before, and one I couldn't see, but one whom I somehow knew. I'd had scary dreams before, but this experience wasn't one of them. This experience was peaceful.

I opened my eyes after what felt like a long blink, and the first thing I noticed was that I was laying down. *When did I lay down? Sure, I closed my eyes, but I didn't lay on someone else's bed!* Then I noticed that the very tall candle was now a short stub. It was still burning, but only barely. *What the heck is happening?*

I jumped off the bed and ran in search of Jeannie. I found her in the kitchen, sitting at a small table.

"How long have I been asleep?" I asked frantically.

"Girl, you were knocked out. I came in there to tell you I was done searching the house, so you could go on home, but you had lain down and was asleep. I didn't want to wake you, so I just passed the time cleaning my house," she said.

"What time is it?" I asked, confused.

She glanced at the watch on her wrist and said, "It's about mornin'. Do you want something to eat?"

"Morning? I've been here all night?" I asked.

"Yep, and you musta needed the sleep, because you didn't move. You looked like you was in a coma. I even had to check on you to make sure you was breathing," she said with a laugh.

"You stayed up all night just to watch me?" I asked softly.

"Yeah, I did, because I was worried about you," she said.

"Why were you worried about me?"

"I dunno. Somethin' told me not to let you go home last night. I don't know what it was, but I knew I wasn't supposed to let you leave here. By the time I ran out of excuses for you to stay, you had done fell asleep, so I just left you alone."

Tears began to run down my face, and Jeannie pulled out the chair next to her and motioned for me to sit down. As soon as I sat, she moved her chair closer to mine and put her arm around me.

"Don't cry. You're going to be OK," she said as she rubbed my shoulders.

I wasn't crying because I was sad. I was crying because I was thinking about how I'd felt the night before, how I had been thinking about taking all those sleeping pills. Who knew if I would have woken up from them? At that time, I hadn't even cared. I knew Jeannie had been right to be concerned. I thought about Jeannie's unusual behavior from the night before, and I was absolutely certain that her actions had saved me.

Jeannie made breakfast, and we sat and ate in silence. I was scared that I had allowed myself to get so sad that logical thought had escaped me. Jeannie looked deeply concerned for her friend. As I took a bite of my pancake, my mind drifted to the dream, if it had even been a dream.

You were such a brave little girl, I thought. *Where is that courage now?*

And that figure, the one traveling beside me, why did he feel so familiar? Who was he? Why did his presence fill me with such peace, both in the dream and even now as I remembered it?

The scenes I'd visited during the dream had all been moments that reminded me that I was not helpless, and I was not a victim. That journey had also revealed to me that I was not alone. I couldn't say for certain that it was true, but I believed that the friend in white who had guided me on my journey was a spiritual being sent to remind me of some very important truths. Such as the fact that God has been with me since before I was created, and He was with me during every moment of darkness. He was there giving me strength; He was there giving me resilience; He was there giving me the courage to keep going; and it was Him who inspired my determination to rise above my circumstances. Somewhere along my life journey, I had forgotten how to rely on Him, but despite that, He had never once failed me. I was very grateful to have been reminded of God's infinite presence in my life.

As the questions swirled in my mind, I let out a quiet sigh before reaching across the table and taking Jeannie's hand. Looking at her solemnly, I said, "Thank you for answering my unspoken call for help."

She returned my squeeze, a warmth in her eyes, and with tenderness in her voice, she smiled and said, "You're welcome."

When my children returned home from Texas, I did everything I could to take care of them. Every evening, we sat down for dinner together, and I listened intently as they shared stories about their days. We spent hours playing learning games, challenging each other, and laughing until our stomachs hurt. Outside, we stood at the edge of the Chesapeake Bay, watching the waves and trying (mostly failing) to skip stones across the water.

Some days, I worried that it wasn't enough. But then I'd see their bright smiles and hear their carefree laughter, and I'd know that it was. They were happy, and that made me happy too.

Chapter 16

What would life be if we had no courage
to attempt anything?

—Vincent van Gogh

Fueled by my reignited faith and deep determination, I began taking action to improve things. The first thing I did was begin the process of petitioning for a divorce and child support. I knew I could not start formal proceedings while Carlos was serving abroad, but I could at least get things started. I didn't have money to pay for an attorney, but I refused to be deterred, so I called more than a dozen attorneys' offices and told them my story. In each case, the person on the other end of the line was sympathetic but ultimately said that they would not be able to assist me. After a few minutes of dialogue, they each concluded that there was nothing they could do until Carlos returned to the US. They also explained their fee structures and the need for a considerable retainer before they would formally speak with me. Work would not begin on my case until after the retainer had been paid and cleared the bank. None of the people who answered the phone at the various firms gave me an opportunity to speak with an actual attorney. They simply told me to call back after things had changed.

As I stared at my list with every name but the last one crossed off, I wondered if it was even worth it to call the last office. I was feeling a bit defeated, but I had known when I'd started that it wouldn't be easy. I was only looking to make a connection with an attorney and get the paperwork started. That way, when Carlos returned to the US, I'd be ready to move forward quickly.

I picked up the phone and dialed the last number on the list. I didn't expect anything different from the last dozen calls, but I was determined to see this through. The phone rang several times, and just as I was about to hang up, I heard a voice on the other end introduce themself and announce the name of their law firm.

"Oh, hello. You caught me off guard. I was just about to hang up," I muttered.

"I'm sorry, dear. I don't move as fast as I used to, and I was clear across the room when the phone rang. How may I help you?" the kind-sounding woman on the other end of the line replied.

"That's OK. Some days, I don't move so fast myself," I said with a smile. "My name is Shoshanna Fuentes, and I'm looking for an attorney," I explained.

"Well, you've called the right place. We happen to have one here," she said playfully. "Can you tell me a little bit about what you need an attorney for, dear?"

I told her the same story I had told everyone else whom I'd spoken with. After having repeated the same story a dozen times,

I recited it from memory, no longer needing my notes. When I finished my narrative, I paused for her to react.

"Well, you've been dealing with a lot," she said. "Let me take a look at Barbara's schedule to see when we can get you in."

"Before you do that," I interjected, "I have to tell you the most important parts."

"There's more?" she asked, curious.

"Yes. Well, two more things, anyway. The most important being that Carlos is stationed in Germany, so we won't be able to start the process right away," I explained.

"And the other?" she asked hesitantly.

I took a deep breath before saying, "I don't have any money to pay a retainer right now, but once the child support payments begin, I will be able to make payments until you are paid in full."

I paused briefly to see if she would end the discussion, but her silence prompted me to continue. "I realize that it probably doesn't work that way, but I'm between a rock and a hard place. I can't afford to pay a lawyer to help me get child support, and I can't get child support without a lawyer," I concluded.

I waited for the same closing that I had received twelve times already: *I'm sorry to hear that, but I'm afraid we aren't able to help you. Please call us back when things change.*

Surprisingly, that wasn't her response. When she finally spoke, she said, "Well, those things aren't that bad. Can you come in on Thursday?"

I wasn't certain that she had heard the part about the money, so I started to repeat it. "I don't have any money ..."

She interrupted me. "I heard you the first time. Now, can you come in on Thursday?"

"Yes, ma'am!" I answered quickly.

I hung up the phone and stared at my list. What had just happened? I actually had an appointment to speak with a lawyer. There was no guarantee that she would be able to help me, but I was very grateful for this small win. Things were moving forward, and that made me happy. I stared at my list that had twelve names that I'd scratched through. A big smile lit up my face before I picked up my pencil and triumphantly placed a large check mark beside the last entry.

I walked into the attorney's office at the appointed time. The office wasn't large and stuffy like I'd imagined a law firm would be. It was a modestly decorated office that was very welcoming.

I approached the receptionist's desk, and before I could introduce myself, she said, "Hi, Shoshanna. You're right on time."

I smiled at the familiar voice as she handed me a clipboard with several forms attached.

"Please complete all these forms, but don't sign any of them. Barbara will explain what they all mean before you sign them, so you know exactly what you're agreeing to," she instructed.

"OK," I agreed.

"You can have a seat right out there," she said, gesturing toward the waiting area. "And I'll take you back as soon as she's ready for you. Would you like some coffee?"

"No, ma'am, I'm fine," I responded politely.

I liked her. I had known her for all of two minutes, but somehow, I already knew that I liked her because she reminded me of a kind grandmother.

I took my seat in the waiting room and began filling out the forms as she'd instructed.

I was completing the last form when the receptionist appeared and said, "Barbara will see you now."

I gathered my things before standing and following her to an office in the back. When we approached the door, she stepped in front of me and said, "Barbara, this is Shoshanna. Shoshanna, this is Barbara. She's a very good attorney, and she also happens to be my daughter."

I stepped into the office, shook Barbara's hand, and said, "It's nice to meet you. Thank you for seeing me."

Barbara and I sat for a long time while going through the details of my situation. I told her when and where Carlos and I had gotten married. I explained when and why we'd separated, and I walked her through my many unsuccessful efforts to get Carlos to agree to voluntarily support his children. She listened attentively and took lots of notes.

When I had finally completed my story, she looked up and asked, "Is there anything else?"

"No, not that I can think of," I responded.

"OK," she said, "I will review my notes and come back to you in about a week with next steps. I have to be honest with you, this will not be easy. Since your husband is out of the country, it will be nearly impossible to get your case in front of a judge. I'm hoping that, given your financial hardship, we will be able to get some leniency. The Soldiers' and Sailors' Civil Relief Act is intended to protect soldiers serving abroad, but it is *not* meant to allow them to neglect their children."

Her voice sounded angry, and I knew in that moment that Barbara was the right lawyer for me. I felt confident that, if there was any way for her to help me, she would.

I worked with Barbara for the better part of a year, and nothing we tried was working. The Soldiers' and Sailors' Civil Relief Act protected Carlos, and no matter how hard we tried, there was no way around it ... *until there was.* I received an unexpected call from Carlos saying that he wanted to speed up the divorce. I explained to him it wouldn't be possible until he returned to the US, but he persisted.

"Don't you have a lawyer?" he asked.

"Well, yes, but she has tried everything, and there's nothing she can do until you return to the US ... which is when?"

"Not for a while, and I don't want to wait until then," he said.

"Why are you in such a hurry all of a sudden?" I asked.

"Don't worry about it," he said.

"I haven't heard from you in I don't know how long. You won't send me any money to help take care of your kids. And now, all of a sudden, you want a hurried divorce? Are you trying to get married?" I asked.

"Maybe," he responded. "Look," he continued, "what I do is none of your business. Just talk to your lawyer and see if there is a way to speed up the divorce."

And, with that, the line went dead. I was so angry. Who did he think he was that he could call and demand that I speed up the divorce because he needed me to? I picked up the phone and dialed my attorney to relay the conversation I'd had with Carlos.

After I replayed the conversation to her, I launched into a tirade. "Can you believe him? Who in the heck does he think he is? We have tried everything, and now, all of a sudden, I'm supposed to jump through hoops just because he says so. Well, we aren't going to do that, are we?"

I heard a sigh through the phone before Barbara responded. "Shoshanna, don't you realize that this is good news?"

I was confused. "How is this good news?" I asked. "Just because he's interested in divorcing me doesn't change the fact that he's protected under military law."

"That's true," she said, "but if you can get him to agree to waive his rights under the Soldiers' and Sailors' Civil Relief Act, we might not have to wait until he returns to the States. I have to look into this a bit more, but I think this is the break we need to move things along. Regardless of the reason, he wants a divorce now—and we need to take advantage of this opportunity before he changes his mind. Do you understand me?"

"Yes," I murmured.

"If he calls you again, tell him that your attorney is working on it and will be in touch soon with the next steps."

As I processed her words, I began to feel hopeful.

"The divorce will include child support, right?"

"Yes, of course," she replied. "But for now, let's take things one step at a time. If we can get a waiver signed, we will be able to litigate the divorce just as we would if he were in the US, which means going after child support and back pay," she said.

I smiled as I hung up the phone. This was wonderful news, but I still felt nervous because the entire plan depended on Carlos relinquishing his rights to legal protection, which was still a wild card. Could he even do that? If so, why would he? And why now? I didn't know why he wanted a divorce so suddenly, and I didn't care. The only thing that mattered was that, after so long, I might finally get the financial assistance I desperately needed.

Over the next several months, Barbara worked on getting the waiver signed, and I was surprised and delighted when she finally called to say that she had received a signed and notarized copy of the waiver from Carlos.

Once she received the waiver, we began working on the details of the divorce. We met several times before landing on the terms that we felt would offer me and the children the most protection. The child support aspect was pretty straightforward because it was a formulaic calculation that was dictated by the state. Back pay was substantial, so to move things along, Barbara included an incremental payment schedule that would allow Carlos to gradually get caught up.

We finally tackled the most emotionally complicated aspect of the terms: custody of the children. I had just assumed that the divorce would include a joint-custody clause where the children would live with me, but Carlos would have input and influence. However, when I read the proposed document, there was no mention of joint custody. The language in the document read, "It is specifically ordered that sole legal and physical custody of the infant children of the parties, Jasmine Marie Fuentes, born April

12, 1990, and Joshua Jose Fuentes, born on July 7, 1992, shall be awarded to the plaintiff."

I stared at the words in disbelief because I did not intend to deny Carlos access to his children or to deny the children access to their father.

I finally asked Barbara, "What does this mean as far as Carlos's visitation rights?"

"He wouldn't have any. You would be solely responsible for all decisions regarding the children."

"What if he wants to see them?"

"He'd have to ask you, and whether or not he sees them would be up to you."

"He will never agree to that!" I said.

"Maybe not, but it's important that we ask."

"Why?"

Barbara explained, "Because six months or a year from now, when you decide you want to move to another city or make any other decision pertaining to your children, I don't want your ability to parent to depend on his mood. And what happens if he remarries and insists that the children spend time with him and his new wife? Will you be OK with that?" she asked.

"The language in this document will give you the legal right to say no to that, and any other request regarding your children that you don't agree with."

"This doesn't feel right," I whispered.

"Look, Shoshanna, it's my job to protect your legal rights. Whatever access to the children that you decide to allow is up to you. I just want to make sure that it's your choice."

It still didn't sit well with me, and deep down, I didn't believe that he would agree to the harsh terms. I trusted Barbara, and I knew requesting sole custody was the right thing to do, so I gave her my approval to proceed.

Barbara finalized the document before sending it to Carlos by Express Mail.

As we waited for the documents to be returned, I felt an overwhelming sense of grief because the signed document would mean that my marriage was truly over. I knew getting the divorce was the right thing to do, and I was angry that Carlos wasn't fulfilling his responsibility as a father. I also desperately wanted closure. Yet, for some reason, I was very sad. Carlos and I had met when I was barely nineteen years old, and in many ways, he had been my best friend. Over the course of our marriage, we had laughed together at some of the silliest things. We made up funny nicknames for our children, like The Boy and The Girl. He was the first person I'd shared my story with—and he'd loved me anyway. As I thought about my marriage, I decided it hadn't all been bad … there were many wonderful memories woven into our history. As I look back now, I believe we were just two immature people who failed to successfully handle the responsibilities that came with marriage and raising a family.

About two weeks after my attorney had sent the paperwork to Carlos, she received his response by Express Mail. I listened on the phone as she opened the envelope and prepared to read the contents.

After a long stretch of silence, I became nervous and blurted out, "Oh no, he didn't sign it. I knew it!"

"Hold on," she said. "Don't jump to any conclusions. Let me look at it."

I held my breath for what seemed like an eternity before I heard her shout, "He signed it!"

I couldn't believe my ears. "He did?" I whispered.

"Yes, he signed it!"

"He actually signed it? Did he agree to everything?"

"Yes, every page is signed and notarized as instructed," she said joyfully.

"Did he agree that I could have sole legal and physical custody of the children?" I asked.

"Yes, he agreed to everything," she repeated.

"Does that mean my divorce is official?"

"Almost. I need to file the paperwork, but for all intents and purposes, you are divorced. Congratulations, Shoshanna!" she exclaimed.

We briefly discussed the next steps, and before hanging up, Barbara said, "Go do something fun to celebrate."

I expressed my gratitude for her diligence and hard work before returning the phone to the cradle without commenting on her suggestion for me to celebrate. This was wonderful news indeed, but it felt like solemnity was more appropriate for the occasion, rather than celebration.

The divorce was finalized on October 22, 1996.

After my divorce, things finally settled down, and I looked forward to a much-needed fresh start. The child support payments had not begun, but knowing that soon it would be easier for me to take care of my children made me happy. Jasmine, now six years old, was doing well at Saint Mary, and the school renewed her scholarship for the following year. I had made friends at the base, and I had also befriended a few of the parents at the school. Although I was not Catholic, I continued attending Mass every week. Overall, I felt spiritually grounded, and I felt a sense of peace that I had not felt in a very long time.

Chapter 17

No one is so brave that he is not disturbed
by something unexpected.

—Julius Caesar

The alarm clock rang, and I began going through my morning routine with precision and efficiency. *Try to wake the children ... Take a quick shower, brush my teeth ... Try to wake the children again ... Get dressed, and head downstairs to make breakfast ... Stop by the children's rooms on the way and try to wake them again, this time adding the threat of tossing them out of bed ... Feed the children ... Head out the door to start my day.*

As I walked into the office, I was prepared to tackle the large stack of paperwork that I'd left on my desk the day before.

Before I reached my desk, I heard a voice say, "Sergeant Fuentes. I need to speak with you."

The voice belonged to Staff Sergeant Lingo, my direct supervisor. I turned toward him and asked, "Does it have to be right now? I have several orders that I need to process before lunch."

"Yes, it has to be right now," he said.

It was only then that I noticed the grim look on his face. My muscles tensed up, and I braced myself for whatever bad news he was about to spring on me.

As he led me to a conference room, I thought to myself, *What now? I'm finally happy, and now something bad is happening.*

I immediately attempted to cut off the self-pitying thoughts. *Stop it ... that line of thinking is* not *helpful. You don't even know what he's going to say. (I knew the peace wouldn't last.) Stop it! (What if it's something terrible?) Stop it! (If it isn't bad, why is it so urgent, and why does his face look so serious?) Stop ... it!*

I silenced my inner monologue and decided that whatever it was, I would listen; I wouldn't get emotional, and I'd avoid any hasty reactions.

We entered the conference room, and I took the chair closest to the door. Staff Sergeant Lingo sat on the other side of the conference table facing me.

"Sergeant Fuentes, I know that you have had a lot going on, and that you are raising your kids by yourself," he began. "But you know that part of being a soldier who is a single parent is making sure you have a plan for your kids to be taken care of if you are deployed," he said.

"Am I being deployed?"

"No. Well, kind of."

"How can I be kind of deployed? Is there a war happening that I don't know about?"

"No. It's not that kind of deployment."

"Then what kind of deployment is it?"

"You're not being deployed. Let me start over. You have been in the military nearly eight years, and you have never done an overseas tour."

"That's right. I haven't."

As I waited for him to continue, I stared at him, my palms sweaty with nervous anticipation. I couldn't quite work out why he seemed so nervous. Being assigned an overseas tour wasn't necessarily bad news, unless ...

"You have received orders to report for duty in Korea within the next six months."

... Unless the overseas assignment was a hardship tour! The commitments I'd made to myself before I'd walked into the conference room began sounding in my head. *Listen, don't get emotional. And avoid any hasty reactions.* They were the only things I could focus on to help me hold it together. If I allowed myself to internalize the words he'd just spoken, I would burst into tears.

"Did you hear me, Sergeant Fuentes? You have been reassigned to Seoul, Korea."

"Yes. I heard you."

"You know that since this is a hardship tour, it's a dependent-restricted assignment, meaning you can't take your children?"

"I know."

"It's not that bad. I have done a tour in Korea, and the time goes by quickly. It's only a year, and they allow you to come home and visit your family after six months."

"Is there anything else?"

"No, that's all. Are you OK?"

"Not really, but I will be."

"Is there anything I can do?"

"No, but thanks for asking."

I left the conference room and headed straight for the ladies' room. As I opened the door, tears filled my eyes. A hardship tour was one of the toughest tours of duty that someone with a family could be assigned. I'd heard stories of hardship tours ruining marriages and breaking up families. The thought of the army sending a single mother on a hardship tour had never occurred to me. But why wouldn't they? Every soldier was expected to fulfill their military duty, and I was no exception.

As I sat in an empty stall, I allowed sadness and grief to engulf me. I leaned into the tears and allowed the self-pitying thoughts to flow freely. I needed this moment, because once I left that stall, I would not cry again. My attention would turn to figuring out my options and finding a solution. However, if there was no way for me to avoid a tour of duty in Korea without ruining my military record, I would go and honor the commitment I'd made as a soldier.

When I returned to my desk, I had a package from the personnel office that included a list of things I needed to do to prepare for my change in duty station. The first thing I was required to do was to go to the personnel office as soon as possible and formally accept the new assignment. I decided that could wait, and I would tackle the to-do list the next day. I went through the rest of the day on autopilot and tried not to allow myself to think about the news or panic.

As soon as I got home from work, I fed the children, and then I called my mother.

"Hello," the voice said after the third ring.

"Hey, Ema, it's me."

My mother instantly picked up on my tone and asked, "What's the matter, Shoshanna?"

"I got some not-so-great news at work today. I'm being moved to Korea for a year."

"Do you not want to go to Korea?"

"It's not that," I said. "It's just that Korea is a hardship tour. It's called a hardship tour because I have to go alone, meaning I can't take the kids with me."

"Oh."

"I don't want to leave my children for a year. Plus, I don't have anyone to take care of them while I'm gone. Carlos is in Germany, and besides, he's not fit to take care of them, anyway. I could probably send them to his mother in Texas, but I'm afraid I would never get them back. Things were finally going well, and then this happens ... Why?!" I exclaimed.

"You could send them to me," my mother said softly.

"I know that, but I don't want to be a burden to you. You already have enough going on, and I don't want to add to it," I said.

"It wouldn't be a burden. I love my grandkids, and I'd happily take care of them." My mother and I had mended our relationship after the fallout with Rebecca, and while I appreciated her offer, I didn't want my children living in Chicago.

"Thank you, Ema. I appreciate your support," I said.

"Can you get out of it?"

"I don't know. I have to meet with the personnel office tomorrow so they can tell me what I'm supposed to do. Ema, I don't want to leave my children. I am all they have, and they are all that I have."

There was a long silence before I heard her speak. "Don't worry, Noonie. The Father will make a way. You just have to trust and believe," she said softly.

"I do believe; it's just so hard. I'm trying to be strong for my children, but every time I solve one thing, it seems like something else pops up. No matter what I have to face out in the world, coming home to my children's smiling faces makes it all worthwhile. If I end up in Korea, I won't have that."

My mother listened before finally saying, "You are not alone, Shoshanna. I will help you however I can. Go to that personnel office tomorrow and write down everything they tell you. Even if something seems small, write it down anyway. Then call me when you get home, and we will figure this out together."

My mother's voice was soothing. It was almost as if I could feel her hugging me through the phone.

"OK, Ema. I will," I said.

"I love you, Noonie."

"I love you too, Ema."

The next day, I went to the personnel office to meet with the person overseeing my relocation. I wrote my name on the sign-in sheet and took a seat next to a gentleman in civilian clothes who was also waiting. He was holding a folder that looked exactly like the one I had.

As I sat down, he glanced over at me and smiled. "What's up, Airborne? Fort Bragg, right?" he asked.

"Huh?" I inquired.

"You were at Fort Bragg before coming here, right? I figured you must be from Bragg since you are a paratrooper. Plus, you have that 82nd look about you."

Returning his smile, I replied, "Oh. Yes, that's right, I was at Bragg." I glanced at the folder he was holding. "Are you being relocated too?"

"Yes, just found out yesterday," he said with a smile.

"Where are you headed?"

"Stuttgart, Germany," he said.

"Germany? Wow! Are you excited?"

"Heck yeah! I have a lot of friends over there, and they love it. My wife is pretty excited too; she wants our kids to learn German. Hey, let me ask you something."

"What's up?"

"Is it true that y'all be jumping with tanks and shit?"

I laughed. "Yes, that's true. Tanks, howitzers, Humvees ... you name it."

"How do you do it?"

"First, they tie the tanks down on skids, and then they rig it up with lots of para—"

"Not that," he interrupted. "I mean, how do you jump out of a perfectly good airplane? I always wanted to be Airborne, but *shit*, I'm too afraid of heights."

"Oh, that ... you just do it."

"There has to be more to it than *just do it*. Aren't you afraid?"

"Not really. I'm not afraid, because when I'm in that aircraft, I'm part of something that's bigger than me. There are other soldiers to my left and right who are counting on me to jump. There are also soldiers on the ground who are counting on me to jump, get on the ground, and do my job. The success of the mission depends on me jumping and playing whatever role is assigned to me. So, no, I'm not afraid, because when I'm in the aircraft, my only focus is the mission; nothing else matters. Doing my job, and not letting my team down, takes precedence over any fear."

"Wow, that's cool. Do you miss it?"

"Yeah, I miss it."

"What brought you to Fort Monroe?"

"Orders, just like you."

"Would you go back?"

"To Bragg? Sure, if the military sent me. I have two children now, though, so I wouldn't volunteer to go back."

"I feel you. Where is this relocation taking you?"

"Korea."

"No shit?"

"Nope, no shit."

"Is your husband going to stay with your kids while you're over there?"

"No, I'm divorced. Besides, he lives in the barracks in Germany."

"The army is sending a single mother on a hardship tour to Korea?"

"Yeah, it looks that way."

"Damn. I'm sorry."

"It's all good. I get out of the army as soon as I get back. I just have to hold my breath for a year."

"What do you mean?" His brow crinkled in confusion.

"I only have eight months left before my ETS. If they extend my term a few months so I can go to Korea, I'll leave the army as soon as I get back. It'll be my expiration of service."

He looked at me with a grim expression on his face. "It doesn't work that way," he said. "They won't extend your term for a couple of months. You'll have to reenlist for another full term. You need to have at least six months left on your term when you return to the States, and since you are near your ETS date, you'll have to re-up before you go."

I stared at him blankly. Whether to reenlist for another four years was a decision I hadn't made yet. I knew my ETS date was approaching, but I figured I had more time before I had to decide whether I wanted to commit to another four years.

He saw the disappointment on my face. He leaned in closer and asked, "Do you want to go to Korea?"

"No, I don't," I said honestly.

"Then listen to me, and don't ever tell anyone I told you this. I work in personnel, and I know how you can get out of going to Korea."

"How?!"

"*Shh* ... lower your voice!"

"Sorry," I muttered. "*How?*"

"Don't reenlist."

I looked confused. "I have to reenlist. Korea is a twelve-month tour, and I only have eight months left on my term," I said.

"That's the point. If you don't have enough time left on your term, and you don't reenlist, they can't send you overseas. You are not allowed to ETS while stationed overseas," he said.

"Won't I get a dishonorable discharge if I refuse a relocation?"

"Yes, and that is why you will not refuse the tour. When you meet with your counselor, accept the duty change, and start doing whatever they tell you to do to get ready. Do everything as if you are going, and then when it comes time to reenlist, just tell them you are not going to reenlist. They will have to cancel the orders."

"Really?" I shook my head in disbelief.

"Yes, really. The trick is that you *must* accept the assignment. Don't mention anything about not wanting to go. Make childcare plans for your children, just as you would if you were going. If you are OK with leaving the military, this is the perfect solution for you. If you aren't, then you have to reenlist and go to Korea," he said.

"If it means not leaving my children for a year, I'll gladly leave the military."

"Well, then you have your answer," he said with a wink.

"Why are you helping me?"

"Because I don't think families should have to be separated. Plus, you seem like cool peeps," he added with a smile.

"I can't thank you enough. I really appreciate you," I said.

We waited together and continued to talk until I heard the attendant call my name. I stood to walk toward the reception desk, and then I turned back.

"Thanks again for your help."

"No problem."

"By the way, what is your name?"

"Gabriel. My name is Gabriel."

"Well, Gabriel, I believe you are my guardian angel. Good luck in Germany. I hope you and your family love it there."

"Good luck to you, too, Airborne."

I turned and walked toward the waiting attendant with a huge smile on my face. My mother had been right. By the grace of God, I was *not* leaving my children.

Chapter 18

Hope is being able to see that there is light
despite all of the darkness.

—Desmond Tutu

I met with the intake counselor, and just as Gabriel had instructed, I agreed to everything.

"It looks like you are heading to Korea, Sergeant Fuentes. Is
that correct?" the sergeant asked as he flipped through the pages
of my paperwork.

"Yes, Sergeant," I said.

He leaned forward, his eyebrows raised. "How do you feel
about going to Korea? Aren't you a single parent?"

"I am a single parent, but I'm also a soldier, so I don't feel
anything about it. Besides, I've never been to Korea, so it'll be a

new adventure." I spoke in an even tone, trying not to let my voice betray the ball of panic that was building inside of me.

What if he sees through me? I thought.

Gabriel had been very clear that I could not reveal any signs of concern or hesitancy. He'd told me I needed to appear to be fully on board, and when they presented my reenlistment paperwork, I was to smile and say, "I want to go to Korea, but I'm planning to ETS as soon as I get back to the States, so I'm not planning to reenlist for four years." That was the response that would put everything else in motion to spare me the pain of leaving my children. It was important that I was convincing, so no one could accuse me of refusing a new duty assignment.

"I know several people who've been stationed in Korea, and they say it's not bad," the sergeant said in a matter-of-fact tone as he punched information into a computer and made notes in my file.

"When I was younger, my brother was stationed in Korea," I added. "He had custom tracksuits made for everyone in my family ... they were pretty cool."

"A lot of people do that because everything over there is so cheap. OK, let's talk paperwork," he said as he turned and slid a stack of papers in front of me. "You'll need a few vaccinations before you leave, and I have to review your long-term childcare plan. Do you know who your children will live with while you are overseas?" he asked.

"Yes, Sergeant, they will stay with my mom in Chicago."

"Great. We'll need to make sure your long-term power of attorney is up to date, and that the permissions for medical care and school enrollment are in place."

"OK," I said.

"Your household goods will be placed in storage unless you want them shipped to your mom," he continued.

"Storage is fine. Where will the storage location be, and will my things be safe?"

"That's up to you," he said. "Your things can be stored here in Virginia and then shipped to your next duty station when you return from Korea, or we can store everything in your hometown. You don't have to decide right now, but I will need to know in the next few weeks so it can be arranged."

"OK. I'm almost certain that I will want my things stored in Virginia, but I'll let you know for sure in a week or so. What will happen to my vehicle?" I tried to ask thoughtful questions to show my full commitment to the journey.

"Your vehicle will be stored here as well. Although most people either leave their vehicle with a family member, or they sell it before they leave," he added.

"Why?"

"Because it isn't good for a vehicle to sit for over a year without being started or driven. So, by the time you come back, it will probably need a lot of work before you can drive it again. Plus, if your vehicle isn't paid for, why would you continue to pay for a vehicle that you can't drive when you can just as easily buy another one when you return to the States?"

"That makes sense," I said. "Is there anything else, Sergeant? I have to get to work."

"No, we're good for now. I'll go make copies of everything, and then you can be on your way. Let's connect again after you finish the medical stuff, and then I'll review your childcare documents. After that, I'll schedule your reenlistment. Sound good?"

"Fine by me," I said cheerfully.

He rose from his seat and headed to the copier. As he walked away, I sat and prayed that what Gabriel had told me was true. According to Gabriel, now wasn't the time to tell the sergeant that I wasn't reenlisting. I was supposed to act surprised when he presented me with a four-year reenlistment contract. I would then explain how I'd thought my reenlistment would only extend long enough for me to complete my tour in Korea. "Make it seem like nothing more than a misunderstanding," Gabriel had told me. He said that, if I did exactly what he'd told me, everything would be fine. I hoped and prayed that he was right ... and, for some reason, deep down inside, I knew without a doubt that he was.

As soon as I got home that evening, I called my mother so I could tell her the good news. I eagerly pressed the buttons on the keypad and smiled to myself as I waited for her to answer. The receiver clicked as I heard my mother say hello in a distracted tone.

She immediately recognized my voice. "Hello, Shoshanna."

"You sound busy. Is now a good time to talk?"

"Yes, it is. I was just getting ready to cook dinner when the phone rang, but I've been waiting to hear from you all day. How did it go?"

"I think it went well, Ema. I also think everything is going to be OK."

"Why do you think that?"

"Because I got some really good advice before I went in to meet with the counselor."

"Advice from who?" she asked with a bit of edge in her voice. My mother wasn't very trusting of people in general, but she was especially leery of random strangers.

"When I was waiting for my turn to speak with the counselor, I met a guy in the waiting room, and we started talking."

"What guy?" she interrupted.

"A guy who was also waiting to meet with a counselor so he could begin his reassignment paperwork. He is in the process of transferring to Germany."

She huffed into the phone, and I could hear her nails tapping impatiently against the table. "So what does this random-ass stranger have to do with your situation?"

"I'm trying to tell you, but you keep interrupting me," I said impatiently.

"Do *not* get smart with me, little girl. I'll ask as many damn questions as I want!" she fired back.

"*Sorry*. I'm just trying to get through the story so you'll know what happened."

"Well, go on, then … tell me what happened," she said a bit more softly.

"OK, so I was sitting in the waiting room, and the guy next to me started talking to me."

"Why did he start talking to you?" she interrupted again. "Was he hitting on you?"

"No, he wasn't hitting on me, Ema. He was just making small talk while we waited. He asked where I was being transferred to, and I told him Korea. When he asked if I wanted to go to Korea, I told him I didn't want to go because I didn't want to leave my kids."

"Why would you tell a complete stranger all of your business?" she asked, her voice sharp.

"I didn't tell him *all of my business*. Telling him that I have children, which I do, is hardly telling him *all of my business*. Anyway, I told him I didn't want to leave my children, and he said that he didn't think that it was right for a mother to be separated from her children. He went on to tell me that he worked in the personnel office, so he knew pretty much all there was to know about duty transfers. I asked him if he had any tips for me, and then he gave me some very helpful information that might keep me from having to go to Korea," I said. I raised my inflection at the end in an effort to sound enthusiastic. I was hoping my joy would be contagious, and that my mother would respond accordingly. However, I had no such luck.

"Tips? What tips? Some random guy that you don't know gives you some *tips*, and now all of a sudden you don't have to go to Korea?" she asked incredulously.

"That's not what I said," I snapped, annoyed that she wasn't excited by this glimmer of hope like I was. "I said that I *might* not have to go. It's still very much a question, but based on what he told me, I feel like I have a good chance of not having to go, which is more than I had before I talked to him."

"Fine. Go on and tell me the rest," she said.

"He explained to me that, in order for me to go to Korea, I must have at least six months left on my tour when I return to the States. Right now, I only have eight months left total, which means that, in order to go to Korea, I have to reenlist. So, while I can't refuse the tour in Korea and maintain my honorable discharge status, I *can* decide not to reenlist without penalty. If I do that, they won't send me to Korea. Instead, I will just leave the army when my term ends in eight months."

"So you would get out of the army and move back home?"

"Yes, I would get out of the army, but no, I would not move back to Chicago," I said firmly.

"Why not?" she demanded. "Why would you leave the army and not move back home? It hasn't been the same since you left, and now you can move back, but you won't?"

"Ema, I only just now learned that I might get out of the army, and I haven't thought about what I want to do next. It's a big decision, but whatever I decide, I'm not moving back to Chicago."

"Why not?" she asked.

"I left Chicago for a reason ... so I could make it on my own. There is an enormous world outside of Chicago, and I want to experience it. A world that I want my children to experience. I'm sorry, Ema, but I'm not moving back to Chicago," I said gently.

Grasping at straws, I abruptly blurted out, "I think I might want to go back to college and finish my degree." The thought hadn't crossed my mind before, but as soon as the words left my mouth, it suddenly felt like a good idea.

It struck me then how little I had thought about my future after leaving the army. I had been so focused on *not* going back to Chicago, that I hadn't really considered what I *was* going to do. The idea of going back to college seemed right, but how could I make it work? How would I juggle being a full-time student, a single parent, and unemployed? The eventual child support payments would help, but would they be enough? Maybe I could even get a scholarship. I was determined to forge ahead. *And if I'm blessed enough to avoid having to leave my children and go to Korea*, I thought, *I'm going to figure out how to make the most out of that blessing.*

"They have excellent schools here," my mother's voice broke into my thoughts, pulling me back to the moment.

"Yes, they do. They also have great schools in Virginia, Boston, and North Carolina," I replied. "There are excellent schools all over the country. I'll do my research and see if I can get a scholarship for one of them."

"Fine, then. I'm happy that you have a plan, and I hope it works out just as your random stranger described."

"Me too. Gabriel felt confident that his plan would work, and I—"

"Who is Gabriel?" she said, cutting me off.

"Oh, that's the name of the guy I was telling you about. The one I was talking to in the waiting room who gave me the tips."

"His name was Gabriel?"

"Yes, why?"

"No reason. It's just that's a very special name. You know God puts the right people in our lives when we need them, right?"

As I listened to her words, I was reminded of my dream. I thought about the spiritual guide who had accompanied me, the figure whose presence had filled me with a peace I couldn't explain. *Was Gabriel another example of God sending someone to help me?* The thought stirred something deep within me, a swell of emotion I wasn't prepared for.

"I know," I said, doing my best to maintain my composure.

"It's a blessing that guy—*Gabriel*—was in the office at the same time you were, and that he happened to have the exact information you needed. *Todah La'El*," she whispered. "That was *not* a coincidence. That was the Most High at work in your life," she said reverently. "*Todah La'El*," she said again.

"Yes, *thanks be to God*," I whispered back.

The next day at work, I had lunch with my coworker Donna, who was also a trusted friend. I told Donna that I was thinking about leaving the army and going back to college to finish my degree in psychology.

"What's stopping you?" she asked. "If you leave the military, you will need an education to get a job. Your military experience will be helpful, but a degree will set you apart. Besides, with all the classes you have already taken, you can't be that far from finishing your degree," she added.

"Do you think the classes I've taken will count?"

"I don't know if all of them will count, but I know schools accept credits from other colleges, as long as they are from accredited colleges."

"Oh, I didn't know that. How do I find out if they will accept my credits?" I asked.

"Do you know what school you want to go to?"

"No."

"Well, start by figuring that out. Once you decide on a few options, you can call the schools' registrar and find out which credits can be transferred," she advised. "Are you thinking about going to school in Virginia? Hampton University is an HBCU, you know."

"What's an HBCU?"

"You don't know what an HBCU is?" She shook her head in disbelief.

"No. Should I know?"

"Yes, you should!" she exclaimed. "An HBCU is a historically Black college or university. HBCUs were originally founded to educate African Americans. They are great learning institutions where you learn a lot more than just the education needed for your degree."

"That sounds nice," I said. "I have to figure out what schools I can get into. I also have to think about where the kids will go to school. Whatever school I attend will have to be in a city that I can afford to live in, and it has to be in an area where the kids can go to a good school. I will also need some sort of scholarship to help with tuition and living expenses. Given all of that, I might apply to Hampton, but I have to look beyond Virginia schools."

"You absolutely should. I'm not telling you to put all of your eggs in one basket. Do what's best for your situation," she said.

After talking to Donna, I had a plan. I spent the next several days researching colleges and universities, and I narrowed it down to two that I would apply to: North Dakota State University and Southern Illinois University Carbondale. I had already taken several courses in psychology, focusing on child psychology, driven by my desire to help children. So, after researching several schools, those two topped my list. They offered the most scholarship money, had impressive psychology departments (which aligned perfectly with most of my completed coursework), and were willing to accept most of my transfer credits. However, both schools had pros and cons.

North Dakota State University offered almost a full scholarship, and the overall tuition was pretty inexpensive ... pro. The university was in a state I had never been to before, and living there would offer a fresh start ... pro. I knew someone who lived in a nearby city who would help me get settled in ... pro. Fargo, North Dakota, gets extremely cold in the winter ... con. Overall, North Dakota is one of the Whitest states in the US with a tiny percentage of African American residents ... very *big* con!

There was also Southern Illinois University in Carbondale, Illinois. I'd learned that, because I was a veteran and a resident of the state of Illinois, I could attend any public college or university essentially for free by leveraging the Illinois Veteran Grant (IVG) Program ... pro. The school not only had a first-rate psychology program with respected professors, but it also had a very large research department, which interested me ... pro. Between the IVG and the GI Bill, my tuition and housing would be completely covered ... pro. Tuition included a university-sponsored medical program, so the kids and I would have medical benefits ... pro. I would only be a few hours from Chicago, so my relatives could randomly visit ... con. The public school that was closest to the university where the children would attend was not good at all ... con. If accepted, I would need to be on campus one month before my military term expired, or I would have to wait a full semester with no income or medical benefits until I started school ... *huge* con!

I decided I would start by applying to both schools to see where I would be accepted. Once I knew what my actual options were, I could then make an informed decision. I applied to both schools by the specified deadlines, and then I anxiously waited for their responses.

While I pursued the path to higher education, I continued to work my way through the list of things I needed to do to prepare for my move to Korea. I had completed my medical exam, and it was now time for my follow-up meeting with my counselor to discuss storage of my household goods, finalize my long-term childcare paperwork, and schedule my reenlistment.

As I entered the waiting room, I hoped I would bump into Gabriel again, even though I knew it wasn't likely. The waiting room was empty, so I picked up a magazine and began mindlessly flipping pages while I waited for my name to be called.

I didn't have to wait long before I heard, "Welcome back, Sergeant Fuentes. Did you get through the list I gave you?"

I looked up to see the same sergeant who had initially assisted me. He was smiling in my direction as he waved his hand toward the office.

"Yep. I finished everything on the list, Sergeant."

I rose from my seat and fell in step with him as we walked to his office.

"Well," he began, "everything from this point on is pretty straightforward. I have already looked at possible dates for you to reenlist, and we can get it scheduled for as early as the end of this week. I just need a few pieces of information from you, and I'll have you out of here in less than an hour."

"Sounds like a plan. Just let me know what you need."

We walked into the office, and I took one of the small chairs positioned in front of his desk. He sat in a much larger chair situated behind the desk.

He grabbed a thick folder and said, "Let's see what we have. OK, first things first, where are we shipping your household goods?" he asked.

"I'd like to store them here in Virginia."

"OK, that's easy enough." He scribbled a few notes on a sheet of paper and then slid it to me. "Sign here and here. Then initial here, here, and here," he said as he pointed to several places on the page.

I took the pen that he'd handed me and signed and initialed accordingly.

"I've looked over your long-term childcare documents, and everything is in order. Please review each of these pages and then sign and initial the bottom of each page," he instructed as he handed several forms to me.

I briefly reviewed each page and then signed and initialed each of them. With each signature, I felt increasingly sick to my stomach. As I read the words on the temporary power of attorney—"I hereby grant power of attorney and full legal and physical custody of ..."—I heard a voice inside my head scream, *What are you doing?*

What *was* I doing? I was signing over the responsibility and all decision-making rights for my children to someone else. This did not feel like I was going through the motions. This felt very real. If Gabriel's advice proved to be faulty, I would lose my children for a full year of their lives, and I had just signed the forms that would allow it.

The room suddenly felt hot, and my hands started shaking.

"Are you OK? You're trembling!"

"Yes, I'm fine. I just haven't eaten all day, and I feel a little lightheaded," I said.

"I have some crackers in my desk drawer. Do you want them?"

"That's very nice of you, but no, thank you."

"If you're worried about them being stale, I just put them in there this morning, and you are more than welcome to have them."

"I appreciate the offer, but I'm fine, honestly. Besides, as soon as I leave here, I'm heading home, and I'll get something to eat as soon as I get there."

"OK, then let's get you out of here as quickly as possible," he said as he began swiftly flipping through the papers on his desk.

I had lied. I wasn't fine at all. Panic was setting in, and I felt like I was going to crack. My mind raced with thoughts of doubt. What if the plan didn't work like Gabriel had said it would? For the last couple of months, I'd convinced myself that I would be spared a tour of duty in Korea. I'd forced myself to believe that the things Gabriel had told me would work, and that there was nothing to worry about. It had sounded like a brilliant plan, and I wanted so badly for it to work. But, as I signed the paperwork to pack up my home, ship off my children, and move seven thousand miles away for the next year, I wasn't afraid that the plan wouldn't work. I was terrified.

"We're almost done," I heard the sergeant say as his voice broke into my stream of consciousness.

Settle down, and keep it together, I coached myself.

"The paperwork for your reenlistment is right here. I just have a couple of questions before we get it scheduled," he continued.

I took a couple of deep breaths to calm my nerves and steady my breathing.

When I didn't immediately respond, the sergeant continued. "Is there anywhere in particular where you would like your reenlistment ceremony to take place?" he asked.

"No, I don't think so. We can have the ceremony wherever it's normally done."

"That's really up to you. Some soldiers have their ceremony as part of a celebration, while others just go to the commanding officer's office and have it done there. You have time to decide. We can conduct the ceremony anytime, as long as it is done at least ninety days before your ETS, which won't be an issue because you will be on your way to Korea before then.

"Have you decided who you want to administer your reenlistment oath? Any commissioned officer, active-duty or retired, can administer it."

I shook my head as I said, "No, Sergeant, I'll just do what everyone else does."

"You're assigned to DCSCD, right?"

"Yes, I am."

"Would you like one of the officers that you work with to administer your oath?"

"That would be OK," I said with a forced smile. "What do I need to do to arrange that?" I tried to mask the shakiness in my voice.

"All you have to do is ask them. After they agree, just let me know who is going to do it. I will take care of everything else."

"OK. I have a couple of officers in mind. I'll ask one of them and then let you know," I said.

"Great. Is there anyone who you would like to invite to the ceremony?"

"I didn't realize that I could invite people. The last time I reenlisted, it was pretty much just my commanding officer and me," I said.

"You can invite whomever you like, but if they are out of town, they need to be able to get here in time for the ceremony, which needs to happen relatively soon. Reenlisting is a special honor, and some soldiers really make a big deal out of it. I know you are on somewhat of a tight schedule, but if you want to do something special, we can try to make it work," he said with a smile.

"I'll give it some thought and let you know."

"Now, one last thing, and then we can get you out of here so you can get some food. How long would you like to reenlist for? The minimum is three years, but you can reenlist for up to six years. What are you thinking?"

This is it! This was when I was supposed to tell him about my plans to leave the military immediately after my tour in Korea. *Breathe, breathe, breathe.*

When I felt that my voice was steady enough to speak, I said, "I really want to finish college, so I'm planning to leave the army as soon as I get back from Korea, so I'd like to reenlist only for the twelve months I need to complete my tour of duty."

I felt my stomach doing cartwheels, and I held my breath as I waited for the sergeant to respond.

"Are you planning to leave the army?"

"Not yet," I said. "I want to go to college and finish my degree, so I am planning to get out as soon as I return from Korea." The shaking in my hands increased, and I began to sweat.

"You can finish your degree while you are in the army. Lots of people get degrees while they are on active duty. Sometimes, the army will even pay for the courses," he said. "I'm not sure how many classes you can take while you are in Korea, but you can definitely take classes when you get back to the States."

"That's a good point. It's just that I'd like to experience the full-on college campus life. I enjoy helping people, especially children, so I want to go somewhere that has a good psychology program. Maybe I can even get into a research program." I tried to keep my voice even, giving enough detail to show that I'd thought it through, while avoiding rambling. The sergeant began drumming his fingers on his desk.

"Well, we might have a problem on our hands," he said.

"Oh no! What's the problem?"

"The minimum time that you can reenlist for is three years, which means that you would not be able to leave the army as soon as your tour in Korea ends. You would have about two years left. You could ETS after that, assuming you aren't assigned to another overseas tour, which isn't likely. And, like I said, you can take your college courses while you are on active duty," he said.

"Hmm ..." I said thoughtfully. "What are my options, then?"

"You really only have two options. You can either reenlist for three years, go to Korea, and ETS after your term expires, assuming that you would still want to. Or, if you don't want to reenlist, we won't be able to send you to Korea, and you'd exit the army when your current term expires," he said.

"Oh," I said, sounding surprised. "You mean I'd have to leave the army now?"

"Well, not now, but in a few months when your term ends," he said.

"What about Korea?"

"You won't be able to go to Korea."

"What will happen with my orders?"

"Your orders would be voided due to minimum remaining time in service being insufficient," he said.

"Oh."

My hands had steadied, but my heart pounded with exhilaration. Gabriel had been right—it happened exactly as he had said it would! I fought to keep my expression neutral, but on the inside, I was bursting with happiness.

"Look, you have a lot to think about. Let's pause for now and meet again in a few days after you have had time to consider your options," he advised.

"OK, I'll come back in a couple of days."

I stood and walked to the door. I stopped before leaving and turned to the sergeant.

"Sergeant, is leaving the army a bad thing? I mean, will it affect my discharge?" I asked softly.

"Sergeant Fuentes, you have to do what's right for you and your family, and leaving the army when your term expires will not negatively impact you. Many soldiers leave the army every day and do just fine. So think about what you want to do, and we will move forward based on whatever you decide."

"Thank you," I said as I turned and left.

Two weeks later, I received favorable responses from both universities, so I had a credible plan for what to do when I left the military. I decided to attend Southern Illinois University. The Illinois Veteran Grant would help tremendously with my education costs and living expenses. I would be given a stipend, which—along with the child support payments—would allow me to focus on school full-time without the need to work. The university offered affordable on-campus housing where the kids and I would live. I just needed to work out a few details because the spring semester at the university began in mid-January and Jasmine would start school around the same time. However, my ETS date wasn't until mid-December, which did not leave me enough time to establish housing, move to Illinois, register for classes, enroll the kids in school, and have everything we needed before the first day of classes.

I explained my situation to the school registrar and pleaded for an exception to allow me to enroll one month late. Unfortunately, there was nothing they could do to help me. I did not like the idea of sitting out an entire semester before beginning school, but I'd done everything that I knew to do, and the time gap seemed unsolvable. Nevertheless, I took a leap of faith and accepted the offer to attend Southern Illinois University, entering as a sophomore for the spring semester in 1997.

The other matter that was top of mind for me was the children's education. They had only attended Catholic school at Saint Mary, but they would have to transfer to public school when we moved to Carbondale. I was not Catholic, but the faith-based education they had been receiving was important to me. Having prayer and Bible study incorporated into their education had been invaluable. We attended Mass each week, where we found a community where we genuinely belonged. And they wore school uniforms, which meant they did not have to worry about how their clothes compared to their classmates. These were the downsides of leaving the army. Applying to colleges in Virginia had been a consideration, but without considerable tuition assistance, the economics wouldn't have worked out. Even if I were to work while attending school, the cost would have still been too great.

To officially put things in motion, I scheduled appointments with the principal of the kids' school and with my transition counselor, to inform them of my decision to leave the army.

When I met with my transition counselor, I told him of my decision to leave the military at the end of my current term. I explained that leaving was a hard decision to make because I really enjoyed being a soldier. I'd never planned to retire in the military, so embarking on a new chapter felt right.

"I'm not surprised," he said.

"You're not?"

"No. I couldn't say it before, but I can now, since you have already made your decision. Assigning single parents to hardship tours is tough. I see more soldiers exit the army because they don't want to leave their children than I do for any other reason," he said.

"How did you know?"

"Know what?"

"That I didn't want to leave my children."

"I didn't know specifically, but why would you? Look, you are a good soldier, Sergeant Fuentes, and I am sure you would have done well in Korea, but when I saw in your file that you are a single parent and your children are four and six years old, I had my doubts that you would leave them."

"I'm sorry," I said solemnly.

"Don't be. Like I said before, you have to do what's best for your family. What are you going to do when you get out?" he asked.

"I was being honest with you when I said that I want to finish college, so that's what I'm planning to do," I said.

"That's smart. Have you thought about where you want to go?" he asked.

"I have." My body began to feel lighter, as if a tremendous weight had been lifted.

"I've been accepted to Southern Illinois University. They have a great psychology department, and I qualify for a grant that will cover my tuition."

"Wow!" he exclaimed. "That's pretty impressive."

"I'm hoping everything works out, though."

"Why wouldn't everything work out? You have already been accepted, you have some sort of scholarship, and you get out of the army in a few months. What's not to work out?"

"The challenge is that school begins the first week in January, but I don't get out until mid-December, which doesn't leave me enough time to get there, find housing, and get my family situated before the first day of class."

"Oh, I see," he said thoughtfully. "When would you need to leave the army for it to work out for you?"

"If my ETS was a month earlier, I would be set … but it isn't."

"Do you mind if I give you some advice?" he offered.

"Of course. I'll take all the advice I can get," I said.

"Look, you seem like a good kid, and I want you to be successful, but do not tell anyone that this came from me."

"OK, I won't," I said.

"The base commander has the authority to allow you to ETS early. If all you need is a month, that is well within his authority to grant. It isn't automatic; he doesn't have to do it. But if—and it's a big if—you can get an audience with him and explain your situation, he just might grant you an early separation so you can start class on time. Even if he doesn't, at least you will have tried," he said.

My face lit up with a huge smile. "Thank you so much!" I exclaimed. "I think I might cry."

"Please don't," he said, but was smiling.

"It's just that every time my back is against the wall, and I think I am out of options, God sends an angel my way. Thank you so much for helping me," I said.

"Look, I'm no angel—and it might not work. It's just that I would hate to see you miss out on a great opportunity because you weren't aware of all your options," he said.

"You are an angel to me," I said softly. "I promise not to cry, but do you mind if I give you a hug?"

"Sure, but don't get all sappy on me. Besides, I have work to do."

I extended my arms and gave the sergeant a big hug. Despite all his bravado, he gently hugged me back.

As I released him from my embrace, he whispered in my ear, "Good luck, kid."

I left the personnel office feeling like everything was going to work out, and I couldn't be happier. I headed to my office as fast as I could.

As soon as I walked through the door, I hurried over to Donna.

"Donna, how do I get an audience with the base commander?"

Donna looked up from her computer and turned toward me, narrowing her eyes. "Child, what are you talking about?"

I spoke with hurried words as I tried to share my news with her. "Donna, I was worried, but then I heard some news—well, not really news—but I think the colonel might let me go to school—well, not for sure—but maybe he will ..."

Donna interrupted. "Stop! I can't understand a word that you are saying. You're making no sense, child."

I started again, slower this time. "You know how I was worried that I might not be able to start school this semester because my ETS date was so close to the first day of class?"

"Yes, I remember."

"Well, I've just learned that the base commander has the authority to allow me to leave the army early for a special reason, and attending college might be a good enough reason."

"Who told you this?" she asked skeptically.

"That doesn't matter. All that matters is that, if there is even a chance that it's true, I want to give it a shot," I said.

"So you're going to waltz into the colonel's office and expect him to let you out early just because you want to start school?" she asked.

"No, of course not! I'm not crazy! I want to start by seeing if I can even get a meeting with him, and if I do, I will make sure that I'm prepared," I said.

"How do you plan on getting a meeting with him?" she asked.

"That's what I'm hoping you can help me with," I said with a smile.

Donna came up with the brilliant idea of writing him a letter. She and I worked on the letter for nearly a week. We made sure the tone and every word were just right. Donna had a meticulous eye for detail, and she had me write and rewrite sentences until she was satisfied with how they read. Finally, the letter met her approval, and I sent it off.

It didn't take long for me to receive a response. The colonel had agreed to see me!

I met with the colonel the following week. He said that he had been very impressed with my letter. He also appreciated the passion I had for being a soldier and understood my desire to create a better life for my children and me. At the end of the roughly fifteen-minute meeting, the colonel agreed to my petition. He said he would approve my transition from the army one month early so I could begin school in the spring.

I was so grateful that things were working out. After my meeting with the colonel, it was time to inform the staff at Saint Mary that the kids would not be returning after the holiday break. I arrived at the school ten minutes before my meeting with the principal and waited patiently to be escorted into her office.

When the principal arrived, I greeted her with a warm smile. "Hi, Sister. How is your day?"

"I am having an amazing day, young lady. What brings you in to see me?" she asked.

I followed her into her office and sat in the chair across from her. I squirmed in my seat as I began. "Thank you for seeing me on such short notice, but I wanted to meet with you right away. There is no easy way to say this, so I'll just get on with it. I have decided to leave the military and move to Illinois to complete my college degree. I have enjoyed my time in the army, and I really like Fort Monroe, but being a single parent in the military is tough. There is always a risk of me being deployed or sent somewhere that my children can't go. This has been weighing heavily on me for a while, but I have finally made my decision. The kids and I are leaving in November."

The nun stared at me with a thoughtful and deeply compassionate expression on her face. "Dear child," she began, "I can only imagine what it has taken for you to get to this moment, and I applaud your bravery. I have enjoyed having your family as part of our learning and faith community. And, no matter where you go, this will always be your home."

My eyes began to tear up. I had never felt such a strong sense of community. I had finally found a place where my children and I felt at home, a place where we belonged. And now we were leaving to start over in a town where we didn't know anyone.

As a tear involuntarily rolled down my cheek, I looked away from the Sister and said, "This means the kids will not be returning after the holiday break."

"I assumed as much. Do you know what school they will attend in your new town? What is your new town, by the way?"

"We are moving to Southern Illinois, to a town called Carbondale. There is a public school a few miles from where we will live, but I haven't registered them yet."

"Is there anything I can do to help before you leave?" she asked.

"No, Sister. You, Father Joe, and everyone here have been so wonderful to us. The only thing I ask is for your continued prayers."

"That I can do," she said with a smile.

I left the school feeling both lighter and heavier at the same time. I was happy to have taken the last step toward putting our new lives in motion, but I was deeply sad to leave the community and the people we had grown to love.

The following weeks seemed like a blur. I worked out my transition details, secured a three-bedroom apartment on campus, and arranged for my household goods to be shipped to Illinois. I also scheduled a meeting with the university's registrar so I could register for classes, and I arranged for a meeting with the guidance counselor at the local elementary school to get the kids registered.

The months had flown by, and we were within days of leaving. The kids and I headed to Saint Mary for what would be their last day of school there.

As soon as I walked into the building, the secretary came out of the office and waved to get my attention.

"Mrs. Fuentes?"

I turned at the sound of my name. "Yes?"

"Sister would like to speak with you before you leave."

"OK, I will walk the kids to class and stop by on my way out," I said.

"Thank you."

"I don't need you to walk me to class. I know the way," Jasmine protested.

"Me either," Josh agreed.

"I know you don't *need* me to walk you, but I enjoy walking you to class. It means that I get to spend a little more time with you and can say hello to your teachers," I explained.

I escorted each child to their respective classroom—Jasmine in first grade, and Josh in preschool—and greeted their teachers before heading back toward the front office.

When I walked into the office, the secretary immediately rose from her chair. "I'll take you right in," she said.

I followed her into the principal's office and sat down as instructed.

"Ms. Fuentes," the principal began, "have you registered the children for school in Carbondale yet?"

"No. I have a meeting with the school's counselor right after the holidays to get them registered," I said.

"Oh, good. I was hoping you would say that."

My eyebrows raised in a curious expression. "Why?"

"Because I have done something that I hope will make you happy. Are you familiar with a town called Murphysboro, Illinois?" she asked.

"No. I've—"

The principal could hardly contain her excitement as she continued before I could complete my response. "It's a town that is about eight miles from Carbondale. There is a Catholic school there called Saint Andrew. I figured the distance was a manageable drive from Carbondale, so I reached out to the school to see if they had availability for Jasmine and Joshua to start this spring."

I sat up in my chair, feeling butterflies in my stomach and wondering where the conversation was going.

"As it turns out, they do!" she exclaimed.

"That's very kind of you," I interrupted, "but I hadn't planned on sending the kids to Catholic school in Illinois because I truly can't afford it. I'm just so grateful that—"

"Don't interrupt!" she interjected in a stern voice.

I stopped mid-sentence, waiting.

"As I was saying, the school is a short drive from the city you are moving to, and they have two spots for your children. I worked it out with Father, and we can transfer the rest of their scholarships from here to Saint Andrew. I also spoke with the diocese in Illinois, and between them and the school, the rest of their tuition will be covered for as long as they go there. Are you interested?" she finally asked.

All I could manage was to stare at her with a befuddled look on my face.

We sat in silence for a moment before she finally said, "I hope I didn't overstep."

I attempted to speak, but my voice cracked. "No, Sister, you didn't overstep," I muttered through building sobs. "It's just that I don't have the words to express the gratitude I'm feeling."

The more I spoke, the more the tears freely flowed. "What you have done is so incredibly kind," I continued. "And ... and ..." I wasn't able to complete my sentence before the dam of tears I had been attempting to hold back broke free.

She sat and watched me in silence, reaching out for a tissue that she gently handed to me.

Once I had regained my composure, I looked up at her solemnly and whispered, "Thank you."

She looked at me with compassionate eyes and a big smile and responded, "You're very welcome."

I left the office feeling peaceful and happy. It wasn't the fact that Sister Mary Rose had arranged for the kids to have a place at Saint Andrew, or the fact that their tuitions would be covered. Those things were great, but they weren't the source of the peace I felt. The peace I felt was bigger than either of those things. The peace I felt was indescribable.

I knew that the wonderful peace that I felt wasn't from a person, an event, or even a thing—it was the peace that surpasses all understanding; it was the peace of Christ. The peace I felt was my Lord and Savior walking with me, protecting me, and carrying me. He had known me, even when I hadn't consciously known Him.

Chapter 19

Just try new things. Don't be afraid.
Step out of your comfort zones and soar, all right?

—Michelle Obama

It was a chilly day in November when the kids and I arrived in our new town. I'd spoken to my mother before we'd left Virginia, and she was very excited that we were moving to Illinois. We weren't moving to Chicago, but the five-hour drive between Chicago and Carbondale was much closer than when we'd lived in Virginia.

As soon as I'd told my mother that I had selected Southern Illinois University, she'd insisted that the kids and I come to Chicago to spend Thanksgiving with the family. I'd initially resisted and told her I didn't want to take a long road trip as soon as I got there. There were things I needed to do to get settled in my new home, and I had little time before class began. My mother had firmly insisted and made it clear that her request was not actually a request, so I'd agreed.

I had mixed feelings about going to Chicago for Thanksgiving. I looked forward to seeing my mother and my sister Miriam, but there was also a level of discomfort. I was no longer the teenager who'd left home nearly a decade earlier. This version of me was a mother and a veteran, and I'd been a wife. Not only had the military changed me, but life had changed me. I didn't expect that I would relate to my siblings much anymore, but because me being there was so important to my mother, I'd agreed to go.

Our new apartment was small but pleasant. It was conveniently located on the campus and was only a few miles from the kids' new school.

As soon as we entered the apartment, both kids raced inside to claim their rooms.

"I get first pick!" Jasmine yelled as she shoved her brother out of the way and ran toward the back of the apartment.

"Settle down, you two. I will decide which room you each get!" I yelled after them.

As the kids raced off, I stood in the center of the apartment and looked around. It had three modest-sized bedrooms, a cozy living room, and a small dining area large enough to hold a table and six chairs. The kitchen was small with simple, white appliances and was oriented in a galley-style format.

I felt a smile spreading across my face as I took it all in. This was our new home ... the place where we would begin the next chapter of our lives. The thought of starting a new journey was scary, but it was also very exciting.

I walked to the back of the apartment, where the children were still bickering over their room choices.

"Mom, I should get to pick first because I'm older, and that means I'm in charge!" Jasmine exclaimed.

"In charge of what?" I asked.

"I'm in charge of Josh and me." The tone of her response suggested, *Duh, what else would I be in charge of?*

"He's little, and I'm big, so that means I'm in charge," she explained.

"I'm not little!" Josh countered in between the cartwheels he was doing in the middle of the empty room.

"You're not in charge, Jasmine ... And, Josh, *stop flipping*," I said firmly as I looked in his direction.

I turned my attention back to Jasmine. "I'm in charge, and I will assign the rooms."

"Well, can I have that one?" she asked as she pointed to the largest of the three bedrooms.

"No."

"Why not?"

"Because that's my room."

"Oh ... then which room is mine?"

"I don't know yet. I will decide when the movers get here."

As if on command, the doorbell rang. I walked to the front of the apartment and saw the large moving truck parked in front of the building.

"The movers are here!" I yelled to the kids. "Come in here and stay out of the way."

"What are we supposed to do?" Josh asked in his deep, froggy voice.

"Sit over there in the corner and read a book."

"On the floor?"

"Yes, on the floor."

"I don't want to sit on the floor," he protested, but he curled up against the wall on the floor, anyway.

"Josh!" Jasmine said. "You'd better sit on the floor before she makes you stand in the corner."

"I'm not going to make him stand in the corner."

"But he's not listening, so you should make him stand in the corner," she said.

"I'm listening, Jas! See? I'm sitting on the floor," Josh said.

I let the movers in and walked them into each room, explaining where things should go.

It took several hours for the movers to unload the truck, and when they were done, it looked like a cardboard factory had exploded in the apartment.

"This is it, kids. Now we get to unpack," I said after the movers had left.

"I'm hungry," Jasmine said in a tone that suggested she might faint.

"This took all day, and I'm hungry too. Can we have McDonald's?" Josh added.

"I don't even know if this town has a McDonald's."

"They do!" Jasmine yelled frantically. "I saw it when we were driving."

"OK, OK. McDonald's it is. Go put on your shoes and grab your jackets."

As the kids ran off to get ready to leave, I grabbed my purse and looked inside my wallet. I only had three hundred dollars left from my last check from the military and my travel allowance. Other than a few dollars that I had in the bank, that was it. I grabbed my planner and looked at the date. I was due my first child support payment in a few days, which would help a lot. I made a mental note that I would need to be very frugal because the money I was expecting from Carlos wouldn't count until it was in my hands. With the money I had, I could buy groceries and a few school supplies and still have enough left over for the trip to Chicago. Beyond that, I would be broke until the child support check came.

The kids ran into the living room, dressed and ready to go.

As we drove to McDonald's, I looked around the town and took note of the different street names. There was a large Walmart near the center of town that was also a grocery store. It was the largest Walmart that I'd ever seen, and it appeared to be the most affordable place to buy groceries. I thought it was somewhat strange that Walmart sold groceries. *Why would I want my socks in the same basket as my meats?* Strange or not, I had to admit that being able to buy everything I needed for the house in one store would be pretty convenient.

The kids and I went through the McDonald's drive-through and picked up two Happy Meals and a sandwich for me. We headed back to the house, where we had a picnic dinner in the middle of the living room.

As the kids ate their dinner and examined the toys that had come with their meals, it occurred to me that, if I did not receive the child support check on time, I would be out of money in a few weeks. I would not receive any money from my school grants until after my registration was fully complete, and even then, the disbursement wouldn't be immediate.

Following the separation and divorce, Carlos and I were not in a good place. We never spoke to one another about the kids or anything else—partly because he was living in Germany, but also because things had ended so bitterly. I hoped and prayed that he wouldn't allow our grievances to prevent him from doing the right thing for his children. I had an uneasy feeling in my stomach because, court order or not, I was all too aware that Carlos would not be made to do anything that he didn't want to do—and he did *not* want to give up a significant portion of his check each month to pay child support. I pushed the negative thoughts aside, deciding that there was nothing to worry about until there was something to worry about.

The kids and I finished up our living room picnic and then began unpacking boxes.

By the time I had bathed the kids and put them to bed, I was exhausted.

I lay on my bed, contemplating the trip to Chicago. Thanksgiving was coming up, which meant that there would be lots of people, lots of food, and, likely, drama. It was not that I didn't enjoy being around my family; it was just that I didn't feel like I belonged anymore. As I thought about it more, I realized I wasn't sure if I had *ever* actually belonged. I'd always felt like a square peg in a round hole. I had been an ambitious kid who was determined to change the world, and I'd believed that there wasn't anything I couldn't do. Because of this, I'd always assumed responsibilities that were well above what was typical at my age, and I had the bold confidence to question things that didn't make sense to me, such as why the government owed me a debt of restitution because I was an African American born in the twentieth century. Although questions of that nature usually involved a threat of physical violence from my mother for "being flippant," as she would say.

In some ways, being home might feel good. The divorce had taken a toll on me, and sometimes I had an overwhelming feeling of loneliness. Being at home for a while could be a good thing for me and for the kids.

On Thanksgiving morning, the kids and I got up early, loaded the car, and headed north toward Chicago. We had a long, five-hour drive ahead of us, so I packed plenty of snacks and books for the kids to read. It was during this trip that I learned about Jasmine's extreme motion sickness that happened when she was reading in a moving car. After only a few minutes of reading, she felt terrible for the rest of the drive. I had to pull over several times out of fear that she was going to throw up in the car.

Because of all the stops, we arrived in Chicago about ninety minutes later than I'd planned. We were the last ones to arrive, and everyone was ready to eat. After a few greetings and hugs, we headed into the dining room with everyone else.

Dinner was easy, and the food was fantastic. My mom had many talents, but cooking was by far one of her greatest. The kids and I had not enjoyed a meal as bountiful as the meal served that day in a long time … if ever.

After dinner, everyone broke into smaller groups and dispersed. Some people went into the basement to listen to music, dance, and have after-dinner drinks. The cousins went in search of mischief. Others went off to find a quiet place to sleep off the *-itis* (that drowsy, sleepy feeling you get after eating a big meal).

I went to find my mom so we could spend some time catching up. I found her in the living room, laying on the sofa.

"Hey, Ema. Whatcha doing?" I asked as I sat on the sofa next to her.

"Nothing. I'm just relaxing for a while," she replied sleepily.

"You deserve to rest; you made an amazing feast. Everything was *so* good, and I ate way too much, but it was all so delicious!" I said.

She sat up in a reclined position and faced toward me. "I'm glad you came in here. I have something that I want to talk to you about."

"Something like what?" I asked hesitantly, thinking she might bring up the topic of me moving home again.

"You know I depend on you, right?" she began.

"Yeah."

"Well, there is something important that I need you to do."

"What is it?"

"I've been thinking about my will and my affairs for when I die, and I want you to be the one who takes care of everything."

"What?!" A wave of anger surged inside me. "Why would you bring that up? And what on earth makes you think I would—or even could—do that?"

Much to my surprise, she did not match my anger. Instead, her voice remained calm and steady as she said, "Listen to me. I know you can do it."

"I don't *want* to do it!" I shouted.

"You will do it, Shoshanna," she said firmly.

"Why?" I pleaded.

"Because you are the only one who can."

"Ema, if you were to die, I would be devastated. I would not have the mental capacity to deal with you dying, much less to handle your affairs. Please ask me anything else, but not this," I begged.

"Shoshanna, this is what I'm asking. You are strong, and you can do this."

"I don't think I can, and I know I don't want to. What about the others? What about Cain, or Betsy, or even Daniel? Why can't one of them do it?"

"They can't do it. You can. I have a copy of my will here that I want to go over with you. I have already named you as the executor and had it notarized."

"So you're not actually asking me, then. I don't even get a choice in this?"

"No, I am not asking you."

"Fine!" I blurted out. "I'll agree to do it if we can just stop talking about you dying. I don't want to review the will with you. Just give it to me, and sometime way in the future—if I need it— I'll read it then. Just please stop talking about this."

"OK, we can stop talking about it. You are strong, Shoshanna. And no matter what happens, you're my rock," she said, looking directly at me.

I was so angry with my mom. Why would she place this heavy burden on me? It wasn't fair. I had always been expected to be the responsible one, but why this? Why couldn't one of the older siblings step up for a change? My only consolation was that

I knew I wouldn't have to do anything for a very long time, which would give me time to convince my mom that someone else was better suited for the task than I was. All I had to do was figure out who.

Chapter 20

Often it's the deepest pain which empowers you
to grow into your highest self.

—Karen Salmansohn

The kids and I stayed in Chicago overnight before heading back to Carbondale. When we returned home, I got the kids settled at Saint Andrew and completed the registration for my classes.

Although I had been able to leave the military one month before my service ended, by the time I reached the registrar to sign up for classes, my options for a liberal arts class were limited. In order to satisfy that requirement and achieve full-time status, I enrolled in a course on New Testament Christianity. I wasn't a Christian, I had no desire to become a Christian, and I didn't particularly want to study Christianity. Ordinarily, I would not have signed up to take a class on Christianity, but it was the only class available that fit my schedule.

Growing up, I was never allowed to question any aspect of our faith, and I was expected to believe what my parents told me to believe. If I had a question about religion, I'd ask my mother, and whatever explanation she provided was what I believed, without question. My parents had never taught me about Christianity, and I believed that, if Christianity was something I needed to know, they would have taught it to me. Given this, a course on New Testament Christianity was a very unusual class for me to take.

One evening while working on my schoolwork, I was struggling with some of the concepts that had been presented in class earlier that day. As I wrestled with some of the statements the professor had made about Jesus, I decided to do what I always did when I had questions about religion—I called my mom.

As I dialed her number, I silently prayed that she wouldn't bring up the conversation from Thanksgiving about me being her executor.

"Hey, Ema. Do you have a minute?" I asked when my mother answered the phone.

She was happy to hear from me, and I could hear the smile in her voice as she replied, "Hey, Noonie. What are you up to?"

We chatted and caught up for nearly an hour before I got to the reason for my call. "Oh, I almost forgot why I called you. I am taking a course on Christianity, and I have a few questions about some of the stuff the professor said in class."

"What made you sign up for a course on Christianity?" she asked, perplexed.

In an effort to defend myself, I explained, "I didn't want to, but I needed a liberal arts course, and this was the only one available."

Before she could respond or scold me for stepping out on our religion, I went on to ask my questions. "The professor talks a lot about Jesus. He refers to Him as God, and he also refers to Him as the Son of God. Do you know about Jesus?"

"Yes, I do," she said calmly, but she didn't elaborate.

"OK, good. Then maybe you can help me."

I didn't find it strange that my mother knew about Jesus; she was well-read, and she knew a lot about many things. I also knew that her mother was Baptist, so I figured that she had probably heard about Jesus from my grandmother.

I continued with my questions. "Isn't it blasphemous for the professor to call Him God? And how can He be God and the Son of God at the same time? In fact, the Torah says that the children of Israel are God's sons; it doesn't say Jesus is, does it?" I was hoping that she would explain what the professor had been referring to or at least agree with me that he had been wrong.

Her voice remained steady as she said, "That's complicated."

"Complicated? The Torah is very clear. Deuteronomy says the Lord, our God, is one Lord. So how is it complicated?" I asked in complete bewilderment.

This conversation was definitely not going the way I had expected. I had expected my mother to laugh and tell me the professor had been wrong. She was then supposed to equip me with the appropriate verses from Scripture to share in class to demonstrate the errors in the professor's teachings. Except, that's not what was happening at all.

"Are you OK?" I asked. Maybe she was just distracted.

"I'm OK," she said, "but I do have a headache, so I will need to hang up soon."

"OK. You don't have to explain all of the complicated stuff right now, but at least tell me what I need to say to my professor before you hang up," I pleaded.

I had been very sure of myself when I'd boldly approached the professor after class to tell him that I didn't agree with his lesson. When he had asked me why, I'd told him I didn't agree with it because it was wrong. "How so?" he'd asked. "Because there is only one God, and next class, I'll bring you proof," I said. "Great, I'd love to see it."

It had been my intention to approach him during the next class with documented proof of why he was wrong, proof that I'd expected my mother to provide. However, given the way the conversation was going, I wasn't confident that I would get the information I needed. I felt very uneasy and confused by her lack of outrage toward his misinformation about God.

As I waited for my mother's response, I heard her take a deep breath before saying, "I have to tell you something."

"What is it?" I asked hesitantly.

She took another deep breath. "You know," she began, "when I pray now, I pray to Jesus, and I pray to the Father in His name."

Silence. More silence.

My brain was going a hundred miles an hour. Surely, I had misheard her.

"Shoshanna, are you there?" she finally asked.

"Yes, I'm here, but the phone broke up, so I didn't hear you." That wasn't true. I'd heard exactly what she'd said, but I didn't know what else to say.

"I said, when I pray, I pray in Jesus' name," she repeated.

That's when I lost it. "What? What does that mean, you pray in Jesus' name? You've never even talked about Jesus, and now you pray in His name? How long have you been doing this? Do we believe in Jesus now? If so, what do we believe? Do we believe that He's God? Is what the professor said true?"

My mind was flooded with confusing thoughts, and my questions were coming so fast that she didn't have a chance to respond to any of them.

"Do I need to pray to Jesus too?" I asked. "And what exactly should I pray?"

My mother had just dropped a huge bomb that had the potential to completely alter life as I knew it. Her praying to Jesus was big news. It was huge!

"Do my sisters and brothers know about this?" I continued.

"Look," she interrupted, "I will answer all of your questions, but I told you that I have a headache, so I'm going to lie down now."

"Wait," I pleaded. "Can't you just tell me what we believe about Jesus before you go?"

When she spoke again, her tone was firm, suggesting that enough was enough. "We'll talk later. Right now, I said I'm going to lie down."

Knowing better than to push her any further, I softly said, "OK."

Before hanging up, grasping at straws, I said, "We are definitely going to finish this conversation, because I need to know what we believe about Jesus."

She chuckled softly and said, "OK, we will."

There was a long pause, and neither of us hung up the phone.

"I love you, Shoshanna," she said solemnly.

"I love you too, Ema," I said, matching her tone.

The next day in class, shame kept me from taking my usual seat up front. Instead, I slipped into a chair at the back, with my head down, hoping to go unnoticed. When class ended, I made a beeline for the door—until I heard my name.

"Shonna."

I froze. *Crap!* I turned to see the professor walking toward me.

"Did you bring the proof you mentioned?"

"Uh, no, not yet. I was busy yesterday and didn't have time." The excuse tumbled out unconvincingly.

"OK, no rush," he said, his tone kind.

His patience felt like a lifeline, rescuing me from the arrogance I had shown the day before.

"Thanks. As soon as I have it, I'll share it with you," I said quickly.

But I never did.

When I got home from class, the red light on my answering machine was blinking. I pressed "Play" as I gathered ingredients for dinner.

Beep.

"Shoshanna, this is Betsy. I need you to call me."

Beep.

Another message. Betsy again.

"Shoshanna, call me as soon as you get this."

I sighed. *What now?* Betsy only called when she needed something. *I'll call her eventually, maybe after dinner.*

Beep.

The next message played, and I froze.

"Shoshanna, it's me," Miriam said. Her voice was thick with tears. "Ema is in the hospital ... and she won't wake up."

The box of Hamburger Helper slipped from my hands, clattering to the floor. My knees buckled, and I gripped the sink, forcing deep breaths to steady myself.

With shaking hands, I picked up the phone and dialed my mother's house. Betsy answered on the first ring.

"Hello."

"It's me," I said.

"Where have you been?"

"I had class all day. Why is Ema in the hospital?"

"If you'd been home, you'd know."

"Why is my mother in the hospital, Betsy?" I asked, my impatience rising.

"She had surgery for the headaches she's been having."

"Surgery? For headaches?" I asked, confused.

Betsy sighed, then explained. For years, our mother had suffered from crippling headaches, but they had worsened—impacting her vision and making it impossible for her to function. She had finally seen a neurologist, who ran a series of tests and discovered the cause: Chiari malformation. A part of her brain was bulging through the opening in her skull, pressing down on vital areas.

My breath caught, and tears blurred my vision.

"Is she going to be OK?" I whispered.

"Just come home. Now," Betsy said.

I tore through the apartment, frantically throwing clothes into a bag. *What will the kids need?* My mind raced. *How long will we be there? A few days? Longer?*

My hands trembled as I filled the bag, and a wave of emotion crashed down on me. I sank to the floor and buried my face in my hands and sobbed.

"My poor mom. Why do you have to be sick?" I moaned between ragged breaths. "Why won't you wake up? Please ... please be OK."

I forced myself to my feet, wiped my face, and finished packing. There was no time to fall apart. I grabbed my keys and rushed out the door.

At after-school care, the kids ran up to me, their usual chatter filling the space. I took a deep breath before speaking.

"Hey, kids," I said, keeping my voice light. "We're going on a trip."

"Where?" Jasmine asked.

"To Chicago. Ema is sick, so we're going to visit her."

"What's wrong with her?" Josh asked, his face crinkled in a frown.

"I'm not sure," I said, swallowing hard. "We'll see her and find out."

The long car ride was quiet as the kids sensed my unease. When we arrived in Chicago, I dropped them off at my mother's house and left them with Miriam. Then I headed straight to the hospital.

I stepped into the hospital room, and the air was suffocating. The steady beeping of machines filled the space. My mother was still alive, but only because the machines were keeping her that way. Betsy stood by the bed with a nurse, both turning when I walked in.

"Shoshanna," Betsy said, but I barely heard her.

I saw my mother. She was lying motionless, with a tube down her throat, her chest rising and falling in a rhythm that wasn't her own. IV lines snaked from her arms, and the machines beside her hissed and beeped.

The room blurred as tears flooded my vision. A strangled sob tore from my throat, then another. Then I was wailing. Gasping. Struggling to breathe between the loud cries tearing through me.

"Ema!" I screamed, my voice raw with anguish.

Suddenly, Betsy was in front of me, her hands gripping my shoulders. She shook me hard.

"Stop it!" she hissed. "You don't need to be in here crying. You need to be strong for her."

I didn't want to be strong. I *couldn't* be strong.

My sobs continued.

Betsy shook me again, harder this time. "I said stop it!"

A firm voice cut through the chaos.

"Leave her alone."

The nurse stepped between us, her eyes fierce.

"She needs this," the nurse said, her voice unwavering. "She has the right to process her emotions however she wants."

Betsy's face twisted with fury. "This is *none* of your business!"

The nurse stood her ground. "Your mother is my patient, so it is my business. Either leave her alone or leave the room."

Betsy let out a sharp breath, then spun on her heel and stormed out. As she reached the door, she muttered under her breath, "Stupid bitch."

Unfazed, the nurse turned to me. She placed a reassuring arm around my shoulders.

"If you need to cry, cry," she said gently. "I'll make sure no one comes in here and bothers you."

She gave my shoulders a firm squeeze, then stepped out, leaving me alone with my mother.

I pulled up a chair and sat beside my mother's bed, my breath unsteady as I tried to process the sight before me. She looked so fragile, nothing like the fiery woman I knew.

I swallowed hard and reached for her hand, startled by how cool it felt in mine.

"Why didn't you tell me you were sick?" I whispered, my voice breaking.

Tears welled up again, slipping down my cheeks as I squeezed her hand gently.

"I'm so sorry," I choked out.

I sat there for what felt like hours, holding her hand, my fingers tracing the lines on her skin.

I talked to her.

I prayed for her.

I begged her to wake up.

She was only fifty-three. I had never considered losing her. Not yet. Not like this.

It was too soon.

There was still so much we hadn't talked about, so many things that had been left unsaid. My mind raced, and I thought about our last conversation. Suddenly, grief gave way to anger.

"You promised," I said, my voice trembling.

A sob broke free as I tightened my grip on her hand.

"You told me we would talk again," I cried. "You said you would tell me about Jesus."

My vision blurred as the tears spilled freely.

"Wake up, and keep your promise," I begged.

My mother remained silent.

The sound of footsteps startled me. I looked up as a man entered the room. It was her doctor. I wiped my face and stood, my voice hoarse as I introduced myself.

He nodded, then turned his attention to my mother, checking her vitals, his expression grim.

"Is she going to be OK?" I was barely able to get the words out.

"I don't know," he admitted. "We've done everything we can, but she still isn't waking up. There's nothing more we can do."

A lump formed in my throat. "So what happens now?"

"Cain has given us instructions to remove her from life support once all her children have had a chance to see her. You were the last one we were waiting for," he said, his voice filled with compassion.

His words felt like a physical blow.

"What?" I felt a surge of anger. "Why would you take her off life support so soon? He doesn't have the right to decide that!"

"He told us that, as the oldest child, she'd named him her executor. That gives him the authority to make medical decisions on her behalf," he said.

For a moment, I couldn't breathe. Then I remembered her will.

"No," I said, my voice sharp. "That isn't true. I have a notarized document from my mother. She'd made *me* her executor."

The doctor's eyes flickered with surprise. "May I see it?"

"I don't have it with me, but I'll get it. I live in Carbondale. I can bring it tomorrow."

He gave a small nod.

I left the hospital and headed back to my mother's house to pick up the kids to head back to Carbondale. It was late, but I was running on pure adrenaline.

As soon as I stepped through the door, Cain was waiting, his face twisted in fury.

"What the hell do you think you're doing?"

I ignored him and kept walking, my eyes scanning the house for the kids.

He followed me, cutting me off in the living room.

"The doctor called," he said, his voice sharp. "He said you told him not to take Ema off life support."

"Yes, I did." I tried to move past him, but he stepped in closer, his towering frame blocking my path.

"Who in the fuck do you think you are? You want her to lie there and suffer?"

I took a step back. He followed, his eyes burning with rage.

"I want to give her time to get better," I said, my voice shaky but firm.

"She's not getting better, idiot!"

I flinched as spit sprayed across my cheek.

My pulse pounded in my ears as rage ignited inside me. My hands clenched into fists, and instead of retreating, I stepped forward, closing the space between us.

"Do you think I'm afraid of you?" My voice was steady, sharp as steel. "I'm not. You don't control me, and you sure as hell don't get to decide what happens to my mother."

Cain's eyes darkened. His lip curled. "Shut up, little girl, before I smack the shit out of you."

"I'm *not* a little girl." I let the words settle, then took a slow, deliberate step to the side. My fingers curled around the cold metal of the fireplace poker. I lifted it slightly, just enough to make my point. "And I dare you to put your hands on me. If you do, I'll knock the shit out of you and then have you arrested."

Something flickered in Cain's eyes—hesitation, maybe surprise. His nostrils flared, but he didn't move.

The silence stretched between us.

Then, without a word, he turned and stormed out of the room.

"Coward!" I yelled at his back.

I packed up the kids, loaded them into the car, and drove back to Carbondale.

The next morning, I called my college and left messages for my professors, explaining why I'd be missing class. I did the same for the kids' school, then packed up the car. By 11:00 a.m., we were back on the road, heading to Chicago.

I drove straight to the hospital. As I approached my mother's room, I saw that all of my siblings were there—Betsy, Daniel, Miriam, and Rebecca. Even my mother's longtime friend, Lisbeth, was there. Cain stood in the hall talking to the doctor.

I turned toward them, but before I could take a step, Lisbeth grabbed my arm.

"Hey, Shoshanna."

"Hey, Lisbeth." I tried to move past her. "Excuse me, I need to speak with the doctor."

She held on, her grip firm. "I think we should all get together and pray for your mom."

"We will, but I need to—"

She tugged me toward the room. "Let's do it now."

I glanced back, but Cain and the doctor were gone. *Damn it!*

Inside, we joined hands. Lisbeth led the prayer, her voice steady and calm. But something about it felt off. As I listened, unease settled in my stomach. She wasn't praying for healing. She was praying like it was already over.

I opened my eyes, scanning the faces around me. Everyone else had their heads bowed in quiet reverence.

When the prayer ended, a nurse stepped just inside the door.

"Excuse me, folks. I didn't want to interrupt, but I need you all to step out so we can bathe her."

"How long will that take?" I asked.

"With all the machines and wires, I'd say come back in a couple of hours."

"A couple of hours for a bath?" I raised my eyebrows in confusion.

"After we bathe and dress her, the doctor will run a few tests," she said.

"Where is the doctor? I need to speak with him."

"He's grabbing something to eat. You can talk to him when you come back."

I swallowed hard. My stomach felt queasy, and I couldn't shake the feeling that something wasn't right. No one else seemed concerned, so I ignored the feeling.

We all left the hospital and returned to my mother's house. Cain wasn't there. *Good.* I didn't have the energy to deal with him. Exhaustion finally hit me, and I sank onto the couch, barely keeping my eyes open. The phone rang, and a second later, I heard Betsy scream. I bolted upright and ran to her. She was crumpled on the floor, the phone receiver dangling from her hand.

"What happened?" Panic filled my voice.

"She's gone." Betsy sobbed.

"What do you mean, she's gone?" My heart pounded.

"She's dead, Shoshanna."

The words knocked the air from my lungs. The room tilted. My heart felt like it was going to burst in my chest. I collapsed. My world went dark.

Chapter 21

God is in the sadness and the laughter,
in the bitter and the sweet.

—Neale Donald Walsch

Each of us dealt with the grief of losing our mother in our own way. Betsy turned to drugs, her eyes often glazed-over and glassy. Daniel disappeared. Cain raided her house for whatever possessions he could take. Miriam isolated herself to deal with her grief alone. And me? I was left with unanswered questions, like what had happened after we'd left the hospital?

I had the horrible task of making sure everything was taken care of as my mother had specified. I was only twenty-eight years old; I was drowning under a mound of grief, and I didn't have the time, support, or mental capacity to navigate any of it. I was angry at my mother for not finishing the story about Jesus. Why had she bothered telling me at all if she was just going to leave me hanging? I was angry at her for leaving me with questions and no source for answers, not even having the foresight to tell me where to look. I was angry at her for taking away the security of my faith.

My faith was my North Star. It was what grounded me, and it was the basis for the rules that governed my life: I can't eat pork, no work can be done during the Sabbath, I must observe all holy days. My faith was what helped me navigate life's hard moments, and it was the reason for all the good moments. It was my identity, and it was the single thing in my life that I was absolutely certain about ... until it wasn't.

What my mother had said to me introduced the possibility that I didn't know the whole story. Maybe Christianity was supposed to be part of my faith journey, or maybe just Jesus was—after all, He was a Jew. For that matter, if Jesus was a Jew, why was Christianity a separate religion? I didn't know the answers to any of these questions, and the person I had always turned to for guidance was gone. For the first time in my life, I had questions about my faith—big, life-altering questions—and I was now forced to figure them out ... alone.

I was angry at her for not finishing our conversation. But, most of all, I was angry at her for not fighting harder to live. I was very angry!

I felt the kind of anger that, if left unmanaged, has the potential to tear you in half. It was an all-consuming anger that was suffocating. She had said we would talk later, but we never did.

It had been several months since my mom had died, and I was still filled with overwhelming grief. As part of her will, she had left all her Bibles to me. I'd left them in a box that I refused to open, until one day, when I was feeling defeated and hopeless, I was drawn to open the box. I took out the Bible that was on top of the pile of books. I hadn't prayed or spoken to God in a while, but I needed help, and I didn't know where else to turn.

I said a prayer for guidance, closed my eyes, and randomly opened the Bible. When I opened my eyes, I was staring at my mother's beautiful penmanship. I read the words, "I will never leave you." The phrase was a quote from chapter thirteen of the book of Hebrews. As I read the words, I was instantly unnerved and afraid, so I quickly closed the book.

It was a very long time before I mustered up the courage to open the Bible again.

The next time I opened her Bible, I found myself in the Gospel of Matthew. I had never read any of the books in the New Testament, but since I'd opened the book at the Gospel of Matthew, that's where I decided to begin.

As I began reading, I was afraid that I wouldn't understand any of the words. I was intimidated by the journey I was beginning, and I felt very alone. Nevertheless, I started reading anyway: "The book of the generation of Jesus Christ, the son of David, the son of Abraham."

I know those names, I thought. David and Abraham were from the Old Testament. Reading those familiar names gave me hope that what I was reading might not be as difficult to understand as I'd expected. The familiarity was comforting. I smiled and continued reading.

I stayed up all night and into the morning reading the Gospel of Matthew. Once I started reading, I couldn't put it down. I didn't want to put it down. The more I read, the more I fell in love with Jesus. I was in awe of His compassion—how He fed five thousand people instead of sending them away hungry. My heart swelled at His mercy—how He healed the woman who had been hemorrhaging for years, instead of reprimanding her for touching Him. And I marveled at the unshakable peace that filled everyone who believed in Him. With every story, every act of love, I felt my heart awakening, overflowing with joy and wonder.

By the time I reached the end of the book, I felt calm. For the first time in a long time, I felt peace. The words that I'd read didn't conflict with what I believed. The Gospel of Matthew was a continuation of the many stories that I knew, not a contradiction. A continuation that brought me hope and joy.

Encountering Jesus through the Gospel of Matthew was an experience that I will never forget. My heart was filled with so much happiness that I wanted to go into the street and shout, telling everyone about Jesus. In the days that followed, I told everyone whom I encountered about Jesus and what He meant to me.

"Did you know that Jesus walked on water," I would ask, "or that He turned water into wine?"

Some people would smile politely and say something like, "Yes, I'm familiar with those stories," while others would stare at me, likely wondering what I was on.

I was filled with so much love for Jesus, and I wanted everyone to know what I knew and to feel what I was feeling. I continued my journey by reading the other Gospels, the Epistles, and eventually, the rest of the New Testament. I slowly crawled, and then began walking, along the journey of discovering my spiritual identity. The more I learned, the more my anger toward my mother subsided. As I embraced Jesus, I was filled with a peace that I couldn't explain.

I eventually realized that my mother could not have answered my questions that day. My relationship with Jesus was an intimate and personal journey that only I could have chosen. She knew that she couldn't have chosen it for me or told me what to believe. She knew that, if I were to have made the choice to have a relationship with Jesus, my faith would have had to come from a place deep inside of me, and not by way of a parental mandate.

I am grateful for that phone call with my mother, and I am grateful that she had the spirit-filled wisdom not to answer my questions. If she had answered my questions, I would have accepted her responses and looked no further. My mother's final and greatest gift to me was her planting the seed that led me to embark on a faith journey that has forever changed my life. So while the beginning of my faith journey was intimidating, I found the courage to step into the unknown and search for the answers I was looking for because my mother had resisted the urge to guide me.

The kids and I had been in Carbondale nearly a year, and they loved their new school. The teachers at Saint Andrew welcomed us, and just as the principal at Saint Mary had promised, all the details of the scholarships had been in place. I was taking eighteen hours of classes while also working to settle my mother's estate. My military GI Bill and the Illinois Veteran Grant had kicked in, so my tuition, books, and housing costs were covered.

Unfortunately, Carlos still had not started sending child support, which left a deficit that meant I could not pay my car payment and insurance, or consistently buy groceries. I had used up all my savings, and I didn't have any additional money from the military coming in. I called my attorney weekly for updates on the status of the child support payments, but with Carlos being out of the country, the process moved very slowly.

The good news was that, because Carlos had waived his legal protection under the Soldiers' and Sailors' Civil Relief Act, my attorney was able to petition the court for wage garnishment, which she did. The monthly payments were adjusted to account for the missed payments, but it would still likely be several months before I would receive the first payment.

The bills were piling up, and without additional income, I was at risk of losing my car. I had already stopped paying my car insurance, so I was already at risk of losing my driver's license.

Without a car, my difficult situation would be made worse. I wouldn't be able to take the kids to school, go to the grocery store, or do many other essential things. Carbondale did not have a robust public transportation system, and all the buses within walking distance only served the university campus area.

I reached out to the local veterans' office, and after a home visit to verify my situation, they gave me two boxes of food and a $250 cash grant. I was grateful for the help because it meant that I could feed my children and pay part of my past-due car payment, which would hopefully prevent it from being repossessed.

Feeling completely desperate, I tracked down Carlos' phone number in Germany. I worked out the time difference, and at the appropriate time, I phoned his unit.

When Carlos finally got on the line, I heard his familiar voice say, "Sergeant Fuentes."

"Carlos, this is Shonna."

"What do you want?"

"I need help. Without child support, I am really struggling to take care of the kids."

"What do you want me to do about that?" he asked.

"I want you to send me the child support you owe me."

"I don't owe you shit."

My anger simmered as I tried to remain calm. "The courts say that you do. You just got paid. Have you sent the payment for this month?"

"No."

"Why?"

"I spent it."

"Carlos, I am struggling to take care of your kids, and you don't give a shit if—"

The line went dead as I screamed into the phone.

I slid down the wall that I didn't realize had been holding me up. As I sank to the floor, I began sobbing uncontrollably. I didn't know what I was going to do. I hadn't wanted to call Carlos, but having him flat-out refuse to help, and then hang up in my face, hurt more than it probably should have. Deep down, I'd wanted to believe that he would do the right thing, and I was very disappointed that he hadn't. The following week, my car was repossessed.

The next few months were extremely tough for the kids and me. I was struggling with deep depression, and I felt so terribly alone. I tried my best to keep it together for my kids, but I was so exhausted from having to be strong all the time.

The parents at Saint Andrew really leaned in to help, even though I never asked them to or talked about my situation. The parents took turns taking my kids to school. Most days, I was able to get one of my classmates to take me to pick them up. I was always the last parent to arrive at after-school care, but the teachers always pretended not to notice, and they never charged me late fees. The kids were frequently invited to sleepovers where they were fed, and they always came home with extra school supplies.

After one such sleepover, Jasmine came home wearing glasses. Her friend's dad, who was an optometrist, explained that he had noticed that she was squinting a lot and having trouble reading from far distances. He had taken her to his office to check her vision. As expected, he'd discovered that she was extremely nearsighted, so he'd had a pair of glasses made for her.

I listened in disbelief. *Why didn't I know that Jasmine was having trouble seeing? How did he notice that she was squinting, but I didn't?* I had let my situation get me to the point where I was failing as a mother. The sting of tears burned my eyes before drops rolled down my cheeks.

Noticing my tears, the dad, clearly feeling uncomfortable, said, "Don't worry. It was no problem at all. And there is no charge for the glasses."

I looked at him, smiled as best as I could, and choked out the words, "Thank you," as I attempted to hold back the flood of tears.

As soon as he'd left, Jasmine walked up to me and asked, "What's wrong? Why are you crying?"

"Nothing's wrong, sweetie. I'm just glad that you can see better. You look so pretty in your glasses."

Jasmine twirled around in an exaggerated motion. "Don't I look pretty?"

"Yes, you do."

"I can see very far. Pick that up, and ask me what it says," she insisted as she pointed to the newspaper that was laying on the table.

I complied and lifted the paper.

"Move back farther," she insisted.

"OK, OK. How about here?"

"That's good. Stay right there."

I froze in place and held up the newspaper as I listened to Jasmine read every line perfectly. Tears burned my cheeks, but I stifled my sob.

"Well done, Jasmine," I said with a smile.

I spent the next several months filling out forms and pleading with the life insurance company to release the insurance funds from my mother's policy. Another downside of being the executor of my mother's estate was that I was the one responsible for making sure that the insurance money was paid out and that everyone received their shares. My mother had allotted the insurance money by each person's level of self-sufficiency. The least self-sufficient siblings received larger percentages of the total, while the more capable children (i.e., *me*) received less. She'd had her reasons for distributing the money the way she had, but I thought it was an interesting approach rather than just giving everyone the same amount. The least capable siblings would end up with more money to waste, but it was what she'd wanted, so I fought hard with the insurance company to make sure each person received whatever portion she had designated for them. I received weekly, sometimes daily, calls from my siblings, wondering when they were going to receive their money and demanding to know how much they would get. No one volunteered to help; I was just expected to figure it out and get their money to them.

Dealing with the insurance company was not easy. Every time I thought I'd submitted the final round of documents, they'd ask for more. I was running up my phone bill on the long-distance calls to them, and I frequently left class early so I could phone them during business hours. Despite the fact that I was going to receive a smaller portion, I didn't waver in my commitment to carry out my mother's wishes. I think my mother knew that I was the only one who would honor her wishes without reservation. So, even if I'd had more time to try to convince her to select someone else as her executor, I now realize that she never would have changed her mind.

After several months, the insurance company finally released the funds and began distributing checks. The check I received provided the financial relief that I desperately needed. After paying the past-due bills and buying a small used car, I put the rest in a savings account.

Not long after receiving the insurance money, I received the first child support payment. My attorney had been successful in petitioning the court for a wage garnishment order, which she'd promptly filed with the military. The order meant that the payments would automatically be taken from Carlos' paycheck and mailed directly to me each month. They superseded any other deductions, which prevented Carlos from setting up various allotments, which was a common practice among soldiers to avoid paying child support. I was sad that this was the way the payments had to be made, but taking care of my children was my only priority, so I didn't care how the payments were made, as long as they showed up.

Things had gotten much better, but there were new challenges that tested my resolve. For instance, I found out I had a serious medical condition that required me to have a complete hysterectomy at twenty-eight years old. Even though I'd only ever wanted two children, the thought of never being able to bear children again made me feel like I was less of a woman. I'd always believed that bearing children was the one thing that made me uniquely a woman, and that being a life-giver was the source of my femininity. To have that special gift taken away from me at any age, but especially during my prime childbearing years, hurt more than I'd expected.

I had little time to grieve the loss of my uterus because, two weeks after the hysterectomy, I was back in the hospital undergoing emergency surgery and fighting for my life because of medical complications following the hysterectomy. Two more surgeries followed.

As if that wasn't enough, Joshua broke his arm twice that year, prompting the emergency room doctor to call Child Protective Services (CPS). Apparently, the doctor didn't seem to understand the propensity of small boys to flip and tumble. But with Joshua smiling and showing no signs of abuse, CPS had no reason to stay, and the matter was closed.

Between dealing with my mother's affairs and my own medical issues, I missed a tremendous amount of school and fell far behind, jeopardizing my financial support. I was dealing with *a lot*! Out of those dark days came three truths that would stay with me for the rest of my life.

The first was that I felt utterly and completely alone. No family members came to help me. No one showed up to take care of the children while I was in the hospital. No one came to assist me with my medical recovery. I had known it for a while, but this situation made it painfully clear—the only person I could depend on was myself.

The second was that I redefined what the word *family* meant. The people who failed me during that time were my relatives, the people with whom I shared a bloodline. However, it would be unfair to ignore the many people who *did* help me. My cousin Cris and aunt Jan loaned me money, not because I'd asked, but because they knew I needed it. My close friends took turns watching my children while I was in the hospital, and they brought food to the house to make sure we ate after I was released. The families at Saint Andrew took the children to school, helped them with homework, and made sure they had lunch every day. Professors at the university gave me extensions on assignments and, rather than failing me, allowed me to make up missed exams. *These* people were my family—the ones who shared their time and resources willingly, out of kindness and with no expectation of anything in return. They were the people who showed up for me during the most vulnerable period of my life, and I remain eternally grateful to each of them.

The third were the words I had found written in my mother's Bible when I was struggling to hold onto my faith after she died. They were the words of Hebrews 13:5: *"I will never leave thee, nor forsake thee."* No matter how dark things seemed, I was never truly alone. God never left me, nor had He forsaken me. He sent helpers when I needed them, provided food as He had for the Israelites in the desert, and gave me the impenetrable resolve to keep putting one foot in front of the other–no matter how small the step. No, He had never left me. He was always there, carrying me every step of the way.

Chapter 22

Once you eliminate the impossible,
whatever remains, no matter how improbable,
must be the truth.

—Arthur Conan Doyle

When I completed my studies at the university, the kids and I moved to North Carolina. Carbondale had been a nice town, but it had never been my intention to stay there after I completed school.

On a summer trip to North Carolina to visit a friend I'd been stationed with, I met a guy named Phillip. I wasn't interested in dating anyone at that time, so Phillip and I started as friends. We kept in touch when I returned to Carbondale, and eventually, our friendship turned into dating. We had been dating for about a year when I left Carbondale and moved to North

Carolina. Phillip and I moved in together, despite my reluctance to do so. Shacking up was not the example I wanted to set for my children, but I rationalized the decision by saying it was prudent, from a cost-benefit perspective, to live together—and I thought we might eventually get married one day, anyway.

After I moved in with Phillip, I noticed a side of him that either hadn't existed previously or that I'd never noticed. I hadn't realized how much he drank or how much marijuana he smoked. These things weren't great, but having grown up in a household of drinkers and smokers, they didn't strike me as deal-breakers, even though I didn't partake in either. The thing that concerned me most was his temper. It took very little for him to launch into a vicious tirade. I thought his behavior was odd, but he always had a good reason for why the other person had deserved it, so I didn't press the issue. Besides, I had never been the recipient of one of his verbal assaults, so I assumed they weren't random and that he had some degree of self-control.

Phillip had a very strained relationship with his family, especially his mother, which further distorted my perception of him. He told me stories about how his mother had always tried to control him, and about how bitter their relationship was. I'd met his mother, and she'd seemed nice. In fact, I'd liked her a lot. She and her husband didn't have any grandchildren, so Jasmine and Joshua became the grandchildren of the family. As such, they were pampered, spoiled, and treated to a family experience they had never had before. Phillip's sisters and brothers, aunts and uncles, and grandparents all embraced them and made them feel special. When I saw how much they seemed to love my children—despite the fact that they were not biologically related—it melted my heart in a way that made me feel like I had found a family where the kids and I could belong.

We settled into our new family dynamic, and Phillip and I decided to get married. His parents seemed indifferent to the idea of us getting married; they didn't advocate for or speak out against the idea. Until one day, Phillip's mother took me shopping for business clothes to prepare for the new job I was about to start. I had studied psychology in college, but without further education, I couldn't find a job in the field. I needed to work, so I took a position as an administrative assistant for a regional vice president at a large company. After years in the military and then college, I had no experience dressing for the business world, so I was very grateful when Phillip's mother offered to take me shopping. We spent an entire afternoon shopping, and she helped me put together some smart outfits centered on a few staple pieces. She taught me how to start with a few basics from which I could build several outfits by changing my top and adding a bit of jewelry or a scarf to accessorize. We were done shopping for the day, and she was driving me home when she brought up the topic of my upcoming marriage to Phillip.

"Are you sure you want to marry Phillip?" she asked.

Surprised by the unexpected question, I hesitated before responding. "Yes, I'm sure."

She may have mistaken my pause for doubt, because she pressed a bit more. "Are you certain you know everything that you should know about him?"

Still confused by the line of questions, I spoke hesitantly. "I think so. Is there something I should know that you want to tell me?" I asked.

"I wanted to stay out of it," she began, "but I don't want to see you and those sweet kids get hurt."

"Hurt? Hurt how?"

"Well, Phillip has issues. Do you know that he's an alcoholic?" she asked.

"An alcoholic? I mean, yes, he drinks, but why does that make him an alcoholic?"

"Because he can't control how much he drinks, and he acts out when he's drunk."

"Acts out how? I've seen him get angry, but he's never gotten drunk and acted out with me or the kids," I said.

"Not yet," she said.

"If you don't want us to get married, just say so," I said, annoyed.

"I don't want you to get married," she said firmly. "In fact, I'm begging you not to marry him—at least, not until he gets some help and commits to being sober. Phillip is a narcissistic alcoholic. He's mean, verbally abusive, and has no respect for anyone, especially women." Her face looked resolute, but her voice was almost pleading.

I stared at her in disbelief, unable to process what I was hearing. What was she saying, and why would his own mother speak about him that way? Phillip had never verbally abused me or shown me any signs of disrespect. However, I had noticed the disrespectful way he treated others, including her. He would say mean things to her, veiled as humor, followed by, "I'm just playing," or "You know I'm just kidding." I'd always thought the jokes were mean, bordering on cruel, but his parents hadn't said anything about it, and they'd never scolded him, so I'd assumed his behavior was an accepted dynamic between them.

But what his mother was describing to me was different. She was telling me things that, if true, were definitely reasons not to marry him. I could either believe her at her word, take my children and immediately flee, or I could take my experiences with Phillip as the truth and disregard his mother's comments. Alternatively, I could simply ask Phillip what was going on. After much deliberation, I chose to speak with Phillip.

When Phillip got home from work, I told him about the conversation I'd had with his mother.

"Phillip, when your mother and I were out shopping today, she made some strange comments," I said carefully.

"What comments?"

I hesitated, then took a breath. "She told me you are an alcoholic, and that I shouldn't marry you."

"She said what?!"

"She also said you would eventually hurt the kids and me."

Phillip jumped up, his voice rising. "Hurt you and the kids? I would never hurt you guys! What the hell is her problem?"

"Why would she say those things about you?" I asked, my voice filled with concern.

"Because she's a fucking hater, and she can't stand to see me happy."

I stared at Phillip, my mind filled with confusion. Was his mother trying to warn me, or was she just being spiteful?

Phillip grabbed the phone and angrily dialed the number to his parents' home. When his mother answered, he accused her of being manipulative, and he said that she was repeating a pattern of behavior she'd done all his life. He called her hateful and said she didn't want us to get married because I was Black and had two kids. He ended the conversation by telling her that he didn't want anything to do with her ever again. I could only hear his side of the conversation, so I don't know what defense she put up, if any.

When Phillip hung up the phone, he turned to me and slumped to the floor, sobbing. "Why doesn't my mother love me?" he lamented through heavy sobs. "I am finally happy, and she can't just be happy for me. She knows how much I love you and the kids, and that I would never do anything to hurt you. This is the shit I was telling you about that she does to control me."

I had never seen an adult male sob in such a way, and I didn't believe that anyone could fake such a powerful emotion. Was he truly a victim of his mother's manipulation? Was she interfering because she didn't like the fact that he was marrying a Black woman? Had she exhibited signs of racism that I'd missed? *Whatever her reasons, shame on her for trying to steal her son's happiness*, I thought.

My heart broke for Phillip. I crouched on the floor next to him, wrapped my arms around him, and told him we were a team and that I was on his side. And, just like that, I experienced the first of many instances of his expertly crafted, perfectly executed, and sadistically cruel emotional manipulation.

Chapter 23

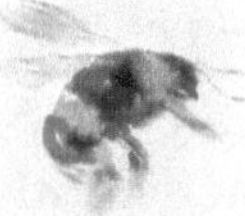

Patience and perseverance have a magical effect
before which difficulties disappear
and obstacles vanish.

—John Quincy Adams

In the spring of 1999, Phillip and I went through with our plan to get married. We went to the courthouse on our lunch break and stood before a magistrate. There were no flowers, no guests, and no celebration. It was just the two of us exchanging vows in a dimly lit courtroom. We moved into a three-bedroom apartment in a very nice neighborhood. The kids went to public school, but it was one of the best schools in the city. In many ways, it rivaled the best private school, but without the exorbitant tuition.

I was the only person of color in the office I worked in, which felt strange, but it didn't bother me. The role had become vacant because my predecessor had moved into a sales support role. I was glad that the person who had previously held the job was still with the company because I believed having her in the same office would speed up my training. However, that wasn't the case.

Sarah, a six-foot-tall White woman with short-cropped hair, a chiseled jawline, and broad shoulders, carried herself with an air of authority. She was used to running the office and having access to anything she wanted. In her mind, nothing was too sensitive or confidential for her to see, even if it didn't pertain to her role. Apart from the boss, anyone who dared question her was met with expletive-filled choice words. She was the self-proclaimed office manager, and no one questioned that designation, even though it wasn't her actual title. Because she was no longer the administrative assistant, many things she was used to having access to were no longer available to her. Especially confidential information.

When I declined to give her my boss's bonus statement because it was confidential, she reminded me that she used to do my job, and then she told me that it wasn't my place to deny her access to anything. *My place? What is that supposed to mean?* I held my ground and didn't share the confidential information she'd requested. Instead, I agreed to speak with my boss to verify what she should have access to.

She wasn't pleased with my response. "I already told you I'm allowed to have access to anything that has to do with this office," she said.

"I'm sure you are," I said calmly, "but I need to verify that with John before I give you access to the information you are requesting."

"You don't need to check with anyone. You work for me!"

"I don't work for you," I said. My voice remained calm. "I work for John."

"We all work for John, but when he isn't here, you report to me," she insisted.

"Since when?"

"Since always, and you'd better not forget it."

Better not forget it. Was this how people spoke to one another in the corporate world?

Her claim was different from the information that had been presented to me when I had been hired. "John never told me that, but I'm happy to check with him when he is back in the office. In the meantime, I can't give you his bonus statement unless he confirms that it's OK."

Sarah stormed off.

The next day, after John and I had caught up on the things I was working on, I asked him about Sarah's claims. He sighed. "I thought this might happen."

"You expected her to ask for confidential information?"

"Not specifically, but I knew she might have a hard time letting go of her old job."

"What do you want me to do?"

"Sarah no longer needs access to confidential information, so don't share confidential information with her or anyone else."

"OK. But do I report to her when you're not in the office?"

"No. You don't report to her, regardless of whether I'm in the office or not."

After that day, I became the office pariah. Apart from John, no one talked to me unless it was absolutely necessary. I ate lunch alone every day. If I happened to enter the break room while my colleagues were eating, they got up and left immediately. Snide comments were frequently made at my expense.

Sarah approached my desk one day when I was filling out expense reports. "Hey, I was wondering," she began.

"Yes, what were you wondering?" I asked as I looked up from the stack of papers I was holding.

"I was wondering why all Black people eat watermelon," she said, laughing.

As soon as the words left her mouth, I heard giggles and laughter from across the office. As Sarah waited for my reply, I took a few deep breaths through my nose to calm my nerves.

I smiled as I looked up at her and said, "I don't know that all Black people do eat watermelon, but I eat it because it's refreshing."

She was not amused by my response, but she was not deterred. "Then why do y'all love some fried chicken?" she asked, shaking her head as she held her hands on her hips in a manner that suggested, *Aha! I got you now.*

"Is there anything that you actually need?" I asked.

"No, I'm just trying to get to know you," she said.

"If you want to get to know me, we can have lunch sometime."

"Like that would ever happen," she said as she sauntered back to her desk.

I had never experienced such overt racism before, and as this was my first business job, I had no idea how things worked or if there was an official way to challenge it. I didn't like being bullied, but I refused to go crying to my boss every time someone hurt my feelings. Instead, I put my head down and stayed focused on my work. After one particularly hurtful series of remarks, I left the office, drove around the corner, sat in my car, and cried.

The hostile behavior continued for months, with Sarah's mistreatment growing increasingly worse. She regularly misplaced my work, spread lies about me to the other coworkers, and constantly reminded me how much better at my job she had been when she had done it. I came to realize that Sarah was an office bully whom everyone was afraid of, and she had decided that I would be the latest recipient of her torture.

My initial approach was to do my job and meet her hostility with kindness. It was very frustrating, but I never raised my voice or made any retaliatory remarks. I focused on doing the things I was supposed to do, and I concentrated on excelling at my job. It wasn't easy, though, because the stress of constantly being bullied was taking a toll on me.

I had once reported Sarah's behavior to my boss, but his only response was, "You two need to work it out." It was clear that he wasn't going to help me, although that's what I thought leaders did.

One day, I was having lunch with a friend, and I told her what was happening at my office. She had worked in the corporate world much longer than I had, so I asked her for advice.

"She actually asked you why we all eat watermelon?" She frowned at me.

"That's the sort of stuff she asks me all the time," I said. "In fact, yesterday, she asked me why all Black people walk so slowly."

"Walk slowly?" she asked. "What did you say?"

"I told her that I'm from Chicago, and no one from Chicago walks slowly, even the Black people."

She burst into laughter so loud that it prompted several people in the restaurant to glance in our direction.

"*Shh* ... you're going to get us kicked out of here," I said.

"Have you reported her to human resources?" she asked.

"No," I said. "How would I do that?"

She explained the process to me, and she told me that what Sarah was doing was wrong and that human resources would have to intervene. She said they would probably write Sarah up for her behavior and put her on notice.

"Won't that just make it worse?" I asked.

"No, because there are laws against retribution, so you are protected," she said reassuringly.

When I returned to the office, I telephoned the administrative assistant for Richard, the head of human resources. I explained to her that I needed to speak with her boss because I wanted to file a complaint. She asked me for a few details about what was happening, so I gave her an overview.

"Oh my gosh, that's horrible," she said. "I am so sorry that's happening to you. I will get this message to Richard right away and will set up a meeting with him."

"Thank you so much. I really appreciate your help and your kind words," I said.

"Richard isn't in the office today, so gimme a couple of days, and I promise I'll get back to you," she told me.

I didn't have to wait a couple of days because she phoned me later that afternoon. "Hi, sweetie. Richard called in to check his messages, so I told him that you were having some issues and wanted to speak with him. I'm sorry, but his response wasn't very kind," she said.

"What did he say?" I asked.

She hesitated before saying, "He said, 'Those people always want something.'"

I could almost hear her holding her breath on the other end of the line.

She finally said, "I'm just telling you because I don't think he's going to help you. If you file a complaint with him, things will probably get worse."

I thanked her for her honesty and told her to disregard my request for a meeting. That was the first and last time I ever attempted to take a personal issue to human resources.

After realizing that seeking help from human resources would be a dead end, I figured I had three options. Option one: quit. Despite the hostile environment, I liked the work that I did, and I was good at it. Option two: tolerate the bullying and do my best to ignore it. This option could only last so long because the mistreatment was mentally exhausting. Option three: stand up for myself.

I chose a combination of options two and three. I refused to let a bully run me away from a job I enjoyed, so I decided I would continue doing my job, being as gracious as possible. I would also try to ignore the immature behavior as best as I could. However, the next time Sarah brazenly disrespected me, I was going to stand up for myself. I had endured much tougher challenges in my life—being in the military, being a single parent, losing my mother, going through major health challenges, and so much more—so I refused to be a victim of an immature office bully who mistook my casual demeanor for weakness.

I didn't have to wait long for Sarah to go too far. One afternoon, after checking in with my boss, who was traveling, I finished up a few tasks, straightened up my desk, and headed for the elevator. I was leaving ten minutes early because I had an appointment across town that I didn't want to be late for. I had cleared it with my boss and made sure that everything he needed was taken care of before I left.

The next morning, when I pulled into the parking lot at 7:30 a.m., I noticed that Sarah's car was already there. Usually, I was the first person to arrive. I got to work early every day so I could open the office and get a pot of coffee brewed before everyone else started arriving. Sarah, on the other hand, usually arrived thirty minutes late. So, because she was there early before anyone else had arrived, I figured something must be up. I headed toward the building, bracing myself for whatever nonsense she had planned.

I walked into the office, and instead of heading to the break room to make coffee, I went to my office, sat at my desk, and began casually reading the paper. I figured that whatever was about to happen, I could at least make sure it happened in the environment of my choosing.

I had been seated for less than five minutes when Sarah appeared at my door. I glanced up from my paper, and before I could say anything, she launched into a clearly rehearsed narrative.

"Who the fuck do you think you are?" she asked, her voice rising.

I assumed the question was rhetorical, so I didn't respond.

"Who told you that you could leave early yesterday?"

Another rhetorical question, so my silence continued.

"This is my fucking company, and I will not let you people ruin it!"

You people? I was the only person of color in the entire region, so I wasn't sure how *we people* were ruining anything.

As she continued her rant, her breathing was ragged, and her hands were shaking. She continued speaking and began walking toward my desk, where I was still seated. "You had better not *ever* leave early again without checking in with me first. Do you fucking understand me?"

By the time she'd concluded her tirade, she was pressed against the front of my desk, only a few inches away from me. I waited for her to continue, but she did not, so I assumed she had concluded her prepared remarks.

I'm sure that when she'd rehearsed this scene in her head, in her version, I would have started crying, apologized, and promised never to disappoint her again.

Well, that was not my response. I might not have been well-versed in how to navigate the business world, but she had just dragged me into the world of insults and aggression. Having grown up on the South Side of Chicago, that world was one that I was all too familiar with.

I set my paper down and slowly rose from my chair. When I had risen to my full height, I began. "Who in the fuck do you think you are, speaking to me that way? Let's get a few things straight right now." I slowly moved closer to her. "I don't work for you, I don't answer to you, and I will *not* tolerate disrespect from you."

As I moved forward, she moved backward.

"Clearly, you have mistaken my kindness for weakness. But to be clear, I am not afraid of you. You may bully everyone else in this office, but you are done bullying me."

She moved backward until her back was pressed against the wall, and I was standing directly in front of her.

"If you *ever* speak to me this way again, do anything disrespectful, or continue to interfere with my ability to do my job, I will show you how we handle disagreements in Chicago. Now, get the fuck out of my office," I said.

I took a small step backward, allowing her just enough room to squeeze past me without touching.

She slid along the wall, turned, and left in a hurry.

I went into the break room and made coffee.

I was certain I would be fired, but I didn't care. Standing up for myself had been the right thing to do. I don't condone violence of any kind, verbal or physical. However, I fully believe in every person's right to defend themselves. What she was doing was wrong, and no job was worth accepting that level of degradation.

By the end of the day, when I hadn't heard anything from my boss, I figured he was waiting to fire me in person.

My boss returned the next day, and still nothing.

Sarah avoided me for the next several days, until Friday, when she randomly showed up at my office door. "Hey. I'm making an office run to Starbucks. Do you want anything?"

One person would gather everyone's orders and then go to Starbucks for afternoon treats. I had never been included in the Starbucks runs before. Why was I being included now? Was she planning to poison me?

In the event that her gesture was a sincere olive branch, I smiled and said, "Sure, thanks. It's very nice of you to ask."

"No problem. What would you like?"

"I'll take a grande cappuccino. Let me get my purse."

"No need," she said quickly. "This one is on me."

I looked confused, but I smiled and said, "Thank you."

Sarah left the office and returned forty minutes later with several Starbucks creations—lattes, caramel macchiatos, iced coffees ... and my cappuccino. Everyone grabbed their drinks and headed to the break area to visit while enjoying their beverages. I headed toward my office.

"Shonna," I heard someone call, "aren't you going to stay and join us?" The voice belonged to Karen, one of my other colleagues.

This was a first. I stopped and returned to the break area.

"Sure. I could use a break," I said as I sat and joined the group.

From that day on, the bullying stopped, and Sarah and I never had another incident.

My other colleagues embraced me as well. I was asked by one of the senior managers to join her on a big project, which allowed me to showcase the many things I was capable of. That project ended up being so successful that I was invited to take on even bigger responsibilities.

Within three years of being hired, a new role was created for me, and I was promoted to the role of sales IT administrator, where I was responsible for the integrity of the global data that was used to calculate monthly commissions. I assumed full responsibility for the annual budgeting process, oversaw large-scale regional meetings, and began developing meeting presentations for my boss.

The coworkers who had once shunned me were now my biggest supporters. They frequently shared details of the work I was doing with their global counterparts, and two years following my initial promotion, I was promoted to the role of project coordinator for global innovation.

Within six years of joining the company, I was promoted twice and was recognized and respected as a leader in my field. All of this had been possible because I had refused to allow my wings to be clipped by an office bully who hadn't even bothered to try to get to know me.

The company I worked for was acquired by a larger company, and my reputation of being a tenacious go-getter followed me. I was just as successful at the larger company as I had been at the original company that had hired me. I was assigned to take on important initiatives, and I was eventually promoted to a project manager. One year following that promotion, I was promoted to the role of global new product manager and presented for the first time to the board of directors.

After I was assigned to take on a global project for one of the company's largest customers, the president of my division said to me, "I have full confidence in your abilities, and I know you will be successful."

"How do you know that?" I asked.

"Because, if you can't go over or around something, you will go through it," he said.

That was one of the greatest compliments he could have paid me.

Chapter 24

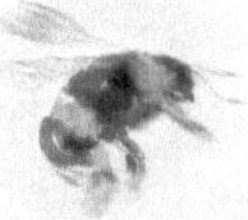

When you're surrounded by a world of constant lies,
manipulation, and deceit, that dark energy
is bound to seep into you eventually.

—Jeffrey Bowyer-Chapman

One day, work had unexpectedly run long, so I was later than usual in getting home. Phillip had called my office several times, but I had been tied up in a meeting, so I had missed his calls.

As I left the conference room and headed to my desk, one of my coworkers stopped me to tell me that Phillip had called several times and that he sounded angry.

"Angry? What do you mean, angry?" I asked.

"I don't know. He just said to tell you to call him immediately."

"Oh. Did you tell him I was in a meeting?"

"Yes, but he didn't care. He just said for you to call him immediately."

I rushed toward my desk.

Phillip answered after the first ring. "Hello."

"Hey. It's me. Is everything OK?"

"No! Everything is not OK."

When he slurred his words, I realized that he had been drinking.

"What's the matter?"

"You're not home, that's what the fuck's the matter."

I took in a deep breath and spoke with an even tone. "I'm sorry that I'm not home yet. My boss called me into a meeting just as I was getting ready to leave. I'm packing up now. Is there something that you need?"

"I need my wife to be home where she belongs," he bit out.

I glanced at the clock and saw that it was almost 6:30 p.m. For some reason, my first thought was, *How is it he's already drunk at 6:30 p.m. when he got off work just ninety minutes ago?* I shook my head to bring my thoughts back to the present.

"I have my things, and I'm walking to the car as soon as I hang up," I reassured him. "Do you need me to pick up anything on the way?"

"No! Just hurry home, you stupid bitch."

As I listened to the sound of the dial tone, I replayed what I thought I'd heard over and over. Had he called me a stupid bitch? Or had he said something else, and I had just misheard him? I couldn't think of anything that made sense that sounded like "stupid bitch," so I turned my thoughts to trying to understand *why* he would call me a stupid bitch.

I had never considered myself to be stupid. In fact, I am the very opposite of stupid. I have a curious mind and an incredible propensity to learn. So, surely, he didn't actually believe I was stupid ... did he?

I drove home in deep thought as I tried to process what had happened. After we had gotten married, Phillip's temper had grown increasingly volatile, and he'd made no effort to control his words or mask his apparent disdain for me and everything I did. If I had a good day at work, it was always at the expense of something that I should have been doing at home. When I had been promoted, he'd said it was because I was Black and the company needed to meet a quota for affirmative action. When I had been chosen to lead a big project that required me to meet with executives in New York, he'd called me a neglectful, unfit mother. No, he was never happy for me. And no matter how hard I tried to avoid making him angry, *everything* I did made him angry.

When I got home, I looked for Phillip so I could ask him about the comment he'd made.

"Phillip, when we were on the phone, you were upset that I wasn't home—" I began.

"Look, don't go bringing up old stuff. I just wanted you to get home," he interrupted before I could complete my sentence.

"Yeah, I know, and that's fine. I was just wondering ... when you were hanging up, it sounded like you called me a stupid bitch," I said.

"What?!" he shouted incredulously. "Why would you say something so crazy?"

"I'm not saying that you did," I said, quickly regretting having brought it up. "I'm just wondering what you actually said."

"Are you accusing me of calling you a stupid bitch?"

"No. I'm not. I'm just wondering what you said, that's all."

"See, that's your problem. You're always wondering about some shit. Why would I call my wife a stupid bitch?" His eyes narrowed as he stared at me.

"Honestly, I don't know. That's why I'm asking."

"No, I didn't call you a stupid bitch," he said in an aggravated tone.

"Then what did you say?" I asked as I continued to press.

"How the hell do I know? You expect me to remember everything I say? I don't remember what I said, Shonna, but I didn't call you a stupid bitch. You need to have your ears checked, and stop making shit up," he said.

He grabbed the remote and turned on the television, effectively ending the discussion.

Was he right? Had I imagined the whole thing? Was that even possible? I remembered hearing the words, and I remembered the sting of pain that had followed. How could I have made that up? Was it *possible* that he'd said something else? I supposed it was. But I had been *one hundred percent certain* of what he'd said. Maybe I wasn't. *Had I imagined it?* Maybe I had.

I went into the kitchen and started dinner. As I rushed around to prepare dinner, I felt his intense stare.

Once dinner was ready, I called the kids down and motioned everyone toward the table. Phillip was the last to join us, but when he did, he greeted the kids with an easy, "Hey, kids," as he took his seat.

Maybe he'd already put the incident from earlier behind him.

I glanced at each of the kids—they were smiling. *Smiling is good*, I thought. Because it meant that he hadn't been cruel or mistreated them. Still, I made a mental note to ask them later.

"Hey, Mom. How was work?" Jasmine asked.

"Yeah, how was work?" Joshua repeated.

"Work was good," I said. "I had an *important* meeting with my boss," I said.

Jas sat up straighter in her chair. She always took an interest in what happened at the office.

"Really? What was it about?" she asked. "Why was it important?"

"Well, my boss wants me to lead a big project that's happening in New York," I said with a smile.

"Yay, Mom! Does that mean you get to go to New York?" she asked.

"It does indeed."

"Will you get to ride in a limo like they do on TV, or will you whistle for a cab like the local people do?"

"Mom can't whistle for a cab like the locals do, Jas," Josh interjected.

"What do you mean I can't whistle for a cab like a local?" I said with feigned insult.

"Because you have to use two fingers, and you can't whistle like that," he explained.

"Neither can you," I teased.

"Yes, I can," he countered.

"Let me see."

He put two fingers in his mouth and blew as hard as he could, but the only thing that came out was air. Jasmine and I erupted into laughter.

Suddenly, Phillip shoved his plate aside, stood up in a dramatic fashion, and announced that dinner tasted like shit and that he wasn't going to eat my "craparole."

Moments later, he was out the front door and in his car, undoubtedly headed to a bar.

Josh looked over at me as I sat quietly, and he whispered, "Proud of you, Mom."

I smiled at him and said, "Thanks, Son."

Jasmine looked at her brother and added, "You still can't whistle," at which we all broke out into laughter again.

It was well after midnight when Phillip finally returned home. I lay in bed with my eyes closed, pretending to be asleep as he climbed in beside me. The overpowering stench of stale alcohol hit me, making my stomach churn. I held my breath and whispered a silent prayer that he would just fall asleep and leave me alone.

Thankfully, he did.

Over the next few years, Phillip's disdain for me became more blatant. His insults became harsher and more frequent. At first, I tried to understand the reasons behind his cruelty. I blamed the alcohol. Maybe it was his daily marijuana use. Perhaps he was just misunderstood. It turned out to be a mix of all those things, and yet, none of them.

Flipping through a magazine one day, I stumbled across an article titled "Are You Being Gaslighted?" The term was unfamiliar to me, so I kept reading.

According to the article, gaslighting is "an insidious form of manipulation and psychological control. Victims of gaslighting are deliberately and systematically fed false information that leads them to question what they know to be true, often about themselves."

As I absorbed those words, a chilling realization settled over me. The *stupid bitch* moment hadn't been an isolated incident—I had been a victim of gaslighting throughout our entire marriage.

Relief washed over me as I realized that I wasn't crazy. There was a word for what he had been doing to me. But at the same time, I felt sad that such a word even needed to exist.

And that's when it hit me. No matter how hard I tried to understand him, he would never change. Change had to come from within, and he seemed perfectly content with who he was.

Realizing that change was unlikely, I considered my options. Leaving him would be the right thing to do—I knew that. But it wasn't that simple. For starters, I wasn't in the best position financially to start over. Another important factor was the relationship the kids had with the rest of his family.

I thought about the many moments they had shared. Camp Granny, when Jasmine went to summer camp while Josh stayed behind because he was too young. The annual tradition of seeing *The Nutcracker*, fishing trips, school concerts, visits to the museum. They were experiencing the kind of childhood I had always dreamed of for them.

How can I leave when they're so happy? I wondered. *Is their happiness worth the cost of my own?* In the end, I decided it was.

Sacrificing my own happiness for the sake of my children was a simple decision because their happiness took precedence over mine. My happiness could come later. I believed it would be OK because, although my marriage was less than ideal, I wasn't completely miserable. There were many things in my life that brought me joy, such as spending time with my children, volunteering at church, my work and growing career, hanging out with the few friends my husband's ill temperament hadn't driven away, and spending time with my in-laws. I believed that I would be OK because finding joy and fulfillment in those things would be enough for me.

Chapter 25

Every new beginning comes from
some other beginning's end.

—Seneca

Everything was not OK. The next seven years were some of the worst of my life. Verbal and mental abuse were regular parts of my day. I was called "stupid bitch," "fat bitch," and other insults as frequently as I was called by my name. The worst part of it all was that he would treat me that way in front of the children. When he yelled and cursed at me, I usually remained silent or tried to appease him because I believed that, if I responded, the situation would escalate and get worse. Despite my silence, the situation *always* got worse because my silence fueled the rage of a shameful bully.

Over time, I tried hard to tune him out because nothing I said or did ever mattered. I had gone from being a self-assured, confident young girl who'd jumped out of planes to a fearful woman with low self-esteem who tolerated abuse and mistreatment. Many times, I wondered how such a drastic transformation had happened. I used to feel proud of my intelligence, and I'd never had body image issues. I used to feel strong and invincible, believing that there were no limits to the heights I could soar to. So why did a destructive narrative from someone who I knew was trying to hurt me cut so deep? It was because, no matter how confident I'd previously felt, the bad stuff was always easier to believe, especially when it was coming from someone who was supposed to love me.

Every day was a challenge as I tried to avoid doing anything that might set him off. The stress was suffocating. I couldn't sleep, so I was always exhausted. Food had lost its appeal, so I barely ate. And I was sick all the time.

One Saturday afternoon, desperate for a brief escape, I stepped into the bathroom and turned on the shower. As I waited for the water to heat up, I caught my reflection in the mirror and froze. The woman staring back at me was unrecognizable.

"What happened to you?" I whispered.

Dark circles had formed under my sunken eyes, and my cheeks were hollow. I looked drained, like a shell of the vibrant, energetic person I used to be.

I stepped under the steaming water, letting the heat soothe me as I reached for the shampoo. Working the lather into my scalp, I closed my eyes. The suds slid down my face as I massaged my temples, trying to will the tension away.

Then, something felt wrong.

Frowning, I moved my fingers through my hair again. A strange texture. A looseness.

I shoved my face under the water, rinsing the soap away, and opened my eyes.

My breath caught in my throat.

A thick clump of my hair sat in my trembling hands.

"No, no, no," I gasped, my voice breaking as panic crashed over me.

I quickly rinsed my hands and began softly pulling small sections of my hair. With each pull, more hair came out. "On top of everything else, now my hair is falling out?" I cried. Overwhelmed with sadness, I sat on the floor of the shower, hugging my knees to my chest. I cried as the water washed over me until it finally ran cold. I stepped out of the water, moving like I was in a trance. I looked in the mirror again and saw the thinning sections of my hair. "No more," I said. "I deserve better than this."

Once I had made the decision to leave, I was fueled by determination. I began carefully planning my departure, considering every detail. I made the choice not to tell the kids. I didn't want them to carry the burden of keeping such an important secret. A year out, I began purging and consolidating the kids' and my belongings. I packed up anything that I didn't need on a daily basis, and I stored the boxes in the attic. Six months out, I opened a P.O. box and forwarded my mail. Three months out, I transferred the kids' and my cell phone plans to my name and started apartment-hunting. Two months out, I rented an apartment in a neighboring city and gradually began moving things there.

I left enough of my belongings at the house so the transition wouldn't be obvious; I knew that, if he discovered I was moving out, there was a high likelihood he would harm me physically. He had threatened me before, saying that if I ever left him, he would hurt me physically and financially. I believed him. Things had gotten so bad that I was afraid to even sleep in the same room with him. I frequently woke up in a cold sweat after having the same recurring nightmare that he'd hurt me while I was sleeping.

Jasmine, now a junior in college, had returned to campus, so I moved across the hall into her empty room. Phillip asked me why I had moved out of our bedroom, and I lied and told him that his snoring was keeping me awake. He didn't like that I was sleeping in a different room, so most nights, he stood at the door yelling and screaming at me for hours until he exhausted himself and finally went to bed. Those episodes terrified me, so I slept with the bedroom door locked and kept a loaded handgun next to me. I lay in bed most nights, too afraid to sleep, thinking, *This is no way to live.*

Moving day finally came. As soon as Phillip left for work, Josh and I began tearing through the house and loading my Yukon Denali truck in a panicked frenzy. We only took clothes, books, and other personal belongings. It would take two trips to get everything, so we knew we had to hurry.

Packing, taking the first load to the apartment, and unloading the truck took much longer than I'd expected. By the time we returned for the second load, it was already midafternoon. We were at the house loading the remaining items as the clock seemed to move in double time.

"Josh, we *have* to leave. He will be home soon, and if he catches us moving, it will be bad," I said.

"I know, Mom. I'm almost done. I have a few more boxes to pack in my room," he replied.

"OK, but let's leave in twenty minutes, no matter what. We will just have to leave anything behind that isn't packed," I said.

"OK, Mom. We'll leave on time."

With ten minutes left, we abandoned packing things in boxes and began throwing anything left directly into the truck.

"It's time, Josh. Let's go!" I yelled.

Josh ran down the stairs with an armful of things and headed for the truck.

I dropped my house key on the living room table, turned the lock on the door before closing it, and jumped in the truck. I turned the key in the ignition, stepped on the accelerator, and sped out of the driveway as fast as I could. My heart was racing, and my hands were shaking. All we needed to do was get out of the neighborhood without running into him. I took each turn as fast as I could without flipping the truck.

"Hurry, Mom," Josh said.

"I'm hurrying. We will be on the highway soon, and then we'll be good."

Josh glared out the windows, making sure he didn't spot Phillip's car.

We finally turned onto the highway, and we both exhaled, not realizing we'd been holding our breath. As I merged into traffic, my cell phone rang. I looked at the screen and saw that it was Phillip calling. He'd gotten home and realized that I'd moved out. If we had left five minutes later, he would have walked in on us moving. I let the call go to voicemail and gripped the steering wheel as I sped down the highway.

It took several hours for Josh and me to unload the truck and get everything settled into the apartment. By the time we were done, I was drained—physically and emotionally. We decided to grab a bite at a nearby restaurant to refuel. Josh was starting his first semester of college the next day, so after dinner, I drove him to campus.

Unlike Jasmine, whose school was more than two hundred miles away, Josh's university was just a few miles across town. The drive was brief, but in those quiet moments, I couldn't help but reflect on the day we'd had.

When we arrived at his dorm, we began carrying his things inside. As we rode the elevator to his floor, I glanced over at him. It had been a long day, and we were both physically and mentally exhausted. Phillip had been calling nonstop, leaving messages until my voicemail was finally full.

"Thank you, Josh. I know today was hard, but I couldn't have done it without you," I said.

He put his free arm around me. "You're welcome, Mom. I'm so happy that you are finally out of there."

"Me too," I whispered as the elevator doors opened.

We dropped off everything, and then he walked me back to the truck to see me off.

"Josh, you don't have to walk me out," I said.

"I do. I want to make sure he didn't come here looking for you."

"He might know the school you're going to, but he doesn't know what dorm you are in," I said.

"I know, but I just want to be sure you're safe," he replied.

We walked up to the truck, and I sat in the driver's seat. I turned to Josh with a serious expression. "Please be careful, Son. He doesn't know where to find me, so the only thing he can do to hurt me is to find you. Please stay out of that neighborhood, and don't hang out in any of your usual spots. Always check your surroundings, too," I said.

"I know, Mom. I'll be careful," he said.

"And don't tell anyone where I've moved to. Not even your closest friends. People talk, and I don't want him to find me."

"I won't, Mom. I promise."

I stepped out of the truck and put my arms around my son, giving him a big hug. As I squeezed him, tears filled my eyes. A heavy load had been lifted, and I already felt lighter.

"I love you, Son."

"I love you too, Mom."

I got back into the truck and drove away while waving at him out the window.

I surveyed my new apartment. We'd filled the two bedrooms with boxes of clothes, and the living room and dining room were completely empty. I'd left all the furniture and dishes at the house. I wanted a clean slate, so I didn't take anything we had bought together during our marriage. The only furniture I owned was an air mattress that I'd purchased from Walmart after I'd dropped Josh off. I'd also purchased a sheet set, blanket, towel and washcloth, frying pan, small pot, paper plates, one cup, and plastic utensils that looked like silver. Just because I was eating with plastic utensils on paper dishes and drinking out of a plastic cup didn't mean they couldn't look nice. The air mattress would be my bed until I saved enough money to buy an actual bed. Since I didn't have a table, I planned to eat my meals sitting on the floor, using a paper towel as a place mat.

I looked around and smiled as I listened to the peaceful sound of quiet.

After inflating the air mattress and putting the new sheets on it, I took a long, hot shower. As the water ran over my body, it felt symbolic of a spiritual cleansing. I was so proud of myself. Everything had gone according to my plan. The kids were safe. I was safe. And, though it would take some time, I was ready to rediscover the strong, beautiful woman I once knew.

I climbed under the covers and glanced at my phone. *Forty-eight missed calls.* The voicemail was full, but I didn't bother listening to any of the messages or turning the ringer back on. I scooched down under the covers and fell into the deepest, most relaxing sleep I'd had in thirteen years.

Chapter 26

First they ignore you, then they laugh at you,
then they fight you, then you win.

—Mahatma Gandhi

The divorce was messy. Despite my leaving Phillip the house and all the contents in it, he still wanted alimony and half of the savings in my retirement plan. Phillip and I had several sessions with a court-appointed mediator to work out the divorce details.

"Why should I give him anything? I've already agreed to give him the house; we don't have any children together, and we are both gainfully employed. What right does he have to anything else?" I asked the mediator in absolute frustration over what I was hearing.

"State law entitles him to half of the money in your 401(k) retirement account. As far as alimony goes, his claim is that, since you make more money than he does, and you cover his health insurance, the divorce puts him at a disadvantage. He also claims that he can't afford the house on his income alone," the mediator explained.

"Then he should sell it!" I shouted.

"Your anger is palpable, Ms. Brackett, and I understand why you're angry, but let's look at this objectively. We've already established that, by law, he is entitled to half of the money in your retirement account, so there's nothing you can do about that.

You can certainly fight him on the alimony, but you will accrue considerable legal fees, and the judge will probably award him some level of support. He won't get much, and likely not for long, but there is a high likelihood that they will award him some support," he continued.

"But he is a full-grown, able-bodied man! He mistreated and tormented me for well over a decade. Doesn't that matter?" I fired back.

"It does matter, Ms. Brackett. You would have the opportunity to tell your story, which might impact the duration of support, but the outcome is not guaranteed."

"I can't believe he has the audacity to sue me for alimony. I hate this!"

"I'm not your attorney, and I'm not advising you against fighting if you feel that's the right thing for you to do. I'm simply laying out the facts so you can make an informed decision," he said. "I suggest you go home and think about how you want to proceed, and let's meet again tomorrow. I also suggest that you speak with your attorney."

"OK," I said.

As soon as I got in my car, I phoned my attorney and relayed the conversation I'd had with the mediator.

"I know the mediator is supposed to be neutral, but it seems like everything he is saying is bad for me. Phillip gets half of the money in my retirement account, plus he also wants alimony, and for me to keep him on my health-care plan during the separation period. Does that sound right to you?" I asked.

There was a long pause before my attorney spoke, during which I resisted the temptation to interrupt with more questions. Right when I thought the line had been disconnected, he started talking.

"Ms. Brackett, I know this isn't what you want to hear, but I'm afraid he's right. I have thought about this in every way possible, and as much as I hate it, what the mediator explained to you is accurate."

"So what should I do?" I asked.

"As the mediator explained, by law, your ex is entitled to half of your retirement savings."

"There's no loophole for an abusive spouse?" I asked.

"I couldn't find one, and the alimony is trickier," he said. "You make more than he does, and you also carry him on your health insurance plan. Plus, there is the fact that you initiated the separation, which he has stated that he is against. It's hard to know for sure what will happen, but I strongly believe that any judge who hears this case will give him some temporary relief to help him adjust. I can't say how much, or for how long, but I believe he would get something. If all of that isn't enough, there's also the matter of the cost of legal fees to fight it."

"I get it. I don't like it, but I get it. And thanks for looking for the loophole to save my 401(k). You may not have found one, but at least you tried," I said.

"I suggest you meet with the mediator again to understand what level of support your ex is looking for. Based on the amount, we can decide if it's worth fighting or not. As a show of good faith, you might agree to giving him half of the 401(k) and offer to contact your financial institution immediately to begin the transfer process," he said.

"I thought you said I don't have a choice?"

"You don't. But if you make the offer, it signals to him that you won't contest it, which works in your favor if we go to court."

"OK, I understand. I'll let you know how it goes," I said as I ended the call.

When I arrived at the mediator's office the next day, he told me that he had an updated proposal from Phillip.

"An updated proposal? I haven't even responded to the first proposal. What does he want now?"

"The transfer process for half of the money in your retirement account has been explained to him. Contrary to his expectations, the financial institution will not give him a check. Instead, they will open a retirement account in his name and deposit the money into that account. If he withdraws any portion of the money before he reaches retirement age, he will be subject to considerable penalties and fees," he explained.

"What does any of that have to do with me?" I asked, confused.

"That's the reason for the new proposal," he explained.

"I have no control over what the bank does."

"He was hoping for cash, which he isn't going to get. And even if he is granted alimony, it could take several months in court before a final decision is made, which means it could be a year or more before he receives his first payment. He will also incur considerable legal fees, that he would be responsible for paying. So, in exchange for waiving any claims to alimony and forfeiting the half of your 401(k) that he is entitled to, he wants you to pay him twelve thousand dollars in cash," the mediator said.

"He wants *what*?"

"He wants a cash payment of twelve thousand dollars, in addition to the house with the remaining contents. He will refinance the house in his name only to pay off the mortgage, which will allow the removal of your name from the deed. After that, you will have no further obligation to him, or him to you," he said.

"Me giving him the house *was* me giving him money. The house is worth far more than it was when we purchased it, so he gets the house, all the equity, and the contents. I could have insisted that we sell it and split the profit, but I didn't … and now he is asking for even more? He knows I have two children in college, and I can't afford to give him twelve thousand dollars," I snapped.

"Mrs. Brackett, I urge you to seriously consider his proposal. Twelve thousand dollars is less than the amount he would get from retirement savings, and if accepting this offer eliminates the possibility of you paying him any alimony, I don't think it's a bad deal."

"That may be true, but I don't have twelve thousand dollars," I said.

"Given the circumstances, you might be eligible to take out a loan from your 401(k) to pay it. You would have to pay the loan back, but they usually give you quite a while to pay it back in small installments. The money goes back in your account, so you would essentially be borrowing it from yourself, and keeping your retirement account intact," he explained.

I sat motionless as he spoke. My mind was racing, considering this new scenario. My emotional side was angry. *Why should I have to give him anything?* My logical side was more rational. *You're not likely to get a better deal. Take it and move on.*

The mediator's voice interrupted my thoughts. "I know this seems terribly unfair, but fighting this in court will cost you much more than twelve thousand dollars, and you will still end up giving him part of your retirement and some level of alimony," he said evenly.

"You're right, this *is* unfair," I said, my voice trembling with frustration.

"I know, and I'm sorry."

I sat still for several minutes trying to regain my composure. I finally looked up at him and said, "Fine, let's do it. I will pay him twelve thousand dollars, but nothing more. Once I accept this proposal, there will be no more negotiating, right?"

"That's right."

"OK, then I accept his proposal. I guess twelve thousand dollars and a house are the price I have to pay for my freedom. It's a lot, and paying it will be tough, but I can't put a price on my mental health and safety. Long after he's spent that money, I'll still be happy and free from him," I said.

I rose from my chair and left the mediator's office without another word.

The rest of the process went smoothly, without any additional contact with Phillip. I followed the mediator's advice and took out a loan for twelve thousand dollars against my 401(k) with reasonable repayment terms. Once I mailed the check, I was relieved that it was over, and I was finally free to move on.

Chapter 27

Hold fast to dreams, for if dreams die,
life is a broken-winged bird that cannot fly.

—Langston Hughes

I had always dreamed of pursuing a graduate degree in business. Obtaining a master's degree had always been part of my education plan, but like with many other things, life got busy and that dream moved to the back burner. Nevertheless, it was something that meant a lot to me, so I thought about it frequently.

At one point, I'd seriously investigated going, and I had brought up the idea to Phillip.

As soon as I told him what I wanted to do, he laughed at me and mockingly said, "Don't be stupid!"

"Why am I stupid?" I asked.

"Graduate school is for smart people, and you're not smart. A business degree is more than just watching a hamster run on a wheel," he remarked, his voice laced with condescension.

The comment about the hamster was a jab at my psychology degree, which he constantly reminded me wasn't a "real" degree.

"I'm smart," I said meekly. The words sounded more like a question than a statement I actually believed.

"Whatever," he said. "Don't embarrass yourself by trying to get into any graduate school."

His discouraging words had lingered in my mind, so I'd never brought the subject up again. I'd rationalized to myself that his words didn't really matter because I was too busy with work and raising my kids to take on graduate school, but deep in my heart, I knew that wasn't true.

After I left Phillip, things changed. I changed. I felt a renewed sense of confidence that inspired me to revisit the idea I'd wanted to pursue more than a decade ago. I knew getting into graduate school wouldn't be easy, and if I got accepted, I wondered if I would be able to keep up with the other students. Despite feeling nervous, I was determined to give it a shot. I made the choice to believe in myself and aim for the stars I had once dreamed of.

After exploring several schools with different programs, I decided that Wake Forest University's evening MBA program was the one I was most interested in. Wake Forest, a prestigious private school, was conveniently located in Winston-Salem, North Carolina, making campus access relatively simple. Another thing I liked was that their program took place in the evenings. I didn't want to give up my job for graduate school, so finding an evening program that aligned with my work schedule was the perfect solution.

I knew that getting accepted into the Wake Forest program would be extremely competitive, so I wanted to learn everything I could about the program before making the final decision about whether to apply. I scheduled a meeting with an admissions counselor, and as I prepared for the meeting, I combated my nerves by thinking, *What do I have to lose? It's just a conversation.*

I met with Janice, the admissions counselor for the evening MBA program. She explained all the pertinent program details, including reviewing the two-year curriculum and admissions requirements.

"You will need two letters of recommendation, and you will be required to write an essay," she explained. "You will also have to submit transcripts from all previous colleges, as well as your GMAT scores." She went on to say that there would be an application fee and an in-person interview.

"I haven't taken the GMAT yet, but I will take it soon if I decide to apply," I said.

"Why wouldn't you apply?"

"I'm just thinking about it at this point."

"I see. What's your hesitancy?"

"Nothing really, I just want to make sure I'm ready for graduate school."

"How will you know when you're ready?"

"That's a good question. I'm not really sure how I'll know."

"What are you afraid of?"

"I'm mostly afraid of failing."

"What else?"

"Well, I'm afraid of not getting in."

"If you apply, and you aren't accepted, the only thing you are out is time and the application fee, but at least you will have tried."

"What if I get in and I can't cut it?"

"If you make it through the application process and get accepted, I'm certain you will rise to the challenge."

"I'm just nervous. I've been wanting to do this for a long time, and I don't want to fail."

"Let me ask you this: what will you do with your time if you don't attend graduate school?"

"I don't know. I guess I would continue working."

"A year from now, do you want to look back and say to yourself, *If I had started the MBA program when I was thinking about it, I'd be halfway through*? Or would you rather celebrate the fact that you *are* halfway through?"

"I'd rather be halfway through."

"Then why wait?"

"I guess there's no real reason to wait. The only issue is that the application deadline is in one month, and I haven't even studied for the GMAT, let alone taken it."

"You're smart, Shonna, and I believe in you. If you want to get the application in on time, I know you will."

"What about the GMAT?"

"Like I said, I believe in you. Reach out to the testing center immediately and schedule your test. Make sure you take the GMAT at least a week before the application deadline, so we can get your scores in time."

"So I only have three weeks to study before taking the test?"

"That's right."

"OK, I'm going to do it," I said.

When I hung up the phone, I felt energized. It felt good to have someone believe in me, and it felt even better to believe in myself. I knew that no matter what, I was going to get my application in on time ... which I did.

The GMAT was difficult, but some areas were a lot easier than I'd expected. While the math was difficult, my performance in writing was exceptional. I submitted my test scores to the school, along with my application, and then the waiting began.

I had my in-person interview two weeks after applying. I was informed during the interview that I would receive the final decision the following week. Despite my nerves, I still felt good.

I'd aced the essay questions, had a great interview, and received decent test scores. Regardless of the result, I was immensely proud of my effort. I'd worked hard and had given it my all, and I'd managed to submit an application that I was proud of, despite the tight timeline.

The phone rang, and I answered it on the second ring. "Hi, Shonna. The admissions panel has made a decision regarding your application," Janice began.

"OK, give me a moment to sit down," I said shakily.

My hands began trembling. I had put everything I had into my application, and now this was it. What if Phillip had been right? What if, after all my hard work, it just wasn't good enough? What if I wasn't good enough? I forced the negative thoughts out of my mind and returned my attention to the present moment.

"OK, Janice," I said as I gripped the phone receiver. "I'm ready to hear the panel's decision."

"Welcome to Wake Forest University!"

"I got in?" I jumped up from my chair, pumping my fist in the air. *Woo-hoo!*

"Yes! Congratulations! You got in. Welcome to the Wake Forest class of 2011!" she said.

I couldn't believe my ears. I wanted to scream, cry, and laugh all at the same time. I'd done it! By the grace of God, I'd actually done it!

Janice and I spoke briefly about logistics and the next steps before I hung up the phone, feeling on top of the world. I was going to graduate school—and not just any graduate school; I was going to Wake Forest University! I couldn't wait to tell the two people that I most wanted to share my good news with ... my children.

When I shared the news with them, they both were as excited as I was. They had been on the journey with me. Jasmine had tutored me in math, and Josh had constantly quizzed me. I had been their support all their lives, and now they were supporting me. I could not have been happier, and happiness felt amazing.

The two years of graduate school flew by. My thinking was pushed, and my mind was expanded in ways it hadn't been in a while. Taking challenging courses and being among highly intelligent students inspired me. My fear of not being able to cut it had been unfounded. I excelled academically, earning A's in most of my classes. Graduate school was great. It felt natural. Every A I got in my classes reinforced my sense of belonging. They were two of the best years of my life, because they sparked the beginning of a transformative rebirth. Those years reminded me of who I was born to be. They reminded me of what I'm capable of. They removed the suffocating doubt in my mind that had the power to hold me back. Those years repaired my broken wings and brought me back to being the beautiful, confident creature that God had created me to be.

It was also during those years at Wake Forest that I met Jeff.

Jeff and I were in the same MBA program. We both loved learning, were highly competitive, and wanted to be at the top of the class. As such, he was naturally my nemesis. During our final year of graduate school, several members of our class visited South America as part of our international business studies. I didn't know Jeff very well, but from what I did know, he seemed to be responsible. I approached him after class one day.

"Hey, Jeff. Are you going on the trip to South America?"

"Yes. I'm looking forward to it," he said.

"I have a question for you. But before you answer, I need you to really think about it."

"What is it?"

"I want you to be my travel buddy for the trip."

"What is a travel buddy?"

"For starters, we never abandon each other. Wherever I go, you go. And wherever you go, I go."

"OK, sure."

"Wait a minute, there's more. Each day, we each get to pick an activity that we really want to do, and the other person has to do it."

"OK, I agree."

"Hold on, there's one more thing. You can't invite anyone else into our group."

"Is that all?"

"Yes, that's all."

"Let's see ... We don't abandon each other, we each get to pick a fun activity every day, and no interlopers. Hmm ..." Jeff made a face in exaggerated contemplative thought. "Yes, I agree to be your travel buddy," he finally said.

We soon became best friends. We did everything together. We laughed at jokes that only we understood. We had entire conversations using only acronyms. And the best part of our friendship was that neither of us was interested in a romantic relationship. Life was great.

As I stood on the graduation stage to receive my coveted hood, two things occurred to me. The first was that I felt an overwhelming surge of pride, a feeling I hadn't experienced in a very long time. Despite the odds that had been stacked against me, I had persevered to achieve what I wanted, much like a determined bumblebee tirelessly collecting pollen from one flower to the next. And, just as the bee's persistence yields honey, my unwavering determination had led to this moment of academic triumph.

As I turned to shake the hand of the professor who bestowed my graduation honors, the applause in the auditorium echoed in my ears.

The second thing was a deep realization: I hadn't pursued graduate school sooner because I had allowed someone else to define what I was capable of. But, as I stood on the stage, I made a silent pledge to myself: I vowed to once again lift my wings and soar, to embrace my full potential, and to never again allow myself to be tethered by others' limited beliefs of what I am capable of.

Following graduate school, my friendship with Jeff continued. Jeff wasn't like the other men who had been in my life. He was kind and empathetic, and he genuinely listened to me. What mattered to me—like my faith—mattered to him. He celebrated my victories as if they were his own, like the time when I got promoted, and he surprised me with a cake. His curiosity mirrored mine, as we spent hours diving into topics, from statistics to game theory. Being friends with Jeff was easy; it just felt right.

A year after finishing graduate school, I was on a business trip to Norway. I had already spent a week there and had another to go before returning to the US. Despite the time difference, Jeff and I spoke every day. I told him about the breathtaking sights, and he kept an eye on my apartment to make sure everything was OK.

On a Friday afternoon, I sat on a train headed to Oslo, eager to spend the weekend exploring. Jeff had helped me map out a weekend filled with fun things I could do on my own. As the train slowed to a stop at the station, my phone rang. It was Jeff.

"Hey, Jeff! Good morning. Are you heading to work?"

I grabbed my bag and made my way toward the doors.

"No, I took the day off," he said.

"Oh, nice! What are you planning to do?"

"I'm going to hang out with you."

"I wish you could," I said with a laugh.

A gust of icy wind hit me as I stepped onto the platform, and I shivered.

"You look cold," he said.

"Huh?" I said, crinkling my nose.

"Turn to your right."

I turned, and there he was, standing on the platform, smiling.

I let out a scream, abandoning my bag as I ran toward him.

"What are you doing here?" I asked, throwing my arms around him.

"I missed you," he said, holding me tightly.

My heart swelled with joy because I had missed him, too. It was then that I knew he was more than just my best friend. Or at least, I wanted him to be.

During our time in Norway, Jeff confessed his feelings for me, and what had once been a deep friendship blossomed into dating.

Our journey together has since spanned fifteen countries, thirty-five US states, and more than seventy-five thousand miles of road trips. Jeff proposed in 2015; and in 2016, by permission of the Pope, we were married in the Vatican. Now eight years into our marriage, Jeff remains not only my beloved husband but also my trusted confidant, best friend, and forever travel buddy.

Chapter 28

Be bold, be brave enough to be your true self.

—Queen Latifah

Two years after Jeff and I were married, I received a promotion and was settling into my new role as a senior director—the biggest role of my career so far. The work was exciting and challenging, and it carried tremendous responsibility. Best of all, it gave Jeff and me the opportunity to move to a new city and embark on a new adventure.

As I was filling my water bottle at the cooler one morning, my coworker Julie approached me.

"Hi, Shonna. You look sharp as usual today," she began.

"Hi, Julie. Thank you. You look nice, too. What are you up to?"

"Nothing really, I'm just taking a break," she said.

I looked up at her and smiled before continuing to fill my water bottle. I noticed that she was still staring at me, so I asked, "Is everything OK?"

"Yeah, everything is fine," she said unconvincingly.

With my water bottle filled, I turned to walk away when I heard her say, "You know, I like you, but I'm scared to death of you."

I immediately stopped and turned toward her, thinking that was such an odd turn for this casual interaction to take.

"You're afraid of me?" I was astonished. "Why?"

"I don't know. You are just so intimidating."

"How so?"

"You just are."

"I see. Well, let me ask you this: have I ever raised my voice to you?"

"No."

"Have I ever yelled at you?"

"No."

"Have you ever heard me yell or raise my voice to anyone else?"

She thought for a moment before responding. "No, I haven't."

"OK, with that in mind, why are you 'scared to death' of me?" I made air quotes for emphasis.

"That's a good question," she said. After a moment of thought, she finally said, "I suppose it's because your presence is immediately felt when you enter a room, even when you don't say anything. You're so confident and always seem so sure of yourself. And you don't seem like you take any crap."

"Do you think I'm arrogant?" I kept my tone soft.

"Oh, dear God, no," she said. "You're very nice."

"Aren't confidence and self-assuredness good attributes for any person to have?" I asked.

"Yes, definitely. I wish I had them. Especially confidence. I'm not confident at all, and when I see you, I am in awe of the fact that you are."

"And that makes you afraid of me?"

"You know what? I guess not. Maybe I'm not afraid of you; maybe I'm just amazed by you."

Caught off guard by her words, I blinked. "Amazed by me?" I smiled. "You know, I amaze myself sometimes too. But, like you or anyone else, I'm just trying to navigate this world the best I can. I show up every day and give my all, but that doesn't mean I don't have doubts or insecurities. I just refuse to let them dictate how I show up."

"I wish I could do that."

"I'm sure you can. There are many things that people admire about you. You just have to see them yourself and embrace them."

"Thank you, Shonna."

"My pleasure, Julie."

As I walked back to my office, I wondered how many people Julie had spoken with and shared the narrative that she was "scared to death" of me.

I didn't have to wait long to find out because, during my year-end performance review a few days later, my manager gave me the *constructive* feedback that I was too intimidating, which made people afraid of me. He went on to say that I should dial it down a bit.

"Dial what down?"

"Your behavior."

"What specific behavior are you referring to?"

"The behavior that intimidates people and makes you unapproachable. Not everyone is as tough as you are," he elaborated.

"Unapproachable? People approach me all the time, many of whom have no problem telling me exactly what they think about my work or anything else. Can you give me an example of the behavior that makes me unapproachable?" I asked.

"I don't have examples," he said. "People mentioned it to me when I asked for feedback on your performance."

"What people?"

"I can't give you names."

"People, as in more than one person, said this?"

"Shonna ..." He said my name in an exasperated tone that indicated the discussion was over.

"OK," I said with a smile, "I'll work on it."

Although I wasn't exactly sure what I was supposed to work on. It also wasn't lost on me that the comment had nothing to do with my actual job performance, nor did he have any evidence to support the accusation. He had no tangible proof or examples to validate the comments he'd heard, but that didn't matter. People's perceptions were their realities, so the allegations were enough to be included as part of my performance evaluation.

I didn't know whether the comment had come from Julie, but that wasn't important. The important thing that was crystal clear to me was that other people's biases can have a profound impact on my career trajectory, whether I realized I was being subjected to them or not. In the best scenario, I would learn about them and take the appropriate steps to mitigate them. In the worst scenario, I would never hear about them and would be left wondering why my career had stalled—or worst, why I'd lost my job.

I was grateful for the conversation I'd had with Julie because it allowed me to see things I hadn't previously noticed or considered before. The great Nelson Mandela once said, "I never lose. Either I win, or I learn." In this instance, I learned that hard work isn't always enough. Managing relationships and interactions with people is just as important, and in some cases, more important. Being mindful of the unwritten rules and unspoken norms is sometimes more valuable than being the best at what you do. Knowledge is power, and with knowledge comes understanding.

I began to understand the complexities of navigating the social structures within corporate America, especially as a woman of color. I didn't stop being confident, nor did I embrace a posture of weakness. Instead, I began to be more aware of occasions that warranted a gentler approach. I honed my abilities to read people, understand situations, and adapt my demeanor accordingly. I became very skilled at blending in with my colleagues, presenting the *appropriate* version of myself during every interaction.

In executive meetings, I mirrored the behaviors of the other women—even if it meant withholding my ideas and opinions. When I spoke, my tone was measured, my cadence smooth, every word intentional. Outside of work, especially when I was around other African Americans, my speech was more comfortable, and my dialect shifted naturally.

One afternoon at the hair salon, I was laughing with my stylist as we were in a heated debate about whether or not ketchup should be refrigerated. "Yes, it has to be!" she insisted.

"Heck no," I said. "Who wants cold ketchup on fries?"

The room was full of laughter when my phone rang. I immediately shushed everyone and answered in a crisp, polished tone. "Hello, this is Shonna."

When I hung up, I noticed everyone staring at me.

"What?"

"Girl, what was that White-girl voice?" my stylist asked with a smirk.

"That's not a White-girl voice," I said.

"Yeah, it is. But if you gotta act White to get yours, you do what you gotta do, boo."

The room erupted in laughter once again.

I knew the truth, though. It wasn't about pretending to be someone else; it was about navigating different worlds and shifting as needed to be seen, heard, and taken seriously.

My ability to adapt served me very well for many years, until one day when I realized that always trying to be *acceptable* was literally killing me. My career was successful, but I was mentally, physically, and psychologically exhausted. Despite exercising regularly, I'd gained nearly forty pounds. Most nights, I wasn't able to turn off my brain long enough to fall asleep. And I was always tired. I had achieved all the career aspirations I had set for myself: move up the ladder, lead a team, become a director, become a vice president, earn a spot on the executive team ... I had done it all, and yet, I wasn't happy or healthy. I was constantly trying to live up to others' expectations of who I was supposed to be, instead of just being myself.

I was once asked in an interview what advice I would give other women. Without hesitation, I said, "Don't be afraid to be your authentic self." Yet I wasn't taking my own advice. I wasn't being fake or insincere, but I had mastered the ability of showing up in the way I was *expected* to show up, speaking the way I was *supposed* to speak, and doing the things I was *supposed* to do.

After many years of navigating this corporate labyrinth, I finally accepted that I could not—nor did I wish to—continue trying to be all things to all people. Being empathetic, kind, and genuine is who I am. Shrinking myself, dimming my light so that others can feel adequate, or showing deference to someone because of their race or gender was not me, and it wasn't how I was going to live anymore.

For the first time in my career, I decided that I would no longer yield to the expectations of others, and I wondered how long it would be before the world around me pushed back.

The answer came sooner than I expected.

Chapter 29

It takes courage to grow up
and become who you really are.

—E. E. Cummings

Three months had passed since I'd lost my job, and I couldn't help but wonder—was that the world pushing back? Since that day, I had cycled through feelings of frustration, self-doubt, and moments of paralyzing fear. Most days, I struggled to find a reason to get out of bed, and when I did, I didn't bother changing out of my pajamas. I just couldn't believe my career had ended so abruptly.

Eventually, the weight of self-pity became unbearable, and I had to do something, anything, to pull myself out of the fog. That's how I ended up at a career networking event, standing awkwardly in a room full of professionals who all seemed to have their lives neatly figured out.

I had barely settled into a conversation when the woman I was speaking to said, "What you do is not who you are."

The words were simple, but for some reason, they unsettled me.

"Excuse me?" I asked.

She had started our conversation with the usual networking opening: "Tell me about yourself." And I had given her my standard response: "I'm a seasoned corporate executive specializing in strategy and transformation." But that wasn't what she had asked.

"What you do is not who you are," she repeated. Her voice was steady and firm.

Since losing my job, frustration had settled over me like a constant cloud. Everything irritated me, but forced small talk at networking events was especially unbearable. I had convinced myself that attending the event would help me find my next role. Instead, I found myself in a strange conversation that felt more like a test than an opportunity.

"I know that," I said, crossing my arms over my chest.

"Do you?"

"Yes, I do!" My irritation was building.

"OK, then … let's try this again. Tell me about yourself."

What was she getting at? I had already told her about myself. "I'm *a seasoned corporate executive specializing in strategy and—*"

She interrupted me. "I didn't ask what your job was. I asked about you."

"Oh!" I said, finally understanding what she was asking.

For as long as I could remember, whenever someone had asked about me, I had given a well-rehearsed elevator pitch describing my job. It had become second nature. But I no longer had a job, so things were different. Embarrassed by the way I had fumbled through her deceptively simple prompt, I lowered my gaze to the floor.

"Why did I even come to this stupid event?" I whispered and turned to walk away.

"Are you leaving? We still have ten minutes," she called behind me.

I stopped and turned toward her. "This was a mistake. I'm going home."

"Did my question offend you?"

"No, you didn't offend me. I'm annoyed with myself."

I turned to leave but felt a gentle tug on my arm.

"Wait, don't go. I'd love to hear your story."

"I don't have a story."

"Of course you do. Everyone has a story."

"I used to have a story, but not anymore, so there's nothing to tell."

"Did you lose your job?"

I didn't respond.

"I lost my job too," she said, breaking the silence.

"You did?"

"Yes, about four months ago."

"You aren't embarrassed to talk about it?"

"I used to be, but I'm not anymore."

"I'm still embarrassed," I said. "I've never been fired before, and I feel pretty humiliated."

"I'm so sorry to hear that." The empathy in her voice was warm and comforting. She paused, as if considering something before she spoke again.

"You want to know how I got over being embarrassed?"

"Yes, please," I said enthusiastically.

"I finally realized that my job doesn't define who I am as a human being."

"It doesn't?"

"No, it doesn't. And if your job was your only sense of purpose, the fact that you lost it might be a good thing."

Her words felt harsh.

"Why would you say that?"

"Because it's true, and now you have an opportunity to discover who you really are and what you want out of life."

"How am I supposed to do that without a job?"

"Try thinking about the types of things that bring you joy, and they will point you to what *really* gives you purpose. Also, practice introducing yourself without mentioning your job. Do you think you can do that?"

"I don't know," I confessed. "Being successful at work made me happy. Without it, I'm not sure what makes me happy."

"Now you have the chance to find out," she said gently.

"What do you say when people ask you about work?"

"I tell them the truth: I'm on sabbatical."

"Sabbatical?"

"Yes. A break from work to pursue my own personal interests."

"I like that," I said with a smile. "Being on sabbatical sounds much better than, 'I'm unemployed because I got fired.'" We both laughed.

The sound of the bell signaled that it was time to rotate partners, but I wanted to continue our conversation. Unfortunately, someone was already approaching us.

"Thank you for the advice, Pam," I said, extending my hand.

"You're welcome, Shonna. But before you go, here's one last piece of advice: when you find what makes you happy, don't anchor it to anything that can be taken away."

Before I could respond, we were interrupted.

"Hi, I'm Jenny," a woman said, introducing herself to Pam.

I gave Pam a quick wave before walking toward the door.

I left the event and walked to my car. Once inside, I buckled up and pulled onto the busy street. *Without my career, who am I?* I wondered. For the first time in my life, I had no plan, no goals, and no sense of direction. The clarity I'd once felt about my future was gone. I had spent decades building a career that had felt like everything I'd ever wanted. It had been my identity, my purpose, my validation. But now, without it, I wasn't only mourning the loss of my job. I was mourning the loss of me.

The car hummed softly as I navigated the familiar streets. While stopped at a red light, I exhaled. *Who am I kidding? I wasn't happy at work. Maybe getting fired wasn't a loss; maybe it was a chance for a fresh start. There is more to me than my achievements, so why am I allowing a job to define me?*

A sharp honk brought me back to the moment. The light was green. With a quick wave of apology, I eased forward—both in traffic and toward a new beginning.

By the time I pulled into my garage, the grief that had clouded my mind was gone. I looked at my reflection in the mirror, and I was already starting to look different. The worry lines on my forehead had softened. My eyes, once filled with sadness, were steady. I didn't just look different. I looked determined. Empowered. Ready.

I knew the journey ahead wouldn't be easy. *What if I fail?* I wondered. I quickly shoved the thought from my mind, refusing to let doubt creep in. Staring at my reflection, I looked ... *happy.* For the first time since losing my job, I wasn't crying. I was smiling.

Chapter 30

Freedom is what you do with what's been done to you.

—Jean-Paul Sartre

Filled with determination, I went into the house and immediately headed toward my office. I reached inside my desk drawer and pulled out my journal, its faded color and worn cover a testament to the turbulent past. When things were tough, I found perspective through journaling. I had begun journaling at the advice of a friend who called journaling her sanctuary, a space where she could pour out her soul unfiltered and without fear. At the time, I shrugged my shoulders in skepticism, but over the years, journaling had become my sanctuary too.

Prior to losing my job, I hadn't opened my journal in a long time because things had been steady. However, two months after losing my job, the grief had become suffocating, my tears unyielding, and the feeling of defeat unbearable. I knew it was time to start rebuilding myself, which meant it was time to return to my sanctuary.

The journal's pages creaked in quiet protest as I opened the book. On a blank page, I wrote in bold, capital letters: **WHO AM I?** I underlined the words, each stroke pressing deeply into the page. It was a simple question, but its weight was heavy. Answering it would require rediscovering the things that brought me joy, the pieces of myself that had been buried beneath years of obligations and endless work.

For once, there were no looming deadlines or an overpacked calendar demanding my attention. Instead, I had been given rare gifts: the freedom to embrace who I am, and the time to enjoy the things that make my heart come alive. They were gifts that I had always assumed would come much later, perhaps in retirement, but here they were, waiting to be embraced. A warm smile spread across my face.

My smile faded as seconds stretched into minutes. The page remained empty as my pen hovered uselessly above it. "Have I really lost myself so completely that I can't even remember what makes me happy?" I asked myself.

I rose from the chair and went to find my husband. Maybe talking it through with him would help me get started. I found him at the dining table, surrounded by a scattered mess of papers, his eyebrows scrunched together in deep concentration.

"Babe," I said, my voice breaking through his focus, "if you could do anything you wanted, without worrying about work, what would you do?"

He tilted his head toward me, his expression thoughtful. "Did we win the lottery in this scenario?"

"No, we didn't win the lottery."

"Am I retired?"

"No, you're just on a break from work. But eventually, you'll go back."

"Well, in that case, I'd travel with you until it was time to go back to work."

His answer was warm and predictable. I smiled before pressing further.

"What if I had to work, and we couldn't travel together?"

He gave me a knowing look. "Are you trying to figure out what to do while you're out of work?" he asked hesitantly.

The last time he'd asked about my plans, the wound of losing my job had been too fresh, and I'd burst into tears. Ever since, he'd avoided the subject entirely.

"Yes, I am. I want to make a list of some of the things I enjoy doing or always wanted to do but never did because of work."

"Well, let's see," he said, nodding thoughtfully. "You've always talked about learning how to swim. Maybe now is a good time to take lessons."

"That's a great idea! I *have* been saying that for years. Why didn't I think of that?"

"How much time are you planning to take off?"

"I'm not sure ... maybe six months?"

"Six months isn't a lot of time," he said, his voice filled with skepticism. "How about you make your list first, and then decide how much time you need to get through it?"

"That's a good idea. How long can we financially afford for me to be out of work?"

"We're OK," he said, pausing for emphasis. "But if you think you'll need longer than a year, let's talk."

"A year! I can't go a year without working. I'll be bored after three months. Six months will be plenty of time," I said confidently.

"We'll see," he said with a chuckle.

I walked back to my office and returned to the blank page, ready to think bigger. I liked the idea of taking swim lessons. I had always been embarrassed by the fact that, as an adult, I didn't know how to swim. During my time in the military, I had only learned how not to drown. If I were ever tossed into water while wearing my battle dress uniform, I could whip up a flotation device in under a minute. But swimming was a skill I'd never mastered. Learning to swim would be humbling, but humility was good. I wrote it down: *Learn to swim.*

Then I paused, letting the pen hover before writing the next goal: *Choose to be happy.* For most of my life, my happiness had been dictated by my circumstances, swayed by the tides of success or struggle. I thought about Pam's advice: "When you find what makes you happy, don't anchor it to something that can be taken away." Her words stayed with me, and I realized happiness wasn't something to chase; it was a choice. A choice that I needed to consciously make every single day.

This was fun. Once I got started, the ideas began to flow. After *Choose to be happy*, I wrote: *Get healthy.* A sense of urgency rippled through me. Just weeks earlier, I had been told for the first time in my life that I had high blood pressure. Both my parents and grandparents had dealt with it, but it wasn't something I'd worried about because I had been careful—mindful of my salt intake and deliberate about my diet. Yet, despite all my precautions, a routine physical had revealed the unsettling truth that my efforts hadn't been enough.

"Shonna, your blood pressure is 180 over 94. That's unequivocally too high," Dr. Carson said, his tone firm but calm.

"180 over 94?" I repeated, disbelief in my voice. "That can't be right. I've never had high blood pressure in my life. Are you sure the machine isn't broken?"

He nodded, understanding my doubt. "I'll take it again manually."

Grabbing a blood pressure cuff, he wrapped it snugly around my arm. "Take a few deep breaths and try to relax."

I inhaled deeply through my nose and exhaled slowly through my mouth, willing myself to steady the worry that was building inside of me. Closing my eyes, I pictured calm waters— still, serene, undisturbed.

The cuff began to inflate, its grip tightening around my arm. I focused on keeping my breath steady as the seconds stretched. Finally, the air hissed out, and the tension released.

"182 over 95," he confirmed.

"How is that possible?" I asked, my voice rising.

Dr. Carson's expression was firm. "The results are accurate, and they're serious. Unfortunately, despite your precautions, you can't outrun genetics."

That same day, I began taking spironolactone to manage my blood pressure.

The next thing I wrote was: *Give back.* Whether donating blood to the Red Cross or supporting families in impoverished communities, helping others had always been an important part of who I am, so it felt essential to make it part of this journey.

The words seemed to come alive on the page as I wrote: *Learn something new,* followed by, *Get involved in my community.*

I hesitated before adding the final entry. My journal had always been my private sanctuary, a safe place for me to pour out my thoughts and steady myself when the ground shifted beneath my feet. But this time felt different. *What if my story is more than just my own?* I wondered. *What if the trials I've endured, the lessons I've learned, and the strength I've found could help someone else?* The thought lingered as my hand rested on the page.

Feeling conflicted, I leaned back in my chair and closed my eyes. My heart wrestled with doubt, but a quiet voice within urged me forward. *What if sharing my story could offer hope to someone else? What if my journey could encourage someone when they need it most?* With a deep sigh of resignation, I decided to take a leap of faith. I leaned forward and slowly wrote: *Share my story with the world.* When I finally rested the pen on the desk, there were seven entries on the page. It was a blueprint for rebuilding my life, and perhaps also a way to touch the lives of others.

My heart raced as I stared at the page of newly written goals. The journey I was about to embark on filled me with equal parts excitement and fear. Could I really do this? I closed the journal, as if sealing a promise to myself, and slid it back into the drawer. I nervously reached for my laptop and opened the web browser. My fingers hovered above the keys, trembling slightly. With a calming breath, I summoned the courage to take the first step and typed into the search bar: *Adult swim lessons near me.*

Epilogue

One year later ...

The two most important days in your life are the day
you are born and the day you find out why.

—Mark Twain

I walked into the pool area of the University of Denver Aquatics Center, which was filled with swimmers of all ages effortlessly swimming laps in the Olympic-size pool. I was wearing a full-coverage swimsuit, but I still felt self-conscious, so I gripped the towel that was wrapped around my waist a little more tightly. I looked around, and based on a quick assessment, I was certain that I was the oldest person in the pool, yet I was there for a beginner's lesson.

I glanced around the area and spotted my swim coach, Coach Max. As if he felt my gaze, he looked up from the student he was teaching to float and gave me an encouraging wave. I smiled in return as I headed for a corner to stretch while I waited for the lesson before mine to end. I had been swimming with Coach Max for about eight weeks, but I was still intimidated by the idea of getting in the water.

In the eight weeks since I had begun taking swim lessons, I had learned to float on my stomach and back, and to travel almost half the length of the pool using a kickboard. I had also learned to glide through the water using my legs to propel me forward. I had not learned any arm movements yet, and the distance I traveled depended on how long I could hold my breath because I hadn't learned any breathing techniques either.

Coach Max walked over to me, indicating that it was time to start my lesson.

"Are you ready?" he asked, once he was close enough for me to hear him.

Coach Max was an excellent swim coach. He was excited for me to learn, and he admired the fact that I was willing to take on the challenge as an adult.

"I think so. Is the water very cold?" I asked.

"It isn't too bad. You just have to take the plunge," he said as he dived into the water.

I took a more measured approach and entered the water much more slowly. I sat on the edge of the pool and let my legs dangle off the side as I moved my feet around in the water. After a minute of testing the water, I slowly slid butt-first into the pool. My teeth began to chatter as my body acclimated to the change in temperature.

Coach Max chuckled and said, "I told you that it's easier to just jump in. Getting in slowly just makes it worse. What would you like to work on today?"

"I don't know. I'll work on whatever you think is best," I replied.

"Do you remember everything we worked on last week?" he asked.

"I think so," I muttered hesitantly.

"OK, let's start with a refresher. Doing some leg work will also help you get warmed up." He handed me a kickboard and told me to push off the wall and swim as far as I could.

I took a deep breath, placed my feet on the wall of the pool, and pushed off as hard as I could. I began rhythmically kicking my legs as I felt my body move through the water. When I finally came up for air, I had traveled nearly half the length of the pool. A big smile stretched across my face as I walked back toward Coach Max.

"Great job!" he exclaimed. "I think you are ready to try some arm movements." He explained to me the fundamentals of incorporating my arms.

"Remember to engage your core, and kick your legs from your hips with a slight bend at the knee. It will be a bit more challenging because you won't have the kickboard to help you float, so don't get discouraged if you don't go that far," he explained.

"OK, I think I got it. Engage my core, kick my legs, slight bend at the knee." As I got ready, I felt my nerves kick in.

"Breathe, Shonna. You can do this," I coached myself. I took a few deep breaths to steady my nerves, and I felt the jitters subside. I looked at Coach Max, and he gave me two thumbs-up with a big smile on his face.

"Don't forget to get a strong push off the wall," he reminded me. As I reached for my goggles, I heard him say, "Try to swim to where I'm standing. And, Shonna, no matter how you do, you should feel proud."

I did feel proud. Eight weeks earlier, I hadn't even wanted to get my face wet. I thought about my sabbatical list. Item number one: *Learn to swim.* Swimming had been something I'd wanted to learn for a long time, but I'd never had the courage to try it, mostly because I was too embarrassed to be an adult who couldn't swim. Because I couldn't swim, I declined any invitation that involved water. I refused to go paddleboarding, white-water rafting, or even kayaking. Canoeing was also out of the question. I would have loved to have done those things, but I was too afraid of being vulnerable in water—even with a life jacket. I worried that I wouldn't be able to save myself if something went wrong, and depending on someone else to save me wasn't an option. Yet, while I was still very much a beginner, here I was in the water, conquering my fear.

I secured my goggles in place, filled my lungs with air, and kicked off the wall as hard as I could. I glided through the water a bit, only kicking my legs. After a few feet, I began rotating my arms. My hands were slightly cupped, and with each water grab, I felt myself being propelled forward. I was actually swimming! I tilted my head a bit and saw Coach Max at the designated spot.

Four strokes later, I swam past him. I felt energized, and I didn't want to stop. I continued moving my arms and kicking my legs. The more I relaxed, the more the water rewarded me with forward progress.

When I had finally exhausted all of the air in my lungs, I let my legs drop beneath me and lifted my head out of the water. I glanced behind me and saw that I had swum nearly the full length of the pool. I looked forward and realized that I was only a few more strokes from the end!

My chest heaved as I took in big gulps of air. Coach Max moved toward me as fast as he could, and when he finally reached me, he raised his hand to give me a high five as he shouted, "Are you freaking kidding me?!" The smile on his face was as big as the smile on mine.

I walked back to the other end of the pool feeling ten feet tall. I thought about my list again, and I felt excited to get home and draw a line through item number one. I had done it. I may not have been Michael Phelps, but I had finally learned to swim.

During the twelve months of my sabbatical, I drew a line through almost every item on my list. I still take my swim lessons, and I continue to get better. The next thing on my list that I drew a line through was *Get healthy*. When I began my sabbatical, I was suffering from high blood pressure, I was overweight, and I wasn't in the best physical condition. I started working with a trainer four days a week, and one year later, I am stronger and leaner, and I have discontinued taking my blood pressure medicine. I have successfully lost forty-five pounds, I've reduced my body fat from 28 percent to 20 percent, and I can easily deadlift two hundred pounds.

Get healthy was followed by *Learn something new*. I joined the local tennis club and began taking tennis lessons. I had never played tennis before, but I really enjoyed watching it. I started off slowly, but within a few months, I moved up a level and began participating in group drills. I continue to play tennis twice a week.

Next up was *Give back*. After reflecting on my career and the many lessons I'd learned, I wanted to help others navigate the various stages of career development by serving as a mentor and coach. I wanted to help young professionals, especially women, by providing mentoring and coaching that I hadn't received until much later in my career. I signed up for an executive coaching program through Saint Joseph's University, and within six months, I became a certified career coach. Within a year, I was certified as an executive coach. Achieving professional certification wasn't about being able to charge for coaching—because I do not—it was about receiving the necessary training that would allow me to be the best coach that I am able to be.

The most important item on the list, which I remind myself of daily, is *Choose to be happy*. Being happy is a choice that I consciously make every day. That doesn't mean that everything always goes my way, but it does mean that, in spite of any given circumstance, I will always search for something to make me smile. On days when that's especially tough, I start with gratitude. There is always a reason for me to be grateful, and as soon as I identify it, I smile, which makes me happy. As you navigate the ups and downs of your life journey, it is my prayer that you, too, can always find a reason to be happy.

By the end of my sabbatical, I had checked off every item on the list, with the exception of one: *Share my story with the world.* However, as you are reading this, I've now checked that item off as well.

My sabbatical may be over, but I will carry the peace it created into whatever the next phase of my journey has in store for me. I now realize that I was born to be the best possible version of myself that I am able to be. I was born to discover how all the many pieces of my life fit together. I embrace the fact that every one of my life experiences has made me uniquely and beautifully me. And, while all of those experiences on their own may seem irrelevant, together, they are moving me toward my God-given purpose. I was born with many gifts and talents that are special to me. The question is, how will I use them? I don't fully have the answer to that question yet, but I do know that I will gratefully and courageously embrace the journey to find out.

I can do all things through Christ
which strengtheneth me.
—Philippians 4:13

About the Author

S.T. Griffon is a former U.S. Army paratrooper turned corporate executive, author, and speaker. Her debut memoir, *She Wasn't Supposed to Fly*, shares her extraordinary journey from hardship to hope, offering inspiration to anyone determined to rise above impossible odds. She lives in Virginia with her husband, Jeff, and their dogs, Jasper and Lola.

Follow her journey:

Website: www.stgriffon.com

Instagram: @stgriffonauthor